THE AMERICAN CONNECTION

THE AMERICAN CONNECTION
U.S. GUNS, MONEY, AND INFLUENCE IN NORTHERN IRELAND

JACK HOLLAND

Roberts Rinehart Publishers
Boulder, Colorado

Published by
Roberts Rinehart Publishers
6309 Monarch Park Place
Niwot, Colorado 80503
TEL 303.652.2685
FAX 303.652.2689
www.robertsrinehart.com

Distributed to the trade by Publishers Group West

Published in Ireland and the U.K. by
Roberts Rinehart Publishers
Trinity House
Charleston Road
Dublin 6

International Standard Book Number 1-57098-261-9

Library of Congress Catalog Card Number 98-89915

Copyright © 1987, 1999 Jack Holland

Cover photograph © Oistin MacBride

10 9 8 7 6 5 4 3 2 1

Manufactured in the United States of America

FOR MY DAUGHTER, JENNY

"Fra le belle tu sei la più bella"

Contents

Preface   ix

Acknowledgments   xi

Glossary of Organizations   xiii

Prologue   1

1. Ireland's Arcadians   7

2. NORAID and the Northern Crisis   27

3. Of Arms and the Man   63

4. Congressional Conscience   114

5. Northern Ireland on Trial:
   Extradition and the U.S. Courts   152

6. Covering the Northern Crisis:
   The U.S. Press and Northern Ireland   196

7. Conclusion: The Decline of the Rebel   236

8. Afterword:
   Northern Ireland in the Clinton Era   244

Chronology of Events   269

Notes   285

Bibliography   289

Index   291

Preface

When *The American Connection* first appeared over ten years ago, the political climate both here and in Ireland was very different. Ronald Reagan dominated American politics; his close ally, indeed mentor, Margaret Thatcher was equally dominant in Britain. Northern Ireland as an issue was still filed under "International Terrorism." In spite of the signing of the Anglo-Irish Agreement in 1985, which many hoped would help create a new dynamic towards solving the long-running conflict, the situation was once more overcome with inertia. The terror of the IRA and the loyalist paramilitaries could not break it; nor did the measures of the security forces seem able to effect a victory decisive enough to bring the violence to a halt. Britain had backed away from many of the provisions in the agreement of three years earlier, and no one seemed able or willing to try and persuade Thatcher that it was necessary to do anything other than hold the line against the "men of violence." A blood equilibrium seemed the best that could be hoped for. But as the political map of the world changed in the late 1980s and early 1990s, so did Ireland, and so did the United States' relationship to it, at least politically.

Along with the break-up of the post–World War Two settlement, the Northern Ireland crisis began to change. It was becoming clear that new opportunities were emerging from within the IRA and Sinn Fein that had the potential to transform the whole situation. The twilight of the IRA's armed campaign, the end of a long and finally futile tradition, was looming before most recognized it.

This new edition is an attempt to explain how and why those changes came about and the decisive role that the American connection played in the process leading to the Good Friday Agreement, and perhaps, finally, the long-hoped-for peace for decades that has eluded the Irish people.

Acknowledgments

Much of the material in the following pages could not have been gathered without the help of numerous individuals. I would like particularly to thank George Harrison for his unfailing cooperation; the staff of the Irish consulate in New York, especially Michael Collins and his predecessor, Ted Smyth, for allowing me the liberal use of their facilities, including their extensive newspaper files; Marcia Simonson in Los Angeles for keeping me up-to-date on West Coast coverage of Northern Ireland; Congressman Mario Biaggi for taking time out from his hectic schedule to answer my questions over the years; to Mary Pike and Steve Somerstein for their invaluable assistance in untangling extraditions and legal complexities; and the editor, publisher, and staff of the *New York Irish Echo,* in the pages of which several of the ideas that are expressed and elaborated in this book found an early platform. Also, I want to acknowledge the hospitality of the many Irish-American organizations that I have met and addressed throughout the United States since 1981. Without such contacts my experience of Irish America would have been much less full, and consequently this book the poorer for it. And, to my wife, Mary Hudson, my thanks for seeing me through yet another book; as always, her contributions, at many different levels, played a vital part in enabling this book to be completed.

Glossary of Organizations

The following list of Irish and Irish-American organizations is concerned with only those groups and parties that are mentioned in some detail in the text. It is obvious, therefore, that the size of any individual entry is not a reflection of the author's estimation of the overall importance of the group or party.

1. Irish

32-County Sovereignty Committee. Formed in late 1997 by dissident Provisionals unhappy with Sinn Fein's role in peace process.

Continuity IRA. Hard-line republican group. Formed in late 1986 and linked to Republican Sinn Fein.

Irish Republican Army (IRA). The main nationalist guerrilla organization since 1919, when it fought the British during the War of Independence. Maintains basic republican goals—a unitary, thirty-two-county, neutral state—but married to socialist politics. Since 1978 it has been dominated by Northern Ireland activists.

Irish Republican Brotherhood (IRB). Formed in 1858, it became the conspiratorial center for Irish revolutionaries plotting the overthrow of British rule in Ireland. After many vicissitudes, the IRB was instrumental in organizing the 1916 Rising from which the modern Republic of Ireland is derived. Linked to the Fenian Brotherhood in America (see below).

Irish Republican Socialist Party (IRSP). A left-wing splinter group formed by former members of the so-called Official IRA, itself a split away from the IRA in 1969. The IRSP was set up in 1974. A companion organization, the Irish National Liberation Army (INLA), was established at the same time to carry out a military campaign against Northern Ireland. Though small, the INLA was violently active throughout the late 1970s and early 1980s.

Three of its members died in the hunger-strike protests of
1981 in the Maze Prison near Belfast.

Northern Ireland Civil Rights Association (NICRA). Founded in 1967
to draw attention to discrimination against Catholics in
Northern Ireland. It did so by passive protests. Went into decline in the early 1970s.

Progressive Unionist Party. Loyalist party linked to UVF.

Real IRA. Dissident members of Provisional IRA who opposed
peace process, formed in late 1997. Linked to 32-County
Sovereignty Committee.

Republican Sinn Fein. Split from Sinn Fein in 1986 over the latter's
decision to recognize the Dail (Irish Parliament).

Royal Ulster Constabulary (RUC). The Northern Ireland police
force, founded in 1922. Its membership was almost entirely
Protestant. It has been the target of much IRA violence.

Sinn Fein. The nationalist party, founded in 1907. Became the political wing of the IRA. In the post-hunger strike period, made
substantial political gains in Northern Ireland.

Social Democratic and Labour Party (SDLP). The main constitutional nationalist party in Northern Ireland. Founded in 1970 by
various nationalist, civil-rights, and moderate left-wing activists,
the SDLP has played a crucial role in Irish political life. Its
leading member, John Hume, was prominent in the developing of the power-sharing initiative in 1973 that led to a
Northern Ireland government a year later: for the first time
Catholics held high political office alongside Protestants.
Later, the SDLP was an important force behind the negotiations that led to the Anglo-Irish Agreement between Dublin
and London in November, 1985. This gave the Irish government a say in the affairs of Northern Ireland for the first time
since the state's formation in 1921. The SDLP commands the
political support of the majority of Northern Ireland's
Catholics.

Ulster Defense Association (UDA). The largest and most violent of the
Protestant paramilitary groups. Responsible for the majority of
sectarian crimes in the 1970s, many of which it claimed responsibility for under the name "Ulster Freedom Fighters" (UFF). In
spite of its violent history, it is still a legal organization.

Ulster Defense Regiment (UDR). A locally recruited regiment of the

British army. Formed in 1970, it has earned a reputation for anti-Catholic bigotry. Many of its member and former members have been linked to sectarian crimes. The SDLP routinely called for its abolition.

Ulster Democratic Party. Loyalist party linked to UDA.

Ulster Volunteer Force (UVF). A violent Protestant paramilitary group formed in 1966 and responsible for much anti-Catholic bloodshed. Unlike the UDA, the UVF is an illegal organization.

2. Irish-American

Ad Hoc Committee on Irish Affairs. Set up by Representative Mario Biaggi in September 1977 at the request of Ancient Order of Hibernians president Jack Keane. Intended to press for open congressional hearings on Northern Ireland and to campaign to reverse the State Department's policy of denying visas to prominent Irish republicans. Ran foul of the Irish government on many occasions, having been accused of supporting the "men of violence" in Northern Ireland. At its peak had about one hundred members, with a much smaller core of activists, but has now declined in influence.

American Congress for Irish Freedom. Formed in the late 1960s by American lawyer James Heaney to publicize civil-rights abuses in Northern Ireland and demand a British withdrawal. Originally supported the Northern Ireland Civil Rights Association but split with them due to NICRA's left-wing bias.

Ancient Order of Hibernians (AOH). One of the oldest and the largest Irish-American groups. Formed in 1836 as a Catholic defense force against militant "Native American" hostility, the AOH spread from its birthplace in New York to any part of the country where the Irish had immigrated. Main Organizer of the St. Patrick's Day parade in New York. Maintains a militantly Catholic outlook; its newsletter states, GOD IS PRO-LIFE, ARE YOU? Was instrumental in setting up Biaggi's Ad Hoc Committee (see above). Has about 30,000 members.

Fenian Brotherhood. Formed in the 1850s as a revolutionary organization linked to the Irish Republican Brotherhood in Ireland, the Fenians were one of the most important Irish-

American organizations ever to exist. Planned the doomed uprising in Ireland in 1866–67 and supplied Irish insurrectionists with personnel, weapons, and money. The Fenians had powerful support in the Union army, and claimed many sympathizers at all levels of American society. After the failure of the '67 rebellion, the Fenians were superseded by the Clann na Gael.

Friends of Ireland. A group of prominent Irish-American senators and representatives that grew out of the "Big Four"—Senators Kennedy and Moynihan, House Speaker Thomas P. (Tip) O'Neill, and former governor of New York Hugh Carey. Irish ambassador Sean Donlon and the embassy's political counselor, Jim Sharkey, were instrumental in forming the Friends in 1981. Every St. Patrick's Day they make regular statements on the Irish situation in support of the Irish government's position. In 1985, the Friends used its influence in support of the Anglo-Irish Agreement. By then, the group claimed as members some twenty-one from the House and twenty from the Senate.

Friends of Irish Freedom. Formed in the late 1980s mainly by former NORAID activists. Politically identifies with Republican Sinn Fein.

Friends of Sinn Fein. Washington-based fund-raiser and lobbying group, formed following IRA cease-fire in 1994.

H-Block Armagh Committee. Established in New York in 1979 to support prison protests in Northern Ireland, where jailed republicans were campaigning for the return of "political status," of which they had been deprived in 1976. Small, with a left-wing slant and links to the leftist IRSP.

Irish Action Committee. A short-lived group formed in 1969 in New York to support Northern Ireland Catholics during the civil disturbances. It was the predecessor of Irish Northern Aid.

Irish National Caucus (INC). Emerged in late 1973 and early 1974. At first had the support of Michael (Mick) Flannery (founder of Irish Northern Aid), as well as of the AOH and various other Irish-American groups. Intended to lobby in Washington for Irish-republican issues. By 1975 was controlled by Northern Ireland-born priest Sean McManus. Close to Representative Mario Biaggi. Split with Irish republicans and their Irish-

American supporters in 1978. Has dwindled in importance in recent years but has managed to maintain public prominence.

Irish Northern Aid Committee (INAC). Also known as NORAID, it has proved the most enduring of all the groups formed in America since the resurgence of the "troubles" in 1969. Set up in April 1970 after consultations with high-ranking IRA man Daithi O'Conaill, NORAID raised funds throughout the 1970s and 1980s; however, by the 1990s its fundraising role had diminished in importance and it was claiming to be a lobbying group. Denounced as a money supplier to the IRA, NORAID countered that its resources went to support only the families of imprisoned IRA men. The Justice Department pressed for it to register under the Foreign Agents Registration Act (FARA) as an agent of the IRA, which it did, with qualifications, in 1984. At its peak could claim more than seventy units throughout the U.S., and two thousand members in New York alone. Estimates vary as to the amounts raised by INAC. Some put it as high as $5 million, though actual returns show just under $3 million collected since 1971. Founding member Mick Flannery, an IRA man in the 1920s, left in 1989 to join the Friends of Irish Freedom. He died in 1994.

PROLOGUE

For six blocks down Manhattan's Third Avenue the crowds stretch, a forest of pickets in their hands. Placards proclaim BOBBY SANDS—IRA FREEDOM FIGHTER; MARGARET THATCHER: WANTED FOR MURDER AND TORTURE OF IRISH PRISONERS; and thousands of others jostle with their slogans of struggle, defiance, and outrage. Two thousand five hundred miles away across the ocean, a macabre death watch nears its grim conclusion as the first hunger striker, Bobby Sands, slips toward death. Imprisoned for possessing a weapon (sentenced to fourteen years), Sands, an IRA man recently elected to the British Parliament, is starving to death in protest of British refusal to recognize him as a political prisoner. The thousands lining the streets around the British consulate on Third Avenue echo his cry. Irish Americans—whose ancestors crossed the ocean that separates them from the scene of the ghastly confrontation between Irish nationalist ambitions and British determination to resist them—angry, sad, and full of foreboding, knowing Sands's end is near, yet full of urgent belief that it should not be allowed to happen, demand that Britain get out of Northern Ireland once and for all. It is late spring, New York City, 1981. But it might be a hundred years earlier, or sixty.

Through crisis after crisis, through rebellion and defeat, through a century and a half marked by famine and war, Ireland's exiled generations in American have provided the protesters, often the passion, and usually the material to enable Irish rebels to continue their quest for the imagined republic.

Between 1845 and 1854, the famine drove one and a half million men, women, and children to entrust their lives to the vast ocean that batters the west coast of Ireland; at least another million and a half died in their mud cabins. Further famine, poverty, and crisis drove to America an average of fifty thousand every year between 1870 and 1900. They halved Ireland's population but gave America one of its largest ethnic groups. "When, after careful study of the history of America, we turn with equal care to the political and social state there, we find ourselves deeply convinced of this truth, that there is not an opinion, custom, or law, nor, one might add, an event, which the point of departure will not easily explain," wrote Alexis de Tocqueville in *Democracy in America,* over a decade before the first famine-fleeing immigrants arrived from Ireland. For Irish Americans throughout the nineteenth century and to a lesser extent throughout the twentieth, the famine, the point of their departure, has proved to be "an emotive furnace" in which the crucial links making up an important part of the American connection were forged.

On that spring morning in May 1981, as their descendants jammed the Manhattan streets near the British consulate waiting for news of the fate of the starving man, the point of departure, over a hundred years before, was all too real. The gaunt ghosts from the Irish past were suddenly alive again in the emaciated form of Bobby Sands.

In 1867, a British member of Parliament lamented that English policy in Ireland had created "a new Irish nation on the other side of the Atlantic, recast in the mould of Democracy, watching for an opportunity to strike a blow at the heart of the Empire." One hundred and fourteen years later, the empire was no more, but the recast Irish nation in America was still mustering its resources, ready to take aim. From the streets of Manhattan to the corridors of Congress, that nation could call on considerable force, at least in theory. The Irish had arrived in America destitute, but had since moved into the places of political power. The Speaker of the House of Representatives, Thomas (Tip) O'Neill, one of the most powerful men in Washington, called on the British prime minister to end her intransigence and recognize the hunger strikers' demands. In the House itself, and in the Senate, where Irish Americans have exercised their authority in the Democratic party for several generations, powerful figures made speeches, hoping for a reasonable outcome. Some pressed President Ronald Reagan, himself of Irish descent, to intervene with the British government and stop the slide toward what seemed like certain chaos. From Ireland came a similar appeal. Charles Haughey, the prime minister, pleaded with Reagan to put pressure on Thatcher. All to no avail. Access to places of power such as has been won by the Irish in America brings with it the complexities of exercising that power. The crowds on the streets might chant, demonstrations grow larger, anger more fierce, despair more bitter, but the mighty juggernaut of American foreign policy, even with Irish-American hands on the controls, would not move against England.

In 1867, when a band of revolutionaries known as the Fenians rose against British rule in Ireland, they did so in the hope that aid and recognition would come from the United States. The Fenians, of American origin, thought they knew America well. Had not Britain recently been on the Confederate side in the bloody Civil War? Did not many in the Union army subscribe to their goals of liberating Ireland and establishing her republic in imitation of the country that had given them a home across the ocean? Surely the United States would see that the injustice its soldiers had so recently fought against on their own soil was little different from what the Fenians were marching against in the cold winter of '67 through the bogs and bleak fields of Ireland. But recognition of the Fenians' doomed rebellion did not come from Washington. The rising went ahead, and was swept away with a gesture as effortless as a lion flicking a fly off its back with its tail. There was aid: from the Fenian organization in America came *Erin's Hope*, a vessel loaded with arms. It set sail in April, bearing thirty-eight volunteers. By the time it arrived, the Fenian rising was over and the handful of rebels who had taken part in it were already being processed in the courts or were in hiding, probably planning to flee to America.

Erin's Hope was as much an emblem of the American connection as was the emigrant's letter with the small remittance sent home to an aging mother or father. Under different names, but with the same intention, it would sail time and time again to Ireland, its cargo of arms ready to be received by eager, outstretched hands.

Nearly fifty years later, another rebellion rocked Ireland. Its waves raced across the ocean to wash against the American shore, bringing the same appeal for aid and recognition. The Easter Rising of 1916 was crushed, but the British brutally executed its leaders and turned what had been a minority-led conspiracy into a widespread resistance movement. By 1919 British soldiers were being gunned down in Irish streets, and members of the Royal Irish Constabulary were meeting the same fate. The party of independence, Sinn Fein, was the most powerful in the country and controlled a rebel parliament set up in defiance of British rule. Yet in 1919, when President Woodrow Wilson presided at the Versailles Conference in the wake of World War I, he stoutly refused to listen to Ireland's plea to be included as one of the small nations whose rights the "Great War" was supposedly fought to uphold. Once again, the American government turned aside Irish-American attempts to embroil it on Ireland's side in the struggle with Britain.

Regardless of their government's disapproval, however, Irish Americans rallied to the cause of the nascent republic. Within six months a victory fund for Irish freedom had raised over a million dollars. Irish rebels belonging to the recently formed Irish Republican Army, which was fighting the British with guerrilla tactics, were welcomed to Irish centers in New York, San Francisco, Chicago, Boston, and Philadelphia. Huge rallies shook the walls of Madison Square Garden, which resounded to the slogans of rebellion. The president reflected, rather dolefully: "The only circumstances which seem to stand in the way of an absolutely cordial co-operation with Britain by practically all Americans is the failure so far to find a satisfactory method of self-government for Ireland." During the spring and summer of 1981, sixty-two years later, President Reagan had cause to agree with him. A satisfactory form of self-government for Ireland had yet to be found.

The British had brought the IRA's guerrilla war to an end in 1921 through the offer of a partitioned, twenty-six-county, autonomous Irish state. The majority of Irish people accepted it, however reluctantly, as a better alternative than the prolonged and all-out war threatened by Britain. For the most part, Irish Americans followed suit. But while partition worked for the twenty-six counties, the position of the other state, known as Northern

Ireland, was not so satisfactory. A large minority of nationalist Catholics was left within its borders. There were enough IRA men and sympathizers in the twenty-six counties, in Northern Ireland itself, and in America, to carry on the republican quest for a completely unified, thirty-two-county Irish republic. For these men, the republic was a Holy Grail never to be sullied through compromise. Their commitment was made more intense by the knowledge that Northern Ireland's Catholic minority were discriminated against and had no hope of achieving full equality with their Protestant neighbors. For these men, there was only one road to the Holy Grail of the true republic—and that was through violence.

In New York in May 1981, a few of them were making ready to finalize one of the largest arms deals they had ever achieved. The arms were destined for the IRA. They worked far from the demonstrators, far from the pickets. But without them the chants of the protesters would have been meaningless and their displeasure and anger without consequence. Through them the American connection runs underground across the country; it runs over the ocean to the back streets of Belfast and lonely lanes of Ulster's countryside. They despise the politicians—Irish American or otherwise—and their pleas in Congress. They regard even the demonstrators marching outside the British consulate with skepticism, asking "Where will they be in a year, when the fuss is over and forgotten?" Of course, they welcomed the crowds demonstrating in support of Bobby Sands. But their years of struggle, of conspiracy, have taught them that crowds melt away. Dedication to the armed struggle is a vocation, and few have it. The commitment it demands is absolute, and they have given it.

The Ireland they seek is a land of the future—the Irish republic that could be if only the struggle were to succeed. It is a land where justice, equality, and peace will reign once the British have been driven out. It is a utopia, and those who struggle toward it are possessed of the belief that it has to be won with arms, through sacrifice. It is not for the faint-hearted, and it cannot be entered into easily. As their witness, they point to the centuries of Irish struggle, death, and defeat.

That spring they hoped to bring it nearer with a purchase of arms consisting of over 350 guns and 50,000 rounds of ammunition.

Another *Erin's Hope* was setting out from the New World to the Old.

Bobby Sands died on May 5, 1981, after sixty-six days without food. The agonies of death by starvation had already been well rehearsed in the media: the rolling eyes, the sickness, the waxen skin, the gut contractions. There were more pleas, more demonstrations, more protests. But the crowds began to melt away, though nine more prisoners were to die of starvation before the autumn. Soon, only a small, faithful knot of picketers would remain on Third Avenue as the busy world of New York flowed around them, enveloping them in its return to normal.*

Yet the American connection remains. It is linked to Ireland by more than utopian aspirations of revolutionary gunrunners. Among Irish Americans it is sustained as much, if not more, by feelings for the past as it is by hopes for the future. For America's relationship with Ireland is a complex, Janus-like one, in which the past and future mingle and often cannot be distinguished from each other, in which the politician has a role along with the rebel.

*Calling itself the Long Green Line, it maintained a presence outside the consulate. In April 1986 it celebrated its fifth anniversary of picket-duty with a luncheon at the Waldorf-Astoria.

1
IRELAND'S ARCADIANS

The English poet W. H. Auden wrote: "Our dream pictures of the Happy Place where suffering and evil are unknown are of two kinds, the Edens and the New Jerusalems."[1] Eden, according to Auden, is the dream place of the arcadian—the person whose perfect world lies in a reverie of the past. It is a world where the contradictions that afflict the present have not yet arisen. "To be an inhabitant of Eden," wrote Auden, "it is absolutely required that one be happy and likeable. . . . Eden cannot be entered; its inhabitants are born there." For Auden, the dreamers of Eden, the arcadians, contrast with the makers of the New Jerusalems, who are utopians who struggle to create a new society located in the future: "The psychological difference between the arcadian dreamer and the Utopian dreamer is that the backward-looking arcadian knows that his expulsion from Eden is an irrevocable fact and that his dream, therefore, is a wish dream which cannot become real." On the other hand, the utopian looks to the future and "necessarily believes that his New Jerusalem is a dream which ought to be realized so that the actions by which it could be realized are a necessary element in his dream." The Irish-American immigrant experience, facing the past and the future, encompasses both the reverie of the arcadian and the dream of the utopian, sometimes—though Auden held this to be in general highly unlikely—in the same individual.

Thomas Brown has observed in *Irish American Nationalism:* "Immigrant nationalism . . . had as one of its sources the all too human melancholia and sense of loss suffered by those who have irrevocably broken with the past that nurtured them. For most, it would probably pass, but for some the ache would remain permanent."[2] He quotes John White, an Englishman who visited the United States in 1870 and observed Irish Americans. "The anti-English immigrant agitator," wrote White, was not, as the British liked to think, a swindler and a demagogue, but "that much more unreasonable animal, a dreamer."[3]

The loss of Ireland is fundamental to the Irish-American experience; in its arcadian aspect it can form the basis for a memory of a distant world of the past—rural, simple, and innocent. Brown quotes an immigrant afflicted with this kind of nostalgia, typical of arcadians: "I would try to recall the smell of turf, and I would think of the streams in which I went fishing, and the place where I found a bird's nest." For this Irish-American outcast, St. Patrick's Day "was a kind of epiphany, in which much was revealed to him," according to Brown. The immigrant, Batt O'Connor, wrote of that day: "I walked in that procession and in the emotion I felt, walking as one of that vast crowd of Irish immigrants celebrating our national festival, I woke to the full consciousness of my love for my country."[4] (O'Connor later returned to Ireland and took part in the 1916 Rising. His book, *With Michael Collins in the Fight for Irish Independence,* was published in 1929.)

For Irish Americans, St. Patrick's Day remains such an occasion, and has much greater significance in America than it ever possessed in Ireland. Among Irish Americans, the sense of a shared experience—harking back to the expulsion from their Eden—binds them together and suffuses the celebration with tremendous feeling, as well as energy.

There is a nice coincidence about the date of the celebration, which has nothing to do with either Saint Patrick or Irish history. The Romans celebrated March 17 as the feast day of the god Liber Pater ("Freedom from the Father"). They celebrated the transition from boyhood to manhood. The boy, come of age, was given the white toga to wear as a sign of his emancipation from the hand of his father. It is certain that when the first St.

Patrick's Day parade took place in New York in 1762, the Irish soldiers serving in a British regiment who spontaneously decided to celebrate it had no idea of the symbolic significance implicit in the coincidence. For St. Patrick's Day has become the day when Irish Americans celebrate the freedom to be Irish. Such a celebration could only have taken place with its customary exuberance beyond the reach of the stern patriarchal rule of Great Britain. In nineteenth-century Ireland, when the parade was reaching its present proportions in America, no such celebration would have been possible. Only in America could the Irish celebrate the freedom to be Irish that in Ireland was denied to them at every level—political, social, cultural, and for a long time, religious.

Deep in the concrete glens of midtown Manhattan, the plangent swell of bagpipes, the roll of drums, and the harmonies of flutes and pipes that fill the streets running east and west of Fifth Avenue are not only the sounds of nostalgic men and women dreaming of the past. The exuberance, noticeable as the parade—the largest ethnic celebration in the United States—moves up Fifth Avenue, on a sixteen-file front, with some two hundred bands and perhaps one hundred thousand people involved in one way or another, is as much a mark of the Irish-American experience as is the arcadian nostalgia. It is an assertion of liberty won in America. It is an assertion also of a powerful conviction that Ireland's destiny would be determined as much by what happened in America as through the changing fortunes of the land the Irish were forced to flee. In that, Irish Americans are not mistaken. The last hundred and fifty years of Irish history cannot properly be understood without taking into account the role played in it by Irish Americans. And this remains as true of the troubled period since 1969 as it is of the nineteenth- or early twentieth-century upheavals in which Irish Americans played a vital, and sometimes crucial, role.

In the Janus-like nature of the Irish-American experience, facing the past and the future, containing elements of the arcadian and the utopian, there are inevitable tensions. The utopia for many is America—the society that gave them the freedom to assert their Irishness. It is a utopia they helped build. The nineteenth-century Irish immigrants arrived at a time of industrial expansion, supplying much of the cheap labor and the unskilled workforce needed for canal construction, in factories, and on the docksides of the East Coast's great ports. According to Lawrence McCaffrey,[5] 72 percent of that human wave settled in seven urbanized states: New York, New Jersey, Connecticut, Pennsylvania, Ohio, Illinois, and Massachusetts. This was one of the largest transitions from rural to urban life ever made by any ethnic group in America. (The post-World War II migration of blacks from the South to the Northeast was another such shift.) The ghettos formed in the big cities were the breeding ground of the Irish-American politician, a pragmatic, hard-fisted, often ruthless figure, the product of the poverty and discrimination he and his fellow Irish faced in the New World. His politics were neither of arcadia nor of utopia but of power and how to hold and wield it. His monument was Tammany Hall. (It should be remembered, however, that John Kennedy's utopian appeal also sprang ultimately from the politics of the ward and the Irish ghetto.)

It was inevitable, therefore, that in the complexities of the Irish-American experience there were tensions between the arcadian longings that were crucial to that experience and the realities of ghetto politics, as there were, in turn, between those realities and the aspirations of the utopians bent on the creation of a New Jerusalem in Ireland.

America "is a plural society determined to set aside the past, its ancient wounds, the dreary accumulation of crimes and corruption which constitutes the history of Europe," according to Denis Donoghue.[6] The exiles who fled famine or failed rebellion in mid-nineteenth-century Ireland could not forget the past or the wounds that the British had inflicted on their country and them. These were a constant ache, a gnawing at the heart of the Irish-American community, a reminder of the past, and a tenacious urging not to abandon the future.

Rebels can be either arcadians or utopians, reclaiming past innocence or proclaiming future goodness. The Young Irelanders were a group of bourgeois, university-educated intellectuals who propounded an almost Rousseauean, romantic view of Ireland and its past. To them the horrors of the famine that they saw around them were a product of the materialistic greed of English civilization. With almost equal horror they rejected "progress" if it meant the success of the industrial revolution: "To make our people politically free," their newspaper *The Nation* declared in 1848, "but bond slaves to some debasing social system like that which crowds the mines and factories of England with squalid victims, we would not strike a blow." They set out to save the remains of the "Celtic" rural world of Ireland as an alternative to the kind of economic and social domination England imposed on their country. Only since the late eighteenth century had the concept of the Celt become something to which romantic notions could be attached; arcadia is empty without its noble savage, and the wild Celt, noble, communal, heroic and poetic, was a powerfully appealing figure to set against the debased materialists of the spreading industrial revolution.

Though their attempted insurrection was a farce, the Young Irelanders' aspirations were sufficiently large and compelling to give a momentum to Irish nationalism that helped create the 1916 Easter Rising before it expended itself. The rebel John O'Mahony came to America after the Young Irelanders' defeat. A stay in Paris had helped acquaint him with continental revolutionary groups, but the concept of Ireland he had learned at home was what dominated his thinking and planning. When he formed a revolutionary organization in America, it was fitting that he should call it the Fenian Brotherhood. The Fenians were the legendary warriors of Gaelic mythology, companions of the hero Fionn Mac Cumhail. O'Mahony was "an Irish gentleman of the old school, of splendid physique, well educated, and an accomplished Gaelic scholar. [He was) descended from the chief of the O'Mahony Clan and recognized as their Chief by the stalwart, fighting peasantry of the mountainous region of the Cork-Tipperary border."[7] O'Mahony was untainted by any connection with Englishness, and the Fenian Brotherhood was his ideal of the national army which, from its base in America, would strike a blow for Ireland's freedom. O'Mahony was the "head center" of the Fenian organization in America, linked to its equivalent in Ireland, the Irish Republican Brotherhood (IRB), established in 1858 on St. Patrick's Day by O'Mahony's co-conspirator in the Young Ireland movement, James Stephens. It was the American impetus that prodded the Irish forward out of the despair caused by the Young Irelanders' defeat.

O'Mahony's broad brow, widely spaced eyes, straight nose, and

firm jaw were the very embodiment of the imagined Celtic nobility. So were his generosity, courage, and unwavering devotion to
the cause that he helped keep alive, through poverty and exile,
until his death in New York in 1877. Those who knew him well
said he was a dreamer—he "lacked some of the essential qualities
of leadership."[8] The dream of Celtic nobility took forms common
in the arcadian view of things. It was identified with otherworldli-
ness, free from crass concern with wealth and fame, more taken
with pondering the nature of eternity, ready to embrace death itself. In Auden's view, in the world of the arcadian death has a
place. "If a death occurs, it is not the cause for sorrow—the dead
are not missed—but a social occasion for a lovely funeral."[9]

The Irish and Irish-American arcadians used the deaths of
their leaders as occasions for a funeral that would remind their
followers of the eternal and vital nature of the ideal in which
those men believed. Such funerals were often historically important, calling on the Irish-American community of nationalists to
show the strength of their commitment to the Fenian goal. When
Terence Bellew MacManus, one of the leaders of the Young
Ireland insurrection, died in California in 1861, his funeral became a demonstration of Fenian power; more than twenty thousand mourners were there to hear the Fenian ideal proclaimed.
From the ashes of death rise the flames of rebellion. (It is significant that the phoenix became a potent symbol of Fenianism, and
remains so among the IRA to this day.)

O'Mahony's funeral was equally impressive as a statement of
undying political commitment. Twenty thousand men marched
behind his coffin in New York as his body was carried to the
steamer that would take it to Ireland and burial. When the most
tenacious Fenian of them all, O'Donovon Rossa, died in New
York, his funeral was one of the most dramatic occasions in Irish
history. O'Donovan Rossa had endured incredible hardship in
British prisons, often spending long periods manacled, naked,
and alone, for he would not wear prison clothes or accept his jail-
er's characterization of him as a criminal for conspiring against
Britain. A poet-scholar, Patrick Pearse, who was also an IRB con-
spirator, gave the graveside oration before a huge, hushed crowd
in Glasnevin Cemetery, Dublin, to which the body had been
brought from America.

We stand at Rossa's grave not in sadness but rather in exaltation of spirit that it has been given to us to come thus into so close a communion with that brave and splendid Gael. Splendid and holy causes are served by men who are themselves splendid and holy. . . . And all that splendor and pride and strength was compatible with a humility and a simplicity of devotion to Ireland, to all that was olden and beautiful and Gaelic in Ireland.[10]

The Fenians had tried to preserve "all that was olden and beautiful and Gaelic" in Ireland through rebellion in 1867. From America had come the rifle-bearing *Erin's Hope:* but it arrived just in time to see the last scattered sparks of that rebellion quenched. More was needed to make that dream a reality than dedication and love of the Celtic past. As he spoke, Pearse was doubtless full of anticipation for steps that he would soon embark on in conjunction with Irish-American sympathizers. "I hold it a Christian thing, as O'Donovan Rossa held it, to hate evil, to hate untruth, to hate oppression, and hating them, to strive to overthrow them." He asserted that the "seeds sown" by the Fenians "are coming to their miraculous ripening today. Rulers and Defenders of Realms had need to be wary if they would guard against such processes."[11]

In this speech, the exaltation of the past becomes a motivation for future action. Arcadian and utopian mingle. One year later, Pearse would assert in arms the spirit he had praised in words by O'Donovon Rossa's grave; the 1916 Easter Rising proved the last insurrection in a tradition that had begun with the hapless young intellectual arcadians of 1848 and motivated the Fenians in 1865, 1866, and 1867. In its crushing defeat, it eventually proved the most successful—a prelude to the struggle from which the modern states of Ireland emerged.

The arcadian dream was strong in a people like the Irish, sundered from the land, forced into the new, alien world of the urban ghetto of the American Northeast in the nineteenth century. In ancient Ireland, Celtic bards had sung of a mythical land to the west, beyond the ocean, where peace and happiness reigned, where the young did not die before the old. Instead, in the words of one historian, the immigrant Irish "had the dubious distinction of pioneering the American urban ghetto, previewing experiences that would later be shared by Italians, Jews, Poles and other Slavs from Eastern Europe, Blacks migrating North from the South, Chicanos and Puerto Ricans."[12] However harrowing the conditions that forced the immigrant to flee, the memory of what was once familiar has an irresistible appeal and can be transformed by the terrors and discomforts of the present into something comforting and desirable. For many, Ireland became the Happy Place, arcadian in its simplicity and warmth, a place of spontaneous friendliness, the "land of a thousand welcomes." Of course, these virtues were not totally imaginary: the Irish are sociable, gregarious, fond of talking and story-telling. But in the arcadian reverie it is only the virtues that survive, for the essence of arcadia is that it be simple, without bothersome contradictions.

Culturally, one can see this in a fairly crude form in movies like John Ford's ever popular *The Quiet Man,* and in the plethora of sentimental ballads played at Irish-American social occasions. Its political effects, though more complex (since other factors are also involved), have often been just as obvious in distinguishing the Irish-American view from the Irish-Irish, and have led in the last century and a half to continued misunderstandings between Irish-American activists and those in the front line in the struggle for Irish independence. Irish rebels not only had to contend with the Irish Americans' arcadian-inspired views, but also had to confront the impatient intolerance of complications, that often sprang from those attitudes. This made Irish Americans suspicious and sometimes hostile to anything that distracted the Irish struggle from the simpler goals of nationalism—which for most of the last hundred and fifty years has meant an obsession with driving out the British.

In the late nineteenth century a powerful movement for land reform grew up in Ireland; its goals were the ultimate abolition of landlordism and the possession of the land by the peasants who worked it. Its leader was Michael Davitt, one of the most influential and powerful figures in recent Irish history. He reserved as much scorn and hatred for Irish landlords as he did for the British, and once swore that "Irish landlords and English misgovernment in Ireland shall find in me a sleepless and incessant opponent."[13] At the time, most Irish Americans supported Charles Stewart Parnell, whose Home Rule party was carrying the banner of constitutional nationalism, with its strong emphasis on parliamentary action as the chief method of winning Irish autonomy. Many were dismayed that Davitt was turning attention away from that goal and toward Irish landlordism. When he came to America in 1882, many influential voices were heard against him, including the important newspaper the *Boston Pilot*. As Brown puts it: "The *Boston Pilot* expressed the American consensus on June 17 when it regretted that Davitt had turned from Irish nationalism to the pursuit of Utopia."[14]

Land nationalization, with its associations with radical European opinion, went beyond the view that all that Ireland needed to be happy was the removal of British rule and links with Britain. It could be seen as utopian because it implied that political change was not enough: social change was necessary to construct a good society. Arcadian-prone Americans have often come into conflict over this with the utopian edge of the Irish revolutionary movement, which has frequently gone beyond simple nationalism into the wilder reaches of socialist or even Marxist thought.

Davitt ran foul of objectors on several occasions on his 1882 trip, and he was forced to dilute his land-nationalization program. At one point, during a gathering in Chicago, Davitt exclaimed after being criticized by a prominent Irish American, "Long" John Finerty, that it was "very easy to establish an Irish nation 3,000 miles away from Ireland by patriotic speeches. I assure you that it is no easy task . . . to do so in dear old Ireland."[15] There was more than a hint of sarcasm in the words "dear old Ireland," a phrase that might fall very easily from the lips of transatlantic patriots in their more sentimental moments but that, as Davitt knew, did not address the complex social and economic realities of Irish life that he and his fellow revolutionaries had to confront daily.

His attacker, John Finerty, was one of those extraordinary individuals produced by nineteenth-century America who seemed to abound within the Fenian movement. Not only had he little time for Davitt's complex land schemes, but he regarded Parnell with small patience. His plan to free Ireland was simple: "If I had my way," he declared, "I would kill every Englishman that came to Ireland as tyrant or ruler."[16] In the 1860s, "Long John," as he was called, was conspiring with the IRB in the bleak Slievenamon

Mountains of Tipperary. The 1870s found him following in the wake of the U.S. cavalry as it moved through the wild hills of Montana; he met Sitting Bull, and in his description of the Sioux chief attributed to him more than an echo of the sort of nobility the Fenians saw in the wild Celts. In Chicago during the 1880s Finerty became an independent congressman, carrying the flag of pure Irish nationalism through the factious battlegrounds of American politics. At this time he founded a newspaper, *The Citizen,* from which he aimed broadsides at Britain and at any American who dared show a trace of the "Anglo-mania which runs high among the bastard British of the seaboard metropolis" of the East Coast.

One of Finerty's Fenian contemporaries, "Pagan" O'Leary, was an even more exuberant individualist. His arcadianism expressed itself in his belief that not only had the English to be driven out of Ireland but the Catholic church must be dismantled and the Irish return to Celtic paganism before they could rediscover their true greatness. According to Fenian leader John Devoy, so thoroughgoing were O'Leary's objections to Catholicism that he refused to be called by his first name, Patrick, because he considered that Ireland's patron saint had turned the noble, heroic, and fearless Irish into a people good for nothing except "thumping their craws and telling their beads." He "claimed that the Apostle of Ireland had demoralized the Irish by teaching them to forgive their enemies. Any man who did that was a poltroon."[17] Pagan O'Leary called himself a "Hereditary Rebel and Milesian Pagan" (in Celtic myth, the Milesians conquered Ireland and were regarded by the old Irish annalists as the first Gaelic settlers). Those who knew him say he believed in Tir-na-nOg, the Gaelic land of eternal youth, and insisted that it was there the true heroes were found, not in a Christian heaven. Tir-na-nOg was a vivid image of arcadia. Nothing but the old Gaelic sports were played; it abounded in fine horses and good hunting dogs, with the Irish heroes for one's companions. The Irish bards sang in the evening when the round of hunting was done, and the heroes enjoyed the company of only the most beautiful women. Life was effortless and contradiction-free, as arcadia must be.

Pagan O'Leary set off from America to join the Fenian uprising in Ireland. He cut an interesting figure: " 'The Pagan' had a number of queer photographs taken in New York before going over on his last trip to Ireland which illustrated the odd character of the man," writes Devoy. "He was dressed in a Garibaldian shirt, but gray, instead of red, and from his belt hung two revolvers and a bowie knife. One of his hands pointed to a black flag, hanging from a horizontal staff, with a skull and cross bones displayed on it, and over them the words, 'Independence or—?'" Devoy refers to him as a "fifth century" Irishman.[18] Yet, for all O'Leary's "Milesian" aspirations, Devoy gives him credit for the work he did in converting Irish-born British troops to Fenianism.

Auden describes arcadia as a "world of pure being and absolute uniqueness. . . . Everyone is incomparable." There can be no dichotomy between what you are and what you seem to be: appearance and reality are one. While few tried, as Pagan O'Leary did, to achieve this state in their everyday lives, it exercised an influence on the Irish-American view of the Irish situation. Ireland was a land of unique characters, where everyone was as Irish as he appeared to be. The arcadian view has very little time for serious consideration of the social structure: "Whatever the social pattern," writes Auden, "each member of society is satisfied according to his conception of his needs."

In the arcadian reveries, social relationships are maintained without any degree of coercion. Though the Celtic arcadia was aristocratic and therefore hierarchical, force played no role in the relationship between the warrior chiefs and their followers. When force was used in Pagan O'Leary's Gaelic dream world, it was directed only against the enemy—the English—when the Gaelic lords went off on a plundering raid to Britain. As has been noted, Michael Davitt's emphasis on Irish landlords and their abusive system complicated that picture. It was not that Irish Americans were unsympathetic to the struggle of peasant against landlord—of course they were not, and their donations helped maintain Davitt's Land League, which was organizing that struggle. But there was a deeper anxiety at work. All arcadias come with their serpents. After all, arcadia is a world lost, from which its former inhabitants have been expelled. To Irish Americans, it was obvious that the serpent that had expelled them from Ireland was British imperialism. Anything that distracted attention from that was regarded with anxiety and suspicion.

The serpent had to be expelled before peace and happiness could return. The problem was that anyone who, like Davitt, focused attention on actual social relationships within Ireland seemed to suggest that the serpent's expulsion would not automatically bring about a return to the dreamed-of world where the Irish, by being allowed to be themselves, would be happy. The Irish landlord's Irishness does not prevent him from making Irish peasants miserable. An arcadian cannot tolerate such contradictions, for they remind him of the impossibility that his dream has—or ever could have—any basis in fact.

Davitt's view was, if anything, utopian. For him, the withdrawal of Britain was the basis from which the construction of Ireland could begin. It did not in itself bring automatic happiness. Later Irish revolutionary leaders who turned to Irish Americans for support in the twentieth century confronted the same problems that Davitt had in 1882. Few of these revolutionaries were arcadians. They knew that independence would bring with it more complications and problems; and from Eamon De Valera, who came to the U.S. in 1919, to Bernadette Devlin, who toured the country fifty years later, they tried to convince Irish-American nationalists that the arcadia of "dear old Ireland" was blighted by more than just the presence of the serpent England.*

The events of this century in Ireland would seem to have compromised the loftiest arcadian view espoused in America. The last Fenian rebellion, the 1916 Rising, was in the old heroic mold: a handful of visionary leaders, among them poets and scholars, taking their stand, outnumbered and outgunned against the might of imperial Britain. Martyrdom followed, and Pearse and the other leaders could join previous generations of Irish heroes in Pagan O'Leary's Tir-na-nOg. But what came after 1916 was of a different character, involving some unfamiliar forces and methods more difficult to integrate into any arcadia.

The defeat of 1916 gave rise to the Irish Republican Army (IRA) and the separatist party Sinn Fein as the chief proponents

---

*However, in stark contrast to his earlier Machiavellian politics, in his old age De Valera enunciated a view of Ireland as simple, rural, and pure as any arcadian could wish for. But it sprang from an old man's nostalgia for the past and his fears of the uncertainty of the future.

of republicanism. The IRA learned from the mistakes of the Fenians before them. Instead of taking a stand, in the hope that help from America would arrive in time to relieve them and join in the final defeat of British forces, the IRA conducted a guerrilla war. It was the war of the weak against the strong. In this war, the weak would choose when, where, and how to fight. It was waged from behind stone walls by mobile columns that would vanish after the attack in the bleak Irish countryside, before the British could concentrate against them. It was often waged by the lone gunman knocking on the door, a pistol under his coat, ready to shoot dead the off-duty policeman or soldier who answered it. It was waged by the bomber throwing his bomb into a truckload of troops as it went down a crowded street. And, unlike the previous Fenian insurrections, it was fought entirely under the control of forces and leaders in Ireland itself. Irish-American contributions, while important, were limited to supplying money and weapons. Irish Americans had no guiding role in the war.

The outcome was a treaty signed with Britain that led to the partition of Ireland into two states. The British retained sovereignty over one of them, Northern Ireland, where the pro-British Protestant population was in a majority. The remaining twenty-six counties were plunged into a civil war between those who accepted partition and those who opposed it. A weary Irish people welcomed the war's end in 1923, when the antitreaty IRA forces called a ceasefire, accepting defeat. Most Irish Americans, appalled and sickened by the viciousness of the civil war, welcomed it, too. The old Fenian leader John Devoy supported the new "Free State," with its autonomous Dublin parliament. It was a far cry from the ideal of the republic as expounded in Fenian propaganda. But it offered a measure of independence, and it had the support of the majority of Irish people. However, a minority of Irish Americans who still clung to that ideal rejected the new arrangements vociferously. They were soon joined by former IRA men fleeing Ireland in the wake of the civil war. Throughout the 1920s and 1930s they came to America, eager to continue the previous generations' fight for an all-Ireland state. But the Ireland left behind was becoming less amenable to the old arcadian reveries that had sweetened their predecessors' recollections of the land they had lost.

Those Irish Americans still active on the Irish question had to confront two major problems. First, there now existed in Dublin a democratically elected Irish government, which, though it might propagandize against partition, was not prepared either to take up arms to end it or to tolerate such action by the IRA. Second, the new state of Northern Ireland contained a Protestant population extremely hostile to the goals and ideals of traditional Irish republicanism. Within the six northeastern counties they formed a majority, and they clearly intended to maintain it by every means at their command. This Ireland, fragmented and embittered, left little room for arcadia to flourish.

In America, Irish-American organizations went into a sharp decline, and relatively few activists remained. Those who did remain betrayed a gradual loss of contact with the realities of the situation in Ireland. Dominant among these was an exiled Ulsterman, Joe McGarrity. McGarrity had left his native County Tyrone at the turn of the century and eventually found his way to Philadelphia. There he became a successful businessman. He joined the Clann na Gael, formed after the Fenian defeats of 1867. Its aims were similar to those of the Fenians, but its methods were intended to be more effective.

McGarrity became prominent in the Clann and met with Irish revolutionaries, including Pearse, when he was in America In 1914, and Eamon De Valera, who came to raise support and money for the struggling republican movement in 1919. Those who knew McGarrity describe him as a man of commanding presence who tended to dominate any company in which he found himself. He raised millions of dollars for the republicans, and also acquired a huge shipment of Thompson submachine guns for the IRA. He grew close to De Valera, and when the civil war broke out supported the antitreaty forces. But McGarrity was bewildered by De Valera's twists and turns through different stages of his political development. From being an enemy of the treaty, De Valera eventually accommodated himself to it. He abandoned Sinn Fein and formed a new party, Fianna Fail (Gaelic for "men of destiny"). These "men of destiny" proved to be in a different, more pragmatic mold than the resonance of their name might suggest. In 1932, De Valera led his party to electoral triumph and formed the government of a state he had previously condemned as a betrayal of republican principles.

McGarrity was bitter but stoical. "Our policy has not changed and will not change until the consummation of our hopes, 'Ireland as a Republic,'" he said. He persisted, even though he witnessed the further loss of many of his supporters who threw their weight and resources behind the new Fianna Fail party. As the base for support of militant republicanism shrank in America, McGarrity's ambitions became more inflated and unrealistic. In 1936 he struck up a friendship with Sean Russell, a leading figure in what remained of the IRA. Though intellectually limited, Russell was absolutely committed to the goal of an Irish republic incorporating all thirty-two counties. He was also convinced that the only way to reach that goal was through physical force. The IRA was in the midst of an ideological crisis, with socialist elements pushing it leftward. McGarrity, like Russell, disapproved strongly of these tendencies. With the faith of a fanatic he believed that the IRA had to keep its attention fixed on ending partition and driving the British out of that corner of the country over which they still held sway, Northern Ireland. Like many Irish Americans before—and many since— for him the only serpent in the garden was England. As for the other complications, the Dublin government and the Northern Ireland Protestants, they did not much concern him. When asked about De Valera's opposition to the IRA's planned campaign against England and the North, he replied: "We shall simply ignore him. . . . We are after the real enemy and the only enemy, and that enemy is England. The fighting therefore will be in the occupied six counties of Northern Ireland and England."[19] McGarrity and Russell were preparing to launch a bombing campaign in English cities in coordination with an expected uprising by IRA units in Northern Ireland, where McGarrity believed there were fifteen hundred volunteers ready to strike. This, like many other of his grandiose ambitions, proved to be a huge miscalculation.

At the beginning of 1939 the IRA sent a declaration of war to the British government. Because the IRA believed itself to be the direct inheritor of the first government of the Republic of Ireland— that constituted and declared by the 1916 rebel leadership—the warning was issued in the name of the government of Ireland. The declaration read: "I have the honour to inform you that the Government of the Irish Republic, having as its first duty towards the people the establishment and maintenance of peace and order, herewith demand the withdrawal of all British armed forces stationed in Ireland." If not, Russell said, the IRA would be "compelled to intervene actively in the military and commercial life" of England. The grandiose diplomatic language offered a startling contrast to the actual means at the IRA's disposal. But the stilted manner of address impressed McGarrity. Something of the unreality that pervaded his view (and Russell's) may be gleaned from McGarrity's correspondence with the IRA leader—whom he now addressed as "Chief"—congratulating him on the wording of the war declaration. McGarrity said it was "forceful and dignified" and "placed your diplomatic correspondence on a high plane."[20] McGarrity himself sent a warning to the British when they showed no signs of responding to the IRA's. He called on the memory of the "blood of the immortal seven"—the executed leaders of 1916—and that of the "unconquered dead" who, along with those still faithful to the republican ideal, will help lead Ireland to that destiny. "We call upon the people of Ireland," he wrote, "at home and in exile, to assist us in the effort we are about to make in God's name, to complete that evacuation" (of the British forces from Northern Ireland) and to "enthrone the Republic."[21]

The quasireligious sentiments of these words could not disguise the cruel incompetence of what followed as bombs started going off in English cities. Innocent civilians were killed—five by one bomb in Coventry—and many were injured. The bombings lasted fourteen months, and led to the arrests of seventy-seven IRA men, two of whom were hanged. McGarrity's distance from Irish and British realities led him to believe he was witnessing the beginning of another 1916 rising. In reality, it was the collapse of the IRA and the end of Irish-American involvement in its struggle for years to come. De Valera outlawed the organization, interning most of its remaining leadership. The Northern Ireland government rounded up many others—though there the IRA had not been nearly so strong as McGarrity had assumed. By now Britain was engulfed in a world war that quickly obliterated memories of the IRA's campaign with far greater horrors of its own.

Before long, the United States would join England to fight the Nazis, further cementing the special relationship that continued to frustrate Irish-American efforts to gain their government's sympathy for their cause. By then, McGarrity was dead. His domination of Irish-American nationalism had represented a narrowing of the movement, both in support and in intellectual outlook. Compared with the flamboyant individualists of the Fenian days, McGarrity appears rather provincial in his dogmatism and unimaginative in his politics. His lack of realism was of an infinitely duller sort than that which occasionally afflicted the nineteenth-century arcadians of the Fenian movement. According to Cronin, "When he died at the age of sixty-six there was no one in America or Ireland to take his place."[22] And Irish-American nationalism entered a period of almost complete inactivity, which lasted, except for two brief interruptions, for nearly thirty years.

The first interruption came with the outbreak of war between Great Britain and Nazi Germany. A short time before, Britain had surrendered the ports it still possessed on the Irish coast. When war came, Ireland under the government of De Valera declared itself neutral. The British prime minister, Winston Churchill, believed that Britain was doubly vulnerable from the loss of the ports and the neutrality of her neighbor. Contacts between the two governments tried to resolve the issue. Churchill was prepared to consider a plan whereby Britain would convince the Northern Ireland Unionists to join a united Ireland in return for the ending of Irish neutrality. He also considered repossessing the ports by force. When rumors reached America that Churchill was considering a new invasion of Ireland, the American Friends of Irish Neutrality came into being. They held rallies and pressured their congressmen to let President Roosevelt know that Irish Americans were concerned over British intentions. America had not yet entered the war, and Churchill was anxious not to do anything that might prolong American neutrality or make it more difficult for Roosevelt to aid the British. A British attack on Ireland would certainly have made it more difficult for the United States to come in on Britain's side as the defender of small nations against Nazi aggression. At the time, the majority of Irish Americans supported Irish neutrality. Apart from everything else, the previous decade of war had left the country exhausted and ill prepared for another conflict—particularly on the scale of World War II. Undoubtedly, Irish-American opinion, through groups like the Friends of Irish Neutrality, played a part in Roosevelt's cautioning of Churchill over his actions in regard to Ireland. In the end, the British prime minister could neither force the Irish to surrender the ports nor convince the Northern Ireland Unionists to make a deal with Dublin to end its neutrality in return for unity.

The campaign of the American Friends of Irish Neutrality went into eclipse when the U.S. entered the war in 1941. As had happened in 1917, when America joined forces with Britain what little Irish-American activity there was came to a halt. Irish Americans' commitment to the U.S. in its fight with Germany and Japan dwarfed any lingering concern for Irish neutrality. A few former members of the IRA returned their draft notices with statements to the effect that as long as the U.S. stood side by side with the British empire, they would refuse to fight. They were subjected to FBI scrutiny but were never prosecuted.[23] America's entry into the war also brought an end to the arms routes McGarrity had built up to supply the IRA, which continued a sputtering existence throughout the 1940s.

Ireland's neutrality throughout the war caused some resentment in the United States, and perhaps contributed in a small way to reinforcing the "special relationship" with Britain. Certainly the U.S. ambassador to Ireland in the 1940s thought so. He later published a pamphlet defending partition and praising Northern Ireland as a valuable contributor to the war effort.[24] Ireland's prime minister, Eamon De Valera, was aware that some public-relations work needed to be done. After the war he launched a vigorous crusade against partition and in 1949 visited the U.S. to rouse Irish-American support. However, he found a different community from the one that had greeted him thirty years before.

Irish-American nationalism was dormant, and remained so into the 1950s except for a second brief interruption, stirred up by renewed IRA activity against Northern Ireland. But the glorious days of Irish-American involvement seemed to have passed forever. Compared with the efforts of the nineteenth century and early 1920s, the activities of the fifties were small indeed. This was partly due to changes in Ireland: partition was not the burning issue among Irish Americans that Britain's dominion of all Ireland had been. But there were changes within Irish America that tended to weaken consciousness of Ireland's troubles. Throughout the 1940s, and accelerating through the 1950s, Irish Americans had been moving into the middle classes. The old Irish inner-city neighborhoods were being abandoned for the suburbs. Prosperity brought with it political changes, too, and a diminution of cultural activity. The new, more conservative, stable, middle-class Irish-American community was in considerable contrast to that which had nourished the John O'Mahonys, the Pagan O'Learys, the John Finertys, and the John Devoys. The Irish America of the nineteenth century had been a center of political, social, and economic turmoil, with papers like Pat Ford's *Irish World* risking church denunciation in defense of radical programs. In the Irish America of the 1950s, what few newspapers survived (Pat Ford's was one of them, but with a drastically reduced circulation) contented themselves with reporting the routine activities of benevolent organizations such as the Emerald Society and the various Irish county associations. Interest in Ireland for the most part was limited to Irish sports in the Gaelic Athletic Association (GAA), attending the various functions run by the Irish county associations, and marching in the Ancient Order of Hibernians St. Patrick's Day parade. Assimilation was bringing with it the dead hand of conformity; respectability, with its soporific comforts, dulled the old pangs of exile.

Able leaders, such as Paul O'Dwyer, a young Mayo-born lawyer who had emigrated in 1925 and was one of the organizers of American friends of Irish Neutrality, turned elsewhere to pursue the cause of justice. O'Dwyer campaigned on behalf of an independent Jewish state in 1947, and the 1950s found him embroiled in civil-rights agitation in the South. He found little support within his own community when he ran for Congress in the Washington Heights-Inwood section of Manhattan. His campaign was hounded by Irish-American Catholics who denounced him as a "communist" because he had the endorsement of the U.S. Labor party.[25] At one time he was so unpopular among Irish Americans that he remembers two nuns crossing to the far side of the street to avoid meeting him on the sidewalk.

A certain kind of conservatism had always been a feature of

Irish-American life from the beginning. Some trace it to the Jansenistic Irish Catholic tradition. But previously it had been moderated by the political vitality and variety engendered through the support for Irish nationalism. One historian has estimated that between 1848 and 1900, Irish Americans contributed $260 million to Ireland.[26] Another has written: "From the time of the Great Famine in the mid-1840s until the conclusion of the Anglo-Irish War (1921), Irish American fanaticism and money sustained Irish Nationalism."[27] This fanaticism moved Michael Davitt to refer to the Irish American community as "the avenging wolfhound of Irish nationalism."[28] By the middle years of this century no Irish wolfhound's bark could be heard from the suburbs of middle-class America to disturb the British and their dependent Northern Ireland state.

However, the exiles from the struggles of the 1920s and 1930s had dug themselves into the Irish-American community. Though a small group, they proved to be an important one. Men like Michael Flannery, who came to America in the 1920s, and George Harrison, who settled in New York in the late 1930s, did not let the indifference Irish Americans felt for the nationalist cause deter them from their commitment to seeing it triumph one day. They and others remained active at different levels within that community.

They could not have guessed that the coming years would bring another upheaval and the worst violence that Ireland has seen this century. Their arcadian dreams and utopian hopes for a unified Irish nation would be put to the test in the frightening reality of the current Northern Ireland crisis.

2
NORAID AND THE
NORTHERN CRISIS

A cycle was completed when, in 1967, a group of Northern Irishmen formed the Civil Rights Association to protest anti-Catholic discrimination in the Unionist-controlled Northern Ireland state. The cycle had begun well over a century before, when Daniel O'Connell set out to force the British government to repeal anti-Catholic legislation by marshaling huge crowds to take part in passive protests. O'Connell knew and corresponded with Frederick O. Douglass, the black American who worked for the overthrow of slavery. The Irish leader rejected donations to his cause from Irish Americans who were slave-owners, holding that Irish Americans should join the antislavery crusade, which he saw as morally equivalent to his own. But beyond Douglass's admiration for his stand, O'Connell's example of passive resistance was an influential one that by way of Gandhi blacks later followed in their campaign for civil rights. By 1967, young, university-educated Catholics in Northern Ireland, with some liberal Protestants, decided in their turn to follow the recent example of black Americans. Transmuted through black-American experience, O'Connell's tactics returned to Ireland. Demonstrations, sit-ins, and a series of marches were held, all with the aim of calling attention to the anti-Catholic discrimination that made it difficult for Catholics to get jobs and housing on an equal footing with Protestants.

At first these protests were on a much smaller scale than O'Connell's. In America they attracted only a little attention. It was a form of resistance alien to Irish-republican tradition, and so for Irish-American nationalists it was no more than a curiosity. Indeed, for most Irish Americans, the rhetoric of its leading speaker, Bernadette Devlin, was alien in its revolutionary socialist tendency. But on October 5, 1968, Irish Americans sat up and took notice as a civil-rights march in Derry, Northern Ireland's second largest city, was batoned into the ground by policemen of the Royal Ulster Constabulary (RUC).

If the Northern Ireland Civil Rights Association, as it became known, proved unfamiliar to Irish-American nationalists, the tactics of the Northern Ireland police were not. It was merely an example of the British brutality they had denounced for years. The fact that Northern Ireland policemen were wielding the baton did not matter—they were in the service of British imperialism. Friends of the Northern Ireland Civil Rights Association sprang up in New York and other cities. These small groups attracted liberals and left-wingers who were not normally associated with Irish nationalism in America. Paul O'Dwyer, by now a prominent civil-rights activist and popular among more radical Democrats, collected a petition that called on the United Nations Human Rights Commission to investigate possible human-rights abuses in Northern Ireland and to impose sanctions if they were verified.

On the other side of the political spectrum, James Heaney, a Buffalo lawyer, established the American Congress for Irish Freedom. Rallies were held and press statements issued attacking injustice in Northern Ireland. Heaney filed suits before the European Court of Human Rights in Strasbourg, arguing that in upholding discriminatory practices in Northern Ireland, Britain was in violation of the Human Rights Convention of which it was a signatory.

These groups were full of political tensions, however. Heaney's organization was pulled asunder by left-right splits. Among those who joined the American Congress for Irish Freedom was an exile from the Irish struggles of the 1920s, Michael Flannery. Born in 1902, Flannery was already a veteran of Ireland's wars and their connections with America. By 1968, he was one of the most highly respected members of the Irish-American community.

The only hint of vanity about Flannery was the rather incongruous slick of sandy hair that curled above his forehead. He was set very much in the mold of a Catholic stoic. He neither drank nor smoked, and he attended mass every morning at eight in his local church in Jackson Heights, Queens. A former life-insurance salesman, Flannery went about his business in a quiet and undemonstrative way. When ideological troubles shook Heaney's organization, Flannery left to form his own, the Irish Action Committee. Like many similar Irish-American organizations preceding it, this committee set out to raise support for the increasingly embattled Irish nationalists.

By 1969 the civil-rights movement had met with such strident and violent opposition from angry loyalists that rioting became frequent. In August of that year, Britain was forced to send in troops to stabilize the situation. For Irish Americans like Flannery, things were beginning to look a lot more familiar. Soon the civil-rights movement was to be eclipsed by more traditional forms of resistance to British rule.

So far the IRA, the main vehicle for that resistance, had not taken much part in events. The organization's leadership in Dublin was divided as to how to respond to them. Some argued that the time had come to take up arms. Others said no—a political course should be pursued. In late 1969 the IRA split into "Official" and "Provisional" wings; Sinn Fein followed suit. The "Provisional" IRA pressed for an active campaign in the North, and soon became the main guerrilla organization fighting the British. (Hereafter it will be referred to simply as the IRA.) The "Official" IRA eventually faded away, as politics gradually absorbed the attention of its leadership and further splits reduced its size. But in late 1969 both factions wanted to win support in America. It was the leaders of the Provisional wing which made the greatest inroads, however, and utilized the potential energy beginning to emerge among Irish Americans anxious and angry at the course of events.

In late 1969 and early 1970 two leading IRA men came to America. They had two aims: to meet with influential Irish Americans who were sympathetic to the cause and who would help raise money for it; and to reactivate the arms network that had atrophied since the 1950s. Daithi O'Conaill and Joe Cahill were veterans of the IRA's struggle. Cahill, a Belfast man, was the older, with an IRA record going back to the late 1930s. Balding and rather bulbous-nosed, he was frequently seen wearing a cloth cap, part of the traditional uniform of the Belfast workingman. Cahill proved to be a survivor. In 1942, along with five other IRA men, he was sentenced to be hanged for the killing of a Northern Ireland policeman in Belfast. His sentence and four others were commuted; only one man was hanged. When the IRA split in late 1969, there was no question as to which side Cahill would take. He went with the militant wing and was soon a commander of their Belfast brigade. He has remained a prominent figure in the movement for the last seventeen years.

Daithi O'Conaill arrived in New York shortly afterward. His history of IRA involvement went back to 1955, when, at the age of fifteen, he first joined the republican movement. He volunteered to be with the first units to attack Northern Ireland when the border campaign began in late 1956, and his subsequent career made him a legend within the IRA. He took part in an attack on an RUC barracks in County Fermanagh during which two of his comrades, Sean South and Fergal O'Hanlon, were killed. They were idealistic young Irishmen, and their deaths roused much sympathy for the IRA. (The crowds at their funerals would not be equaled until the deaths of the hunger strikers in 1981.) The Irish police arrested O'Conaill after the attack. He was released, then interned again without trial. But he escaped in October 1958 and immediately went back to the border. A year later he was badly wounded in a gun battle with the RUC. Captured, he was put on trial in Belfast, where he conducted his own cross-examination of the police witnesses. At the age of nineteen he was sentenced to six years in Crumlin Road Prison, Belfast. As with Cahill, there was no doubt about which course O'Conaill would take when the choice had to be made between preparing for an active military campaign or following the political road.

The aims of building a support network and reactivating the arms supply were kept separate. They had to be—fund-raising is a public activity, for it needs to appeal to as broad a base of support as possible. The IRA men had in mind an organization rather like the Friends of Irish Freedom, which had collected money and gathered support for the IRA during its war against the British from 1919 to 1921. When O'Conaill came to New York in the spring of 1970 he wanted to meet Irish Americans who would be able to help build such an organization. One of the first he spoke with was Michael Flannery.

The Irish Action Committee already existed and could form the basis of the kind of organization O'Conaill had in mind. Flannery and other Irish Americans close to him did not need to be convinced that as the situation deteriorated in Northern Ireland (O'Conaill predicted there would soon be an all-out guerrilla war), money would be needed to help Catholics. More specifically, O'Conaill foresaw that as the IRA grew and became more active, it would lose more of its volunteers to jails. Since traditionally the IRA has supported the families of jailed IRA men, this would put a great financial strain on the organization. Irish-American money would help alleviate that strain. As they discussed the nature of the proposed organization, it was decided that the name Irish Action Committee would have to be changed. Flannery was anxious that there be no connotations of violence associated with it—that is, it should be recognized as a benevolent organization. They considered calling it "The Dependents Fund," but this was rejected as too vague. Finally they chose The Irish Northern Aid Committee (INAC)—or NORAID, as it has become popularly known.

The founding members were Flannery and two other old IRA men of Flannery's generation, Jack McGowan and Jack McCarthy. McGowan had fought in the IRA's Clare Brigade fifty years before. McCarthy had been a member of the Cork Brigade. Like Flannery, they had come to America in the 1920s after the republican cause suffered defeat in the civil war. And also like Flannery, both men were active in the Irish-American community, with wide contacts in its various organizations and in the labor movement.

Originally, NORAID was linked with an organization called the Northern Aid Committee, based in Belfast. This in turn had been set up by the republicans in the wake of the riots in 1969. Joe Cahill and another leading IRA man, Sean Keenan from Derry, were its sponsors. It was supposed to handle the money sent from NORAID. After a few years, the Belfast Northern Aid Committee was replaced by the Green Cross, which was part of An Cumann Carbhrach, the organization for dependents of IRA prisoners.

NORAID always maintained that its relationship was with these organizations and not directly with the IRA. NORAID's purpose, insisted Flannery, "was to help and clothe the people of the North." But he said that "we have no stipulations as to how the money we send is to be spent." At the same time, he denied that the money went to buy weapons for the IRA. "I am heart and soul behind the IRA," he asserted easily. "We should be shouting IRA from every housetop. It was the only way peace will come to Ireland." But he was quick to add, "At no time in the present have I had any connection with the IRA." He admitted he met with O'Conaill and others, but only as representatives of Sinn Fein, the political wing of the IRA, of which O'Conaill was a vice president.

The U.S. authorities took a different view. They maintained, along with the British and Irish governments, that NORAID was really an IRA front, and that its money went into the pockets of gun dealers and gunrunners. In the early days particularly, money raised by NORAID was difficult, if not impossible, to keep track of, and an unknown amount of it may well have gone to illicit purposes. And undoubtedly IRA leaders like O'Conaill were influential in the formation of the organization. Equally certain is that individual members of NORAID were proved to be involved in gunrunning. Yet, notwithstanding all this, an examination of subsequent events shows that the relationship between NORAID and the IRA was more indirect than the authorities liked to believe.

When O'Conaill and Cahill arrived in America, their visits were monitored. The FBI noted that O'Conaill had come as a representative of the "Provisional IRA" and a "member of the army council," the organization's ruling body. Its source claimed that O'Conaill had become ill as a result of the strain of the U.S. tour he undertook, going from city to city looking for support. The FBI also noted the arrival in April 1970 of Sean Keenan, an IRA veteran and republican organizer from Derry. An FBI memo said that Keenan had come to the U.S. to "consolidate efforts for the INAC."[1] Later that year Cahill returned, and from mid-November to December 6 he visited Chicago, San Francisco, Cleveland, Boston, Yonkers, and Philadelphia. The FBI source named Cahill as a "sponsor" of the Northern Aid Committee in Belfast. On July 10, 1970, when NORAID held one of its first demonstrations, near the United Nations building in New York, the FBI was there to watch.

The FBI sent a special agent to the Bronx to check out NO-RAID headquarters. On August 4 the agent observed the committee's office: "a small store, located in a one-story building in a row of attached stores wedged between apartment houses of several stories in height." He went into the office and noted copies of *An Phoblacht*, the IRA newspaper; handbills; demonstration information; and "other forms of literature having to do with the situation in Ireland." At this time, the authorities' investigation of the Flannery committee was low key. Seven months after the FBI special agent visited INAC headquarters, an FBI memo said that it would continue to "follow activities of INAC on a regular basis, through its normal coverage from an intelligence standpoint. . . . However, in view of what appears to be the responsible and conservative nature of the leadership of this Committee, and the absence of any evidence that the group is involved in subversive activities or activities inimical to the best interests of the national security of the United States, this case will be maintained in a pending inactive status at NYO [New York office]."

The FBI also noted that the INAC had registered under the Foreign Agents Registration Act (FARA) on January 14, 1971, less than a year after its formation. Since 1938, FARA has been used to compel any person or organization deemed to be acting as an agent for a "foreign principal" to register as such with the attorney general. The name of the foreign principal has to be disclosed, as do other details about the relationship to that principal and the nature of the activities undertaken on its behalf. These must be furnished on registration, and every six months following. If money is collected for the foreign principal, the amount raised must be filed, as well as details of how it was collected. All disbursements in connection with the foreign principal must also be disclosed. FARA's statutes demand that any written material of a political nature produced by the agent must be designated as "foreign political propaganda." Registration allows the authorities to mount unannounced searches, without warrants, of the agent's financial records and correspondence. FARA's operations have provoked controversy, because its requirements would be in conflict with First Amendment rights if they were enforced against Americans engaged in political advocacy of causes of their own choosing. Such a controversy soon gathered around application of FARA to NORAID and the pro-IRA newspaper that supported it, *The Irish People.*

When NORAID registered with FARA initially it named the Northern Aid Committee, Belfast, as its principal. But as NORAID's activities in the U.S. increased throughout the early 1970s, the Justice and State departments adopted a more stringent attitude toward it, and stepped up their investigation of the Committee in order to demonstrate that it was in fact acting under the control of the IRA.

According to Flannery, NORAID "spread like wildfire" in the first years of its existence. However, its initial effort to get money across to Ireland was marred by failure. The first check, for $2,500, was sent through a New York bank. It never arrived. (NORAID claims the bank destroyed it because it was told the money was for "subversive" purposes.) The Committee collected clothes as well as money. The Irish airline, Aer Lingus, transported the clothes. "They took tons of clothes for us," according to Flannery. "Hundreds of blankets, baby clothing direct from the manufacturers." But he explained that the Aer Lingus clothes shipments stopped after some of the garments were damaged because the airline had the cargo fumigated.

Some sixteen months after its formation, NORAID claimed chapters in Manhattan, Queens, Staten Island, the Bronx, Long Island, Connecticut, New Jersey, Washington, D.C., Baltimore, Philadelphia, Boston, Buffalo, Chicago, St. Louis, and Detroit. There were soon some seventy branches throughout the U.S. The greatest support was concentrated in the New York area, where the Committee claimed two thousand members. It received steady support from the older, more established Irish-American organizations, such as the Ancient Order of Hibernians (AOH), which runs the St. Patrick's Day parade. NORAID's image was as yet that of an untainted benevolent body, one that even offered money to Northern Ireland's Protestants. But the latter, according to Flannery, "said they would look after their own." *The Irish People* appeared weekly, carrying news of the INAC's activities and stories about the war in Northern Ireland. The paper was outspokenly pro-IRA, and for a time shared offices with NORAID. It took material from Irish-republican newspapers like *An Phoblacht,* giving the IRA's version of events. (The establishment press at the time relied almost entirely on British government sources.) Many of the paper's editorial staff were also members of the INAC.

At this time, contacts with IRA activists and political spokesmen were frequent as men like O'Conaill, Cahill, and the president of Sinn Fein, Ruiari O'Bradaigh, came into the country on NORAID-sponsored tours. They met with prominent American politicians. An American bishop, Thomas Drury, attended a meeting given by O'Bradaigh.

Undoubtedly, British policy and conduct in Northern Ireland were responsible for the rapid growth of NORAID during this period. From 1970 through 1972 the British army went on a full-scale offensive against the nationalist ghettos. Among some of the events that generated sympathy in America were the illegal curfew imposed on the Catholic Falls Road area in July 1970, during which four civilians were killed and many more injured by army gunfire; the introduction of internment in August 1971; and the Bloody Sunday killings of January 30, 1972, when soldiers of a parachute regiment gunned down thirteen unarmed demonstrators in Derry city. There was also news of the constant conflict between the IRA and the army, in which many civilians were killed—often by troops and often in disputed circumstances.

During this time, NORAID was filing six-monthly returns with the Justice Department in Washington, giving details of its fundraising activities. The figures provide a good barometer of Irish-American reaction to British tactics. From August 1971 to the end of January 1972, the INAC reported collecting $128,099. In the next six-month period, ending in July 1972, and encompassing the Bloody Sunday killings, collections of $313,000 were recorded. The next six months showed a considerable drop, with a reported collection of $150,000; the period coincided with the height of the IRA's car-bombing campaign, which resulted in heavy civilian casualties, and may have cost the IRA support in America reflected in NORAID's returns. (American historian Dennis Clark believes this. In *Irish Blood* he attributes the IRA's failure to win widespread support among Irish Americans to their bombing campaign against what the guerrillas called "economic targets.") The committee's returns for the following six months—

January 29, 1973, to July 29, 1973—show another decline, with only $123,000 reported, and the figures for 1974 show that NORAID collected $211,000 for the entire year, much less than fundraising for only the first six months of 1972. Throughout the rest of the decade the returns filed showed a steady decline. However, the accuracy of these figures remains a matter of dispute.

Initially, the INAC sent the money to Ireland in cash amounts ranging from $1,500 to $11,000. For instance, in the six-month period after Bloody Sunday, NORAID registered thirty disbursements, twenty-five of them marked as having been hand-delivered in cash to Joe Cahill. The Justice Department maintained that such cash payments were only those that NORAID chose to register, and that many more were made that the committee simply did not report. Flannery admitted that his committee preferred to send money in cash with people they trusted. "With cash," he said, "the government didn't know how much we sent." Also according to Flannery, the committee asked people going to Ireland if they would be prepared to "take a message" for them. In one instance in 1985 a prominent member of the committee on an Irish trip handed over checks worth $40,000 to the dependents' fund.

In the early days most of the money was collected in bars in the big cities. Sometimes more ambitious schemes were employed. A prominent Irish-born bar and restaurant owner in Manhattan organized a fund-raising concert for NORAID at Carnegie Hall in 1972 that realized $21,500. On another occasion, NORAID raffled off a car and raised $13,000. Beginning in January 1973, the committee held annual fund-raising dinners at the Astoria Manor Ballroom in Queens. Other "testimonial" dinners were held by different units in Boston and Philadelphia, but the New York event was the biggest. Prominent politicians like Congressman Mario Biaggi of the Bronx were frequent guests at the New York affair. Ticket prices for one of the 120-plus tables ranged from $40 to $400. The testimonial was almost always sold out, according to the organizers. All the proceeds, they said, were sent to the prisoners' dependents' fund, the Green Cross.

In the early 1970s, Philadelphia was also a busy center for NORAID activities. Dennis Clark reported that there were nine functioning branches of the committee by 1972. The *Philadelphia Evening Bulletin* estimated that they raised about $10,000 a month

in and around the city, mainly through dances, rallies, and pic-
nics. According to Clark, "One old fellow, a native of County
Clare, took up collections almost full time. Contributors received
a card as receipt with two lines printed on it:

> Though strife in the North fill poor Erin with care
> There are hearts true and trusted toward Erin so fair."

There were visits from prominent Sinn Fein spokesmen like
Ruairi O'Bradaigh. In 1972 a Belfast woman, Margaret Murray,
whose sisters had been killed by British troops firing on their car,
visited Philadelphia. Jack McKinney, a prominent local journalist,
organized a press conference at which Mrs. Murray described the
trials and tribulations of Belfast's Catholics. Not only had her sisters died at the hands of troops, but her husband had been badly
beaten by soldiers during the introduction of internment.
Observed Clark: "The impression she made was heart-scalding to
Irish-Philadelphians, and it prompted many to pledge themselves
to do something to retaliate against the army that could act so
savagely against civilians."[2] Such activities have made Philadelphia one of the strongest centers of NORAID support in the
country. On a state level, Pennsylvania ranks second to New York
in financial contributions to NORAID, according to the Justice
Department.

NORAID took root in places as diverse as Butte, Montana,
where many of Irish descent worked in the copper mines;
Cleveland, Ohio, where Mayo emigrants prepared the ground for
its growth; and on the West Coast in San Francisco, San Diego,
and Los Angeles. California, with an Irish-American population
of about two million, was soon ranking third behind Pennsylvania
in amounts contributed to its NORAID chapter. In a report in the
Los Angeles Times (February 2, 1981), the president of the Los
Angeles NORAID unit, Mike Fitzpatrick, claimed that his group
raised as much as $10,000 a year through "house parties." In a
well-known Irish pub in San Francisco, an old glass jug sat on the
bar. Patrons were asked to put money into it for "detainees and
the internees" in Northern Ireland jails. On the walls graffiti proclaimed UP THE PROVOS, BRITS OUT NOW, and IRA. Such sights were
common in similar bars in cities throughout the U.S.

The level of activity was high enough to cause the authorities concern, and the British and Irish governments were also exerting pressure on them to do something about Irish-American militancy. Already in December 1971, President Nixon and the British prime minister, Edward Heath, had discussed the Northern Ireland problem and its American connection at a meeting in Bermuda. A few months later, while in the U.S., the foreign minister of the Irish Republic, Patrick Hillery, expressed concern to U.S. government officials at the rise in support for the IRA in America.

Though other organizations sympathetic to Irish nationalists were active—an FBI memo of January 1973 lists the National Association for Irish Freedom (a support group for the Northern Ireland civil-rights movement), the American Committee for Ulster Justice (formed in New York in 1972), the Irish Republican Clubs (an older group, made up of ex-IRA veterans), and the Anti-Internment Coalition—only NORAID came under intense scrutiny. By August 1973 the FBI in Cleveland was "developing qualitative and penetrative informant coverage" of the local branch of the INAC.

The FBI's investigation concentrated on getting evidence that would force the INAC to register under FARA as an agent of the IRA. In this way, the authorities hoped, many supporters of NORAID would be persuaded to leave the organization because they would not want to be identified with a subversive group. This course met with some success. "Many INAC members," an FBI memo from early 1973 said, "have become inactive as a result of the Bureau's investigation." Another memo, dated June 29, 1973, gives an example of this effect. Agents were investigating New Jersey's Bergen County chapter after it had collected $10,000. It questioned a member of the chapter, who told the FBI that the money they had raised was given with the intention that homeless and poor people in Northern Ireland would receive food and clothing." The FBI said that it believed that the money went for other purposes, and that the INAC was being asked to declare its relationship to the IRA. The memo noted that agents were later informed that "the membership had been greatly curtailed because members feel that some of the aid given may be used to obtain things to cause destruction." The member questioned told the FBI that he was "divorcing himself from the organization because of the potential problem."

Another member of the Bergen County unit told the FBI that controversy had broken out in it because of the investigation. Some members who were against violence wanted to resign. This man told the agents he would leave NORAID if it was shown to be connected to the IRA. He volunteered his help to the FBI to "locate terrorists."

In the same state, another NORAID unit, formed in January 1972, was dissolved thirteen months later because of the investigation. The FBI noted: "Individuals did not want to become involved in any political type organization which would register or be associated with registration as an agent for a foreign power."

However, these FBI successes did not stop the flow of money through NORAID to Ireland. A memo of September 17, 1973, registers the authorities' concern: "The Irish Problem has become a serious problem and a source of embarrassment to the United States." It also said the agency's investigation was limited to possible violations of FARA and suggested that the CIA and the Alcohol, Tobacco and Firearms Agency become involved because, it claimed, the INAC is "the primary fund-raising organization for the Provisionals [IRA] in the United States."

What is interesting about the FBI's memos is that they show the overriding concern to be stopping the fund-raising activities of the INAC; the interest in finding violations of FARA seems secondary, a byproduct of the effort to curtail support for the IRA. Defenders of NORAID would later argue that the FBI was using FARA as an excuse to infringe American citizens' First Amendment rights to free speech, as well as their right to raise funds for organizations whose political goals they support, which is not against the law.

The memo calling the Irish problem a "serious embarrassment" to the government went on to say that the State Department was "seeking assistance in alleviating" this problem. Two days later, on September 19, 1973, another memo noted: "The State Department has requested any information the FBI might have with regard to the Irish Northern Aid Committee (INAC), specifically any information available regarding individuals who have contributed to the INAC. The State Department additionally inquired whether prosecution was planned or possible against those individuals who had contributed to INAC, which organization State described as a 'terrorist' organization."

Though NORAID was being called a "terrorist" organization, it was engaged in the same activities in 1973 as it had been in 1971 when the FBI referred to its leadership as "conservative" and "responsible." What had changed was the pressure on the American government to do something to reduce fund-raising among Irish Americans for the IRA or the IRA's cause, even though this kind of support was legal. According to lawyers of the American Civil Liberties Union, "The government's attempt to deter and harass such fund raising would still be unlawful," whether or not it were proved that some of the funds would eventually be used for terrorist purposes.[3]

A week after the FBI memo was written, an interagency meeting was held to "coordinate these investigations . . . in alleviating the Irish problem in the U.S." Officials from the State Department, the Justice Department, the FBI, and the Treasury, as well as Brian Ahearn, counsel for the registration unit administrating FARA, discussed the "Irish problem in the U.S." Among the topics touched on were illegal arms shipments and also "the flow of money" from Irish Americans to Ireland. From then on the FARA investigation was launched in earnest, directed not only against the INAC but also against the newspapers *The Irish People* and *The Irish Echo.* As a subsequent memo makes clear, the FBI was still not certain which of these papers was identified with NORAID's policies, in spite of the fact that the *Echo* had been in existence for some forty years and was "moderate" in its views of the Northern Ireland crisis. The FBI requested that two copies of the *Echo* be acquired for dissemination among the agents involved in the investigation. (The authorities did eventually conclude that the *People,* not the *Echo,* was the organ of NORAID.) It is also apparent from memos around this period that the State Department was not the only agency to ask for and receive information on the INAC collected during the FARA investigation. The British and Irish police and their diplomatic services were given documents on the FBI's inquiry into the INAC and *The Irish People* on a regular basis. Both the British and Irish governments were anxious that spokesmen such as Ruairi O'Bradaigh of Sinn Fein be prevented from entering the country to attend NORAID fund-raising dinners. The FBI scanned the columns of *The Irish Echo* and *The Irish People*, which advertise these events, to see who was billed to speak. The State Department would then try to "deny or sufficiently delay"[4] visas for speakers from Ireland to prevent them from attending the dinners. (From about that time until 1994, no prominent spokesman for Sinn Fein or the IRA was granted a visa to enter the U.S.)

The Justice Department's concern continued to be focused not on possible violations of FARA but on the actual fund-raising activities of the INAC. A memo to the director of the FBI reported that "two previous dinners were a financial success and . . . profits were sent to Ireland for the relief of the hard-pressed people in Northern Ireland." The ACLU observes that this report is "inexplicable except on the understanding that the government's pol-icy was to harass and deter such fundraising,"[5] an activity that the ACLU emphasizes was quite legal. FARA provided a ready means of deterrence. An FBI memo of April 1974 notes that a Portland, Oregon, chapter of the INAC folded after it was told of the investigation of the INAC's connections with the IRA. A year later, the FBI directed tax authorities to review the records of a Baltimore INAC unit, after noting that it had netted $10,000 in a fund-raiser, and to "obtain the names of all officers and other pertinent information, such as names of bank account for INAC."

However, as another memo reveals, the government's concerns went beyond those covered by FARA. On March 2, 1974, Henry Petersen, then assistant attorney general, wrote to the FBI: "As members of your staff are well aware, the Department of State together with the British Government have requested the Government of the United States to make all efforts to halt the shipment of weapons and explosives to Northern Ireland and punish those individuals who have violated our criminal statutes by engaging in such activities. I cannot express too strongly the seriousness of this situation."

The authorities were still bent on proving that NORAID supplied money to the IRA directly, as well as being involved in the weapons-smuggling business. In June 1972 the Justice Department subpoenaed five New York members of NORAID to appear before a grand jury sitting in Fort Worth, Texas, to investigate alleged arms smuggling across the Mexican border. All the men were in their seventies, of working-class backgrounds, and had been active in NORAID—attending functions and rallies and picketing the British consulate. Human-rights lawyers, like Paul O'Dwyer, who took up their case, accused the government of deliberately harassing Irish-American activists by forcing them to go some 1,400 miles to testify. "It was the same Department of Justice," commented O'Dwyer in his autobiography, "that had contrived to try nuns and priests in a Ku Klux Klan stronghold, which now had chosen Fort Worth as the appropriate jurisdiction to subpoena . . . before a grand jury a group of New York Irish Americans. When his office inquired as to why his clients were being summoned to Fort Worth, the only reply received from the authorities was that they were wanted for questioning. The men were warned that they would be asked about the activities of their friends in NORAID, who would then perhaps be subject to FBI investigation. The five elected not to answer any questions. They were judged in contempt and jailed indefinitely. According to O'Dwyer, Judge Leo Brewster told them: "If you cooperate, you will be set free. You have the key to the jail in your pocket."[6]

The five New Yorkers were held in the Tarrant County Jail. "The total space that was home, church, dining room, toilet, and sole recreation area of its occupants measured 16 feet by 7 feet. The prisoners were too far from New York to see family and friends, and their only visitor other than counsel was a young Baptist clergyman who acted as chaplain. There was no Catholic service of any kind."[7] Their lawyer had to fight to get them moved to a federal facility. But bail was denied by the judge, an unusually vindictive step.[8]

There was an outcry not only within the Irish-American community but also among civil libertarians. Eventually, bail was granted thanks to the intervention of Supreme Court Justice William O. Douglas, whom O'Dwyer had gone to see personally. After ten months, the five were released. No indictments were ever brought against them.

Another grand jury convened in Philadelphia in 1973 and subpoenaed local members of NORAID. One of them, Daniel Cahalane, was suspected of purchasing twenty thousand dollars' worth of guns and ammunition in Norristown, Pennsylvania. Like the men brought to Forth Worth, Cahalane refused to answer the grand jury's questions, and on July 27 he was jailed for contempt. Defense lawyers alleged that Cahalane and two other local men were the victims of wiretapping. NORAID pickets appeared in front of the federal courthouse in Philadelphia proclaiming BRITISH TERRORIST REGIME ENLISTS SUPPORT OF US JUSTICE DEPARTMENT TO STOP AID TO OPPRESSED PEOPLE OF NORTHERN IRELAND. (According to Philadelphia historian Dennis Clark, "It would be hard to exaggerate the fury, disgust, and contempt for the Nixon government that this affair aroused among the Philadelphia Irish."[9]

Two years later, Cahalane, along with four other NORAID activists, was indicted for conspiracy to smuggle weapons and munitions to the IRA. One of those charged was an ex-steward on the liner *Queen Mary*. He was accused of sending six suitcases of arms and ammunition on the *QE2* with an eighty-three-year-old woman. Other NORAID activists were brought before the courts in places as far apart as Butte, Montana, and Baltimore to face weapons-smuggling charges. On February 14, 1974, federal agents scored a coup in New York. Treasury Department agents arrested James Conlon and Michael Larkin, accusing them of conspiring to smuggle twenty thousand dollars' worth of arms purchased at a Maryland gun shop owned by William Westerfund. Westerfund was also arrested, as were two other Irish-American activists, Harry Hillick and Kieran MacMahon. Involved were one hundred Armalite rifles, which they were alleged to have obtained from Westerfund. All went to prison. (Conlon, who was in poor health, died soon after his release.)

Though individual members might be connected with arms dealing, attempts to link NORAID itself to illegal activities proved more difficult. While the FBI's investigation pressed ahead under FARA, the British government mounted a frontal attack. In late 1975, the British prime minister Harold Wilson accused the committee of "financing murder." He said that "misguided American supporters" of the IRA were responsible for providing "most of the modern weapons now reaching the terrorists in Northern Ireland." At around the same time, the *New York Times* ran a front-page article about NORAID. It quoted "intelligence sources in Washington" who believed that 75 percent of the money collected through NORAID went to purchase arms. The *Times* article quoted a leading NORAID member as saying that as for buying guns, "we've no objections to it if they have money to spare. They've got to get them somewhere."[10]

FBI files also noted other evidence of an IRA-NORAID connection. A memo reports an INAC statement that referred to a communication between the republican movement and the committee. As quoted in the memo, the statement declared: "The leadership of the Republican Movement in Ireland have indicated to us their wish that all fund raising efforts in the U.S. be directed through the National Headquarters of the Irish Northern Aid Committee at 273 East 194 Street, Bronx, New York." This directive was to ensure central financial control of all moneys raised under the committee's auspices and "to discourage parochial efforts by individuals or groups which tend to negate their expressed goal for unity." It added that the movement in Ireland had informed them that the need for aid was "desperately urgent."

From around this time, in the mid-1970s, NORAID's filings show a sharp decrease in funds. In 1975, their returns reveal that for the first time the yearly collections dropped below $200,000. During 1975, $174,000 was reported. The following year the amount fell to $119,500. The decline continued into 1977, when the INAC registered collections of only $108,000. Though the Justice Department believes that these reports are inaccurate, and that more was collected than reported, the decline was a real one. The war in Northern Ireland seemed to drag on endlessly. The IRA was operating its campaign on a smaller scale than in the early 1970s, and it rarely made headlines. When it did, they were invariably reports of some atrocity such as the bombing in early 1978 of a hotel near Belfast in which twelve people burned to death. From 1977 through 1978, collections hit an all-time low.

It was clear that the worse things were for Northern Ireland's Catholics, the better it was for NORAID's fund-raising efforts. From 1977, any British actions that were directed against the IRA and the nationalist community in general were kept much more low key than in the early 1970s. Internment had ended, and while allegations still reached America of IRA prisoners' being abused at the hands of the police, these were obviously not sufficient to rouse anger of the kind that helped fill the coffers in 1971 and 1972. By 1978, even the allegations against the police began to diminish. It was another two years or so before events in Northern Ireland were able to rouse Irish-American indignation to new heights and reinvigorate the INAC's activities.

In the meantime, the Justice Department was not allowing this decline in INAC support to prevent it from pressing forward with its aim of proving the committee in violation of FARA statutes and of reducing its fund-raising efforts even more. Early in 1976 a meeting like that in 1974 was held with officials from the State and Justice departments, along with agents from the FBI and the Bureau of Alcohol, Tobacco and Firearms. The aim, according to an FBI memo, was "to determine what additional action could be taken" concerning alleged gunrunning to, and fund-raising for, the IRA. Not long after this interagency meeting, it was decided that there was now enough evidence to file suit against the INAC to demand that it declare as its foreign principal not the Belfast Northern Aid Committee or the Green Cross, but the Irish Republican Army.

A case was also set in motion to force *The Irish People* to register as an agent of the INAC. Compliance with this demand would have meant, under FARA, that any written material of a political nature in the newspaper would be designated as "foreign political propaganda," the paper would be forced to supply the Justice Department with the names of recipients of a hundred or more copies, and it would be subjected to the threat of "unannounced, warrantless, standardless searches of all correspondence, records, financial records, and other materials" concerning the activities for which registration has been ordered." It was hoped that this would help depress the paper's circulation in the same way that the investigation under FARA had discouraged many INAC members and influenced them to leave the organization.

An attack on NORAID was also launched from a different quarter. The year 1977 witnessed the first St. Patrick's Day appeal from the most powerful Irish-American politicians—Senators Kennedy and Moynihan, New York State Governor Hugh Carey, and House Speaker Tip O'Neill—directed at Irish Americans, asking them to stop supporting organizations connected to violence. Though

NORAID was not actually named in their statement, it was obviously the target.

NORAID's lawyers fought back, accusing the government of using FARA as an excuse to interfere with their fund-raising, which, as the ACLU repeatedly emphasized, was not in itself illegal. It would only become so if it could be proved that the INAC was fund-raising under the direct control of a foreign principal without declaring that relationship, which would place it in violation of FARA's statutes. And NORAID's lawyers argued that the government had failed to prove either that it was under the direct control of the IRA or was financed by the IRA to promote the aims of the guerrillas. On the contrary, the argument went, the members of the INAC were American citizens acting on their own initiative, of their own free will, without direction from abroad, to propagate views that they held and that under the U.S. Constitution they had a right to express. It was also within their rights to raise money on behalf of any organization that shared those views.

NORAID lawyers quoted FBI memorandums to prove that the office of the attorney general had set out to use FARA against NORAID because of the committee's views and political activities in support of the IRA. Had not the government in 1973 described NORAID's fund-raising as a "problem" that had to be "alleviated"? And had not the memos demonstrated clearly that the primary concern was a political one, heightened by the Department of State's anxiety over the continuing "embarrassment" of the "Irish problem" and its sensitivity to British government pressure to do something to help resolve it? As the ACLU later argued on behalf of *The Irish People*: "The government's attempt to 'alleviate' that problem, through use of FARA against the defendant, is plainly improper."[12] It claimed: "Unlike groups whose services are essentially purchased and against which FARA was directed, politically active Irish Americans are a committed, mutually reinforced, and self-motivated source of indigenous American expression." Their dedication to the IRA was a product of deeply held political views.

There was also a strong sense that NORAID and *The Irish People* were being singled out for attention when other groups engaging in similar activities were left alone. For example, it was suggested that if the government's interpretation of FARA in the NORAID suit were to be strictly applied, then the Roman Catholic hierarchy in the U.S. would have to register as the agent of the Vatican, since the church leadership plainly espoused the Vatican's views on abortion, divorce, and nuclear warfare, and advocated that they be politically adopted by the United States government. Likewise, various Polish-American groups that supported Solidarity, and Jewish-American groups whose goal was to increase support for the policies of the Israeli government, would fall under the same strictures, as would the organizations raising money for the Contras in Nicaragua. Yet FARA had not been interpreted against them in this way. The inescapable suggestion was that the government pursued NORAID and *The Irish People* solely for political reasons. The battle was waged in the courts for four years. In 1981, the courts found against NORAID, ordering it to register as an agent of the IRA. While appeals were heard, NORAID refused to file returns, in protest.

However, the dispute dragged on for another three years. Under FARA, filings are made under penalties of perjury. NORAID asserted that since it did not believe itself to be an agent of the IRA, if it filed as such it would be committing perjury. The wrangle lasted until the Justice Department threatened to sue NORAID for contempt of court in late 1983. Early in 1984, the court gave the committee ninety days to comply with its ruling. Finally, something of a compromise was reached. NORAID agreed to file as an agent of the IRA, but with the stipulation that it be allowed to add that it had done so only under court order. The court agreed, and NORAID registered in the summer of 1984, naming its foreign principal as the IRA "as ordered by the court." Both the Justice Department and NORAID's publicity director, Martin Galvin, seemed happy with the decision. Some members of NORAID felt that it was a victory because it only acknowledged the court's description without actually agreeing with it. However, the Justice Department's cause for satisfaction would seem more certain. While NORAID supporters might claim a moral victory of sorts, the authorities could now say that the committee was a front for a foreign "terrorist" organization, and so discourage concerned Irish Americans from associating with it.

The case against *The Irish People* was handled by the ACLU. A ruling that found that the paper was an agent of the INAC was handed down in 1985, the judge finding, according to the ACLU, that the "Irish Problem" was not "legitimate political activity" or even political fund-raising, but solely a matter of "gun-running and terrorism."[13] (The court also found that there was no connection between the government's admittedly illicit motive in using FARA to deter pro-IRA fund-raising in general and its action in seeking to register *The Irish People* as an agent of the INAC.) This decision was appealed, but NORAID was finally forced to register as an agent of the IRA; however, by 1994 it had ceased to file under FARA, saying that it was not the same organization that had originally registered.

During the period in which NORAID was facing the court order to file as an agent of the IRA, it was undergoing the greatest resurgence of sympathy and support it had ever experienced. As usual, this was entirely due to events in Ireland. After the lull of the late 1970s, tension began to increase again in 1980. Republican prisoners were protesting against the British policy of refusing to recognize them as "political prisoners." They refused to wear prison clothes, adopting much the same attitude as the old Fenian O'Donovon Rossa had over a hundred years before. Instead, they wore blankets, and became known as "the blanket men." Things deteriorated when, as a result of a dispute during which prison orderlies allegedly dumped the prisoners' chamber pots over their cells, the protesters refused to clean their cells out but instead smeared their excrement over the cell walls. The blanket protest became "the dirty protest."

In the fall of 1980 NORAID smuggled two former protesters, Fra McCann and Liam Carlin, into the U.S. to talk about conditions in the jail. They toured American cities, hosted by one INAC unit after another, giving interviews to the press and other media. Slowly interest began to revive, not only through direct contact with the prisoners who had been brought over, but also because Irish Americans could see the increasingly large demonstrations that were being reported from Belfast and Dublin—demonstrations in favor of the prisoners' demands for recognition of their political status. The change was reflected in the increase in the funds NORAID reported—almost $70,000 for the period between July 1980 and January 1981, as compared with just over $50,000 for the previous six months.

The dirty protest led to the hunger strike, the ultimate weapon of prison resistance in the tradition of Irish republicanism. An initial hunger strike had been called off in late 1980 when it was thought that the British were going to make some concessions. When they failed to do so, Bobby Sands, who as IRA commander in the prison took responsibility for the setback, began refusing food on March 1, 1981. (It was five years to the day since the British had abolished the privileges that till then were accorded to paramilitary prisoners and which constituted in their eyes "political status.") The news of the start of Sands's hunger strike received only a brief mention in the mass media. Yet within months the situation was transformed, and the world's press focused its attention on Northern Ireland as it had never done before. Sands won a seat to the Westminster Parliament in an election at the beginning of April, demonstrating the increasing level of support his fast was winning for the republicans. The protest crowds grew in numbers throughout Ireland. And in America, NORAID pickets began clustering outside British consulate offices from New York to San Francisco. As Sands weakened, the pickets grew in strength. In Los Angeles, NORAID supporters gathered near the British offices to chant the rosary as the prisoner's life ebbed away. By that time, the protesters in New York stretched for six blocks down Third Avenue. Never before had the INAC's activities attracted comparable support and interest.

Sands's death created a momentum that was continued by a series of other hunger strikers who followed him to the death—nine in all before the protest ended five months later. Sinn Fein, the IRA's political wing, found itself propelled into electoral victory when it contested the seat Sands had held until his death. And the INAC found itself able to command large audiences and marshal overflow crowds at its pickets.

When Prince Charles arrived in New York in June to attend a Royal Ballet performance of *The Sleeping Beauty*, he was greeted by enormous crowds of protesters organized through the INAC. The performance was memorable only for the vehemence and size of the protest crowds. According to NORAID's publicity director, thirty thousand people were there to greet the prince outside Lincoln Center in Manhattan (the police say five thousand). They were chanting, "Prince of death must go" and "Parasitic royalty must go," as well as the usual pro-IRA slogans. As the elegant guests attired in evening wear stepped out of their sleek silver and black limousines, they were greeted by an unusual but ear-splitting noise—one that was more familiar in the narrow streets of Northern Ireland's Catholic slums: the clash and clatter of trash-can lids being slammed against the pavement. Catholic women used this method to alert the area of the approach of British troops or police. But it would be hard to conceive of a more unsuitably cacophonous overture to the melodious sweetness of *Sleeping Beauty.* Even inside the prince and the other concert goers were not safe from the protesters. They were no more than ten minutes into the performance when a man stood up in the hall shouting support for the IRA. He was hustled out. However, at intervals three more stood up, denouncing the prince. One shouted at Charles: "You are murdering the Irish!" An angry guest screamed "Kill the bastards—they're ruining the whole evening!"

The hunger strike brought feelings to a pitch, and militants on both sides of the Atlantic were eager to transform the anger into more tangible evidence of support. INAC had already organized successful tours by prisoners on their release from Northern Ireland's jails. As sympathy increased in the spring of 1981, the committee organized a tour by the relatives of the starving men. It was obvious that this would be the most effective way to bring home to Americans the trauma of the hunger strike.

Sands's immediate successors on the hunger strike were Francis Hughes, Ray McCreesh, and Patsy O'Hara. Hughes died on May 12, McCreesh and O'Hara nine days later. Sands's brother Sean, and Malachy, the brother of McCreesh, were available to come to the United States. And O'Hara had a sister, Liz, an attractive and vivacious young woman who was at the same time outspoken and articulate—on the surface, an ideal person to tour the United States. However, there was a complication.

Like Sands, McCreesh and Hughes were both members of the IRA. But Patsy O'Hara belonged to the smaller, left-wing Irish National Liberation Army (INLA), which had been formed after a split with the Official IRA in 1975. Left-wing connections were a liability in Irish-American circles. Some INAC activists feared that the "Marxist" taint would counteract the kind of support the hunger strike was producing. NORAID was always sensitive to British allegations that republicans were left-wing revolutionaries who duped simple-minded Irish Americans into supporting them. Also, some members of NORAID did not like the idea of the INLA plugging into its network, which was designed to support the IRA struggle. As a result, objections were raised to Liz O'Hara's presence on the tour. Couldn't someone with more pure "republican" connections be found? Ironically, at the same time that some of NORAID's leaders were expressing these objections, *The Irish People* was praising Patsy O'Hara as a martyr. In the end, Malachy McCreesh and Sands's brother refused to go on the tour unless Liz O'Hara accompanied them. Whatever INAC's objections were, they had to be put aside in the interests of solidarity with the hunger strikers.

Other men had already replaced Hughes, McCreesh, and O'Hara on hunger strike; one of them, Joe McDonald, had been fasting for a month when the relatives arrived in the U.S. in mid-June to begin the tour. They hoped, as did McDonald's family, that if American indignation were aroused strongly enough, perhaps Britain's prime minister, Margaret Thatcher, might be yet convinced to meet the prisoners' demands and so avoid any further sacrifice. The goal of raising money was, as far as they were concerned, a very secondary matter.

The relatives visited about twenty-six cities in four weeks, conducting one of the most successful tours ever on the Irish-American circuit. It was exhausting and emotionally charged; the relatives had to deal with a myriad of Irish-American dignitaries—labor leaders, politicians, and so forth—hoping that somehow something might be done to save the next hunger striker from death, while from home came constant reports that he was weakening, and that there was yet no sign of any movement from Britain.

For Liz O'Hara it proved especially trying. She went to America with vivid memories of her brother's last days as he was wasting slowly to death. She had been there, at his side. The contrasting experience of the American trip could not but be startling. The INAC treated them like celebrities, and she found the ever-present sentimentality about Ireland difficult to tolerate. At times, the fund-raising was done in ways that were vulgar and exploitative.

Often, the hunger strikers would be invoked by INAC leaders at the same time as others passed around large buckets in which supporters were eagerly stuffing fistfuls of dollars. Emotion was being translated directly into cash, a kind of reductionism that seemed to obscure or even obliterate the nobility of the cause for which her brother and his comrades had died, and for which others were dying.

The vexing question of exactly how much cash was raised was made even more complex than usual with NORAID at this time. Because it was in dispute with the Justice Department over the registration issue, the committee was refusing to file its six-monthly financial returns. The last period for which those figures were available before 1984, when the dispute was resolved, was January–July 1981. For this period, the committee disclosed that it raised $92,800, a startlingly small sum considering the huge swell of support it was then getting.

According to sources close to the tour itself, the three relatives raised about a quarter of a million dollars—more than the INAC had been able to collect in any year since 1972, at least according to its official returns. (These were not always in line with what its spokesmen told reporters.) But the INAC alleged that no more than $200,000 was collected for the whole year, and that the relatives' tour was only a small part of the overall campaign. The question of how much money was contributed was to have other ramifications when it came to deciding how it should be divided up, and whether or not the INLA and its political wing, the Irish Republican Socialist party (IRSP), were entitled to a share.

O'Hara found herself in frequent dispute with the INAC, who insisted on referring to her brother Patsy as an IRA man. Though she was told she could not refer to "socialism" or "communism," she says she always made it clear what her brother's affiliations were. She also undertook her own initiatives. She tried to get powerful trade-union figures to support the hunger strikers' demands, and appealed to Teddy Gleason, head of the Longshoremen's Union, with whom she met on several occasions. However, he was not responsive to her request for a strike in support of the prisoners. Gleason told her that the Reagan administration had made it clear that any such move would not be helpful. And Gleason was a strong supporter of Ronald Reagan. Reagan had already rejected an appeal from the Irish prime minister, Charles Haughey, to intervene with Thatcher, and pursued a policy of neutrality.

By the time the tour ended, Joe McDonald was dead and another hunger striker, Martin Hurson, was ebbing fast. All attempts at mediation in America and in Ireland were failing. The vigor of the protests could not be kept up; weariness was setting in on both sides of the Atlantic. As defeat became more real, bitterness was inevitable. O'Hara returned from the tour disillusioned about the INAC. Its image of the Irish struggle was hopelessly simplified. The political commitment of socialists like her brother had no place in it—indeed, was seen as threatening.

The last two hunger strikers to die were Tom McIlwee and Michael Devine in August. Devine, like O'Hara, was a member of the INLA, and the third member of that organization to die on hunger strike. (The other, Kevin Lynch, died earlier in August.) The Catholic community in Northern Ireland was weary and exhausted; the thought of further deaths became intolerable— more so since it was blatantly clear that Thatcher would not concede. The hunger strike was finally over by the beginning of October. Already the recriminations had begun. The INLA's political wing, the IRSP, met with Sinn Fein and demanded a slice of the $250,000 cake that the IRSP claimed had been produced by the tour. However, Sinn Fein reportedly told the IRSP that it must address its requests to the INAC.

The IRSP sent over one of its leading members, Sean Flynn, a Belfast city councilor, to meet with INAC officials in New York in September. He was asking for one third of the money, since in the cold arithmetic of death, approximately one third of the ten men who had died were INLA members. Flynn also pointed out that Liz O'Hara had played an important part in the tour which raised the money.

Flynn met INAC officials in New York. He told them that the families of two of the dead INLA men still owed money for the funerals of their sons. In one case, they didn't have enough to cover the cost of their electricity bills and traveling expenses. When Flynn went to the home of a prominent INAC member he was told that NORAID knew nothing about giving money to the IRSP. Their meeting deteriorated into a shouting match, and

Flynn was asked to leave. He later accused NORAID of hypocrisy in praising the INLA men who died on hunger strike while at the same time refusing to help their families. But NORAID maintained that the issue was not its responsibility; its money goes to the Green Cross which administers it to the families of jailed IRA men, over which it has no say. The dispute left bitter feelings between IRSP/INLA and the IRA and its American supporters.

While Flynn was in America, he undertook a tour of his own. But as far as getting money was concerned, he did no better on the tour than he had with the INAC. The tour was organized with a small left-wing support group, the H-Block Armagh Committee, based in New York. (The name refers to the women's prison in Armagh and to the Maze Prison in Belfast, where the cells are grouped in "H" configurations.)

Outside the INAC circuit, Flynn spoke to mainly small, radical groups, not prime fund-raising sources. However, INAC people would occasionally show up. On one occasion, on the West Coast, Flynn met a NORAID supporter who was a millionaire warehouse owner. The wealthy Irish American at first assumed that Flynn was just another IRA or Sinn Fein activist on the stomp looking for dollars, not realizing his left-wing background. Flynn mentioned the need for funds to cover the funeral expenses of two of the hunger strikers; the millionaire generously offered to write a check out the following morning for whatever the cost was. Flushed with this offer, the IRSP spokesman invited the would-be patron along to hear him speak that evening. The millionaire showed up, only to find himself in the company of radicals, blacks, and various leftist politicos. He was appalled when Flynn spoke, comparing Northern Ireland Catholics and their struggle with that of the blacks in South Africa. The millionaire got up to leave. He told Flynn their morning appointment was canceled. Shocked, Flynn asked why. "I don't like niggers," he was told.

Flynn's experience was similar to that of Bernadette Devlin when she toured the U.S. in August 1969 in the first days of the crisis. Her avowed Marxism perplexed Irish Americans, and her support for black civil rights disturbed the racist inclinations among those who were more conservative.

The INAC attracted many conservative Irish Americans who could only see the Irish problem as a British-versus-Irish struggle;

anything deeper than that, especially with a social and economic analysis smacking of socialism, was rejected angrily.

The INAC was aware of this. They knew that if republican left-wingers had their way in America, supporting blacks and Palestinians and Salvadoran guerrillas, it would alienate many Irish Americans. It would also play right into the hands of the British, who tried to paint the IRA a bright red. As it happens, the IRA was no more a bright red than it was an untarnished shade of emerald green. As a revolutionary movement, it always had a socialist tendency—James Connolly, one of the leaders of the 1916 Rising, was arguably the most articulate and cogent Marxist writer that the British Isles has ever produced. (Ironically, the Rising received unequivocal support from only two sources: Irish Americans and Vladimir Lenin, who defended it against left-wing criticisms that it was a mere "putsch" and not a proper revolution at all.) But this tendency, while influencing the political outlook of the IRA, did not change the fundamental nature of it, which was nationalist and republican. The fact that it was left-wing was only a reflection of the nature of liberation struggles in the late twentieth century, for which the most appealing ideology was Marxism in some shape or form; it offered an immediate termi-nology and model for struggle which the liberal democratic ide-ology of western capitalism could not offer. For the IRA this meant that it must face two ways, toward the utopian socialism in one direction and toward the arcadian nationalism of Irish Americans in the other. It knew that by overemphasizing the one, the other might well be sacrificed.

In America, those contradictions were easily resolved by being ignored. The chief platform which the INAC had for expounding republican views was *The Irish People*. Though it was not in any sense owned or run by NORAID, it was edited by NORAID's pub-licity director, and its policies generally supported those of both the IRA and the committee. The bulk of *The Irish People's* material came from Sinn Fein's weekly newspaper *An Phoblacht* ("The Republic"), published in Dublin, from which it reprinted articles and reports. But there was an interesting difference between what appeared in one and what was selected by the other. *An Phoblacht* carried abundant reports and features on third-world struggles: South Africa, Nicaragua, El Salvador, Chile, and the Middle East all receive attention. The paper was invariably sympathetic to the Sandinistas, the Salvadoran guerrillas, the African National Congress, and the Palestine Liberation Organization. It was extremely hostile to the policies of Ronald Reagan, with whom it linked Margaret Thatcher in an unholy and reactionary alliance as enemies of republicanism in Ireland and freedom and democracy everywhere.

A reader of *The Irish People* would have found little of this. The left-wing world view of *An Phoblacht* was not evident from the selections that appeared there. Though South Africa-related stories were occasionally reprinted, the Sinn Fein-IRA attitude on most other liberation struggles, which *An Phoblacht* expressed, was in general omitted.

In November 1985 Sinn Fein President Gerry Adams made a speech at his party's yearly convention that was run in full in *An Phoblacht*. The speech strongly identified the IRA's struggle with that of third-world liberation struggles, and berated Reagan, Thatcher, and the Irish government. Soon after the beginning of his address, Adams went on the attack: "It is no accident that the Dublin government finds common ground with Thatcher and Reagan in their attitude to liberation struggles. Dublin's attitude on these issues is but an extension of its attitude to the British presence in this country. The natural and logical place for Ireland is alongside the Palestinians, the Chileans, Salvadorans, and Nicaraguans. A government which truly represented the Irish people would be in opposition to Reagan's backing of repressive regimes in Central America, in opposition to Israel's policy of genocide against the Palestinian people, and in opposition to the British partition of this country."[14] Adams went on to speak of the threat Sinn Fein radicalism represented to the Irish government, and spoke of their fears that it would help rouse the Irish working class. The approximately ninety paragraphs of the address dealt with Sinn Fein's role in fighting various social evils like drug abuse in Ireland, and its support for social reforms such as divorce, which is outlawed in Ireland.

A week later, *The Irish People* ran an excerpted version of the speech, some seventy-six paragraphs in length. Among the most prominent omissions were the remarks by Adams quoted above, the appeal of Sinn Fein as a radical alternative, and the section on social reform. Though *The Irish People's* version did include Adams's expression of support for the African National Congress, it tended to emphasize what was traditionally republican—eulogy of recent IRA martyrs, abuse of the British, and attacks on the moderate constitutional nationalists of the Social Democratic and Labour party (SDLP). That is, it focused on the most nationalist aspect of the IRA-Sinn Fein program and tended not to dwell on the social and economic policies of the movement. In this, it was in keeping with Irish-American activism from the mid-nineteenth century onward, what was called here the arcadian view. The conflict between that and the utopian (of which Marxism is the most militant example) was ever threatening to the solidarity that *The Irish People* wanted to build up for Irish republicans. To reprint *An Phoblacht* articles of a left-wing slant dealing with Central America or the Middle East would have caused problems, according to *The Irish People* editor, Martin Galvin.

"The word socialism means something different here than it does in Ireland . . . Americans aren't aware of what socialism means in a European context," he said. He picked only items which he believed were of interest to Americans—clearly, the IRA's third-world views and commitments would not be.

The traumatic months of the hunger strikes fused Irish-American emotional sympathy with the IRA's struggle against Britain in Northern Ireland. NORAID went through a resurgence that saw an immediate increase in the number of members. Galvin claimed that from that time onward NORAID was able to raise about $150,000 every six months, double or triple what it was collecting in the years before the protest. He also noted that now, for the first time, the number of American-born members exceeded those of Irish origin. (The organization kept no recruitment figures, so it was not known exactly how many people were involved.)

Of its founding members, only Michael Flannery was still alive. He remained steadfast in his identification with the IRA, even when they carried out attacks, such as that outside Harrods department store in London, in which innocent people died. His attitude: "I wait to hear what the IRA have to say. When it happens in London it's good propaganda. I've no qualms when they take the war to England. . . . Innocent people get killed in all wars." Not surprising from a man who knew and supported Joe McGarrity's bombing campaign in England in 1939. He saw the struggle as purely between the IRA and the British. Northern Ireland's Protestants had little role in this view of things. Of them Flannery said, "They have no right to be against a United Ireland whatsoever. They're there three hundred years so they're Irish and there should be no dispute about it." He met with the Ulster Defense Association (UDA), the largest of the loyalist paramilitary groups, three times. He was appalled at the suggestion that Protestants might want to remain with Britain because of economic self-interest. "Because they've a good thing going there!" he exclaimed. "My God—that's the most immoral thing I ever heard." The role of Ulster's Protestants was given little further serious consideration. How could it be? Irish-American arcadians could not possibly deal with the possibility that there might be more than one serpent in the Garden of Eden; that the problem would be easily solved when the British were expelled was a reverie that must not be interrupted by the reality of Protestant hatred of the republican cause and determination to resist it.

He admitted readily that NORAID's support depended not so much on its political views as on British atrocities. As proof of this he claimed, "We collected more in three months during the hunger strike than we do in a normal year—over $300,000."

In the end this was the most essential truth about NORAID. Like the IRA, it would exist as long as Britain had troops in Northern Ireland or maintained any kind of connection with it. The U.S. government's efforts to curtail its activities had less impact than the brutalities Britain was seen to be committing or not committing on the streets of Derry and Belfast.

The long squabble over registration and the result, which had the committee noted as the IRA's agent, did not prevent some Irish Americans from continuing to contribute. A potentially more serious move in 1984, which would have made it possibly illegal for Irish Americans to support the IRA, failed when the necessary legislation proposed by Secretary of State George Shultz got snarled in Congress. (One of the proposed bills would have outlawed American involvement in "support services" for any organization deemed "terrorist" by the State Department.)

In the meantime, NORAID went on, its New York testimonial dinner attracting as many politicians as ever, its pickets still present—though in smaller numbers—outside the British consulate in New York, and its spokesmen still launching forth at every opportunity against British actions in Northern Ireland. And the major question, which had been hanging over the organization since its foundation in 1970, was still being asked: Does the committee's money buy guns for the IRA?

To begin with, it is almost impossible to estimate exactly how much was raised. A lot of the early money was sent in cash, hand delivered, often to Joe Cahill. In 1984, a Justice Department official expressed the authorities' frustration. "We've seen six-thousand-dollar checks made out to cash and payable in this country," he said. "We can't keep track of that. You can't tell much from their financial records."

The organization itself put out contrary statements on its collections. In 1981, NORAID told the *Los Angeles Times* that it had collected $230,000 in 1980.[15] But its returns filed with the Justice Department show only $157,300. Witness the confusion over the amount raised during the 1981 relatives tour. One source claimed that at least $250,000 was collected in one four-week period alone. Flannery claimed over $300,000 was raised in three months. Another spokesman told Sean Flynn when he came in September to claim a share of it for the IRSP/INLA that only $200,000 had been raised so far for that year. Meanwhile, the (admittedly incomplete) records for 1981 show that a mere $92,800 was reported raised between January 29 that year and the end of July—which was the peak fund-raising period. In one of the committee's poorest years, 1977, the records show only $39,000 collected in one six-month period. However, authorities claimed that the amount raised was double the amount filed that year. As a general rule of thumb, it would seem, both the U.S. and British authorities regarded doubling the official returns as a way of arriving at some approximate idea of how much was actually collected. Using this means of calculation, one arrives at an approximate figure of $4 million raised by the INAC between 1971 and 1981, when the last returns were filed. And by 1986, according to the INAC, about $150,000 had been collected every six months, which would have added another $1.2 million to the total, or $2.4 if the authorities were to be believed.

It is in this uncertain context that the dispute about money for guns is placed. NORAID spokesmen consistently denied that their organization was providing the funds for IRA weapons. Martin Galvin was categorical: "It matters to me very strongly that when I say this money goes to dependents that it does so—I don't want to deceive people," he affirmed in 1985. "But morally I support the IRA's struggle." The spokesman for NORAID in San Francisco, Seamus Gibney, told the *Los Angeles Times:* "We can't prove the money doesn't go for guns. But the British government never offers proof when it says that it does."[16]

Mick Flannery, the founding member of the committee, was adamant that there was no IRA connection. He said that at "no time in the present" did he have any connection with the IRA. (He refused to sign the INAC's returns to the Justice Department because it listed the committee as an agent of the IRA. His lawyer signed for him.) He did concede that when the INAC was founded, there was influence from Sinn Fein, the IRA's political wing. There is also evidence that IRA leader Daithi O'Conaill was influential in the discussions in New York in 1970 which led to the setting up of NORAID. Subsequent visits by leading IRA–Sinn Fein figures like Joe Cahill, Sean Keenan, and Ruiairi O'Bradaigh were concerned with consolidating the committee's work. Individual members of the INAC were charged and convicted of arms smuggling. In September 1981, Mick Flannery himself was arrested and charged with contributing money for a weapons haul. Though this and other evidence was deemed enough for the Justice Department to successfully argue that NORAID was an agent of the IRA and should be registered as such under FARA, it was still not totally persuasive. There was weight to the Opposing arguments that such contacts did not prove the IRA directly controlled the INAC, and that INAC members were doing no more than exercising their constitutional rights when they raised money and spoke out on behalf of the republican movement in Ireland.

In one way, the dispute about whether or not INAC money went directly to buying arms is scholastic. This is so even from a legal point of view. As ACLU lawyers pointed out, even if it were true that some of the money sent to Ireland went to the purchasing of arms, it would still not be unlawful for American citizens to make contributions to NORAID. But the money that the INAC contributed to the Green Cross fund was vital to the IRA simply because it freed other funds which were in turn used in the purchase of arms.

In the 1970s British intelligence estimated that the average yearly income of the IRA–Sinn Fein was £950,000. The British found that the bulk of its money—some £550,000—came from theft in Ireland. Overseas contributions accounted for £120,000, of which officially the INAC remittances amounted to £55,000; but, unofficially, the British calculated it to be at least double that amount—i.e., £110,000. In other words, the INAC in the 1970s was by far the largest overseas contributor to the republican movement. The IRA–Sinn Fein expenditures were estimated to involve £180,000 for the Green Cross. If the authorities' unofficial figures for NORAID's contributions are approximately correct, it would mean that throughout the 1970s, the committee funds made up about two thirds of the IRA–Sinn Fein's expenditure on prisoners' dependents. As a result of this and other contributions, the IRA, according to the British, was left on average with £170,000 free to spend on arms, ammunition, and explosives every year.

There was no similar breakdown of the IRA's balance sheet for the 1980s. However, it would seem that it was able less and less able to rely on theft, such as bank robberies, for its income, as security tightened over the years.

In the early 1980s, the IRA turned to kidnapping for ransom. But this, too, had its dangers. In 1983, the Irish police mounted a massive manhunt searching for an executive whom the IRA had kidnapped for a reported million-dollar ransom. It threatened to disrupt the IRA command network in the south. Intensive searches can lead to the uncovering of arms dumps and the flushing out of IRA men on the run.

Meanwhile, in Northern Ireland, the authorities were cracking down on other sources of income, such as alleged protection rackets. The 1980s also witnessed a large influx of prisoners into Northern Ireland's jails as a result of the use of highly placed informers (so-called supergrasses). Increased political activity by Sinn Fein as well, which was comparatively dormant in the 1970s, no doubt put an increased strain on the movement's financial resources. Under these circumstances, NORAID's contributions would become ever more crucial to the smooth running of the republican organization, including its capacity to free sufficient funds for purchasing guns. Without the constant supply of weapons, the IRA would be lost and the whole republican structure would quickly break down.

Throughout the late 1980s and early 1990s, NORAID declined and, in 1994, was superceded as a fundraising organization by the Friends of Sinn Fein, which opened an office in Washington in the wake of the first IRA cease-fire. (See Chapter 8)

The most persuasive evidence that NORAID had little direct connection with arms acquisition comes from the fact that to sustain its weapons supplies the IRA turned to other contacts, among whom the most important was one man. He was a loner, a revolutionary who was never a member of NORAID, content to remain for the most of his life in the shadows, where he plotted to bring about the defeat of Britain and the destruction of the Northern Ireland state.

3
OF ARMS AND THE MAN

Three flights of creaking stairs led to the narrow, dusty landing of the top floor. To the right a patched and peeling door opened into the small, cluttered, but strangely bare apartment of George Harrison. It ran from the front of the house to the back. The bedroom overlooked the bustling activities of a Brooklyn avenue. But the back room was quiet. Its window gazed down on a wild, overgrown garden, which was steeped in quiet as surely as a monastery garden. The walls of the back room were almost bare, except for photographs of Bernadette McAliskey (née Devlin), the former civil-rights leader, and Archbishop Romero of El Salvador (assassinated in 1981), and near the door, ten buttons with diminutive photographs of the ten dead hunger strikers. And beneath them was a slogan from a Belfast ghetto wall: "For those who understand, no explanation is necessary—for those who don't understand, no explanation is possible."

An old, somewhat threadbare couch, a few chairs, a small coffee table, and a larger table set between the two windows overlooking the untended garden comprised the furniture of the back room in which George Harrison spent much of his time when in the apartment. On all of them were stacked piles of pamphlets addressing every liberation struggle currently unsettling rulers and governments. Pamphlets and handbills and posters spilled onto the floor, along with newspapers in Spanish, notices of demonstrations outside the South African consulate, the Filipino consulate, and the British consulate. Occasionally, old handbills peeked out proclaiming their slogans from some past meeting, gathering dust under the more recent accumulations of the printing press. Beyond this room the profusion continued into the bedroom at the front of the house. Boxes of books and newspapers and pamphlets sat on the floor in that room darkened by the drawn blinds that were never raised. For all its quiet, the apartment seemed oddly alive, thanks to this profusion of papers, the detritus of political passions that gave the feeling of hectic, ceaseless activity, the product of some perpetual political meeting where militants proclaimed their cause and slogans vied breathlessly with slogans.

Yet at the center of it all was the stone-cut demeanor of George Harrison, with all the calm of certitude. And at the heart of that certitude lay his commitment to a thirty-two-county Irish socialist republic and the end of British rule in Northern Ireland. It was a commitment that had led him to become the IRA's principal source of arms for almost thirty years. Most of the weapons from America reaching the hands of the IRA first passed through his. They were the large hands of a working man. In their strength and coarseness could be traced the lines of his father, who was a stoneworker, as were several other members of his family. But George did not follow that trade. Instead, he worked as a security guard with Brinks until his retirement in 1983.

In the tiny kitchen off the back room he fended for himself like any Irish bachelor alone in a London flat or New York apartment. He breakfasted on scrambled eggs and ran in the nearby park to keep fit. Though he had not set foot in Ireland for nearly fifty years, he still spoke with a brogue that took the listener back to another world, beyond the urban backyards and gardens of Brooklyn to the small, poor farms and stony fields and bleak, treeless hills of the west of Ireland.

George Harrison's roots lay in the shallow, gritty soil of County Mayo, where he was born in the village of Shammer in 1915, one of ten children (two died in infancy). While his father hewed stone, his mother ran a small shop in the village. Shammer was set in one of the most impoverished and bleak stretches of Irish countryside. Infertile fields merged into miles of undulating bogland, the surface of which, if it was watched long enough, seemed to roll and heave like that of the ocean. Outcrops of rough, rock-strewn mountains broke the horizon. This was the land of Croagh Patrick, the steep, stony hill that is a pilgrim's path; every year thousands of them come from all over Ireland to crawl on their hands and knees to its summit, their bleeding skin a penance for their sins. Mayo exacts hardships not only from its pilgrims but from its people too. In the first decades of this century, when Harrison was growing up, the memory of the great famine still cast its shadow over their lives, which were bare and hard as Mayo's stony fields.

Though Shammer had only fifty houses, it was divided into two areas. One was called Shammer Dubh ("Black Shammer") and the other Shammer Ban ("White Shammer"). It is not certain why these names arose, but it is surmised that it had something to do with two different types of flowers that flourished in Shammer Dubh and Shammer Ban. The village economy depended largely on the money earned by its young men, who went to England in May or June to pick potatoes. They came back home in December with a few pounds. Income also came from America, where several Shammer families, including Harrison's, emigrated.

For entertainment the villagers held boxing matches in a near-by field, or tied up a few old socks for a football. Shammer Dubh would compete with Shammer Ban. They could look forward to a fair now and again. A couple of days a week the villagers would gather in Harrison's home for a *ceilidh*—a session of dancing and singing. Shammer had a few good flute players, and there were plenty of people with stories to tell, songs to sing, and poems to recite. Often, the older people would talk about the famine; the conversation would turn to memories and speculations about their relatives in America. But by the time Harrison was a young boy, politics dominated their thoughts. It was more than a topic of conversation—the war against the British was raging, and all Ireland seemed up in arms.

Harrison's first memory of Ireland's political strife was linked to a flagpole that stood directly outside his home. He recalled seeing it flying an Irish tricolor one day. Shortly afterward, some villagers hoisted a Sinn Fein banner. It was estimated to have cost £30—a fortune in those days. It was worded: THE THOMAS ASHE CUMMAN,

SINN FEIN, and proclaimed UNITED WE STAND. It also carried a portrait of Ashe, a 1916 hero who had led a unit of rebels near Dublin and was one of the last to surrender. He was a tall, striking man, and a splendid piper. After his arrest and conviction, Ashe refused to wear prison clothes and went on hunger strike. He was forcefed, and died in September 1917 in Mountjoy Jail, Dublin. A close friend and comrade of Harrison's in later years, Paddy McLogan, had been on hunger strike with Ashe. He often described to Harrison how he saw Ashe for the last time, pale and writhing in agony, strapped to a bed being wheeled down the corridor of the prison to be force-fed.

Soon a company of the IRA sprang up around Shammer, commanded by Martin Casey, who came from the area. It was part of a battalion based in East Mayo under the command of Pat Finn. A Sinn Fein cooperative was organized in the village which Harrison's father joined. Gaelic-language classes were held. Then, when Harrison was five, the notorious Black and Tans arrived. They came to his house and took two capfuls of eggs and some butter from his mother. He was wearing a little green sweater at the time. He remembers the Black and Tan who led the search party snarling angrily at him. But no harm was done to him or to his mother, and they left soon after confiscating the food.

It was not long before the IRA struck. The guerrillas surrounded a local police station in the nearby town of Kilkelly. The police surrendered and were allowed to leave. The IRA set fire to the station and burned it to the ground. Martin Casey had led the attack. Within days, the Black and Tans were back in Shammer looking for Casey. Everyone was questioned, and the soldiers lived up to their reputation as they ransacked their way through Casey's mother's home, so badly manhandling the old woman that she died not long after they'd gone. However, the British found no sign of the IRA leader, nor was any information forthcoming from the villagers as to his whereabouts.

Casey was eventually captured. By then, however, the IRA and the British were making preparations to negotiate. He was freed and came home a hero. Harrison was there along the roadside enjoying the sight of the tar-filled barrels blazing in welcome at Casey's approach. But the mood of celebration was short-lived. The terms of the treaty settled on by the British and republican negotiators confused and troubled many. When it was clear that Ireland was to be partitioned into two states, there was dismay.

"When people asked what kind of state they were going to have, and were told that the North wasn't going to be part of it, they said, Well, this wasn't what the fight was for," said Harrison. Martin Casey led his unit of the IRA into the antitreaty forces. The civil war claimed one Shammer native—Michael Duffy, an IRA man who died of his wounds after a gun battle with Irish government troops. He was a cousin of the Harrisons.

The defeat of the antitreaty IRA was demoralizing, but the republicans continued to organize in and around Shammer. Harrison's first involvement with the IRA came when Martin Casey gave him a few copies of *An Phoblacht* to sell around the village. (Seventy years later, Harrison still read *An Phoblacht* every week.) Soon he was running messages between local IRA units. By age sixteen, he was attending weekly IRA meetings. The IRA was said to be preparing for another campaign, this time against Northern Ireland. Harrison was drilled with other recruits in a disused building. After about a year of "forming fours" and marching around, they were given a rifle. Weapons were scarce and treated almost with awe. It was a Lee Enfield dating back to World War I. The recruits were trained how to fire it. Then the big day arrived. They were taken out to a nearby bog where they would not be seen. Each of them was handed the precious object in turn and permitted to fire two rounds of ammunition. Then they marched back again. A few months later they got the chance to fire another two rounds.

"They were very sparing," said Harrison. "Nothing was wasted in those days." Bullets were as precious as gold to a miser. Without them and the weapons to fire them, the road to the Holy Grail of a united Irish republic was forever blocked. With the frugality and dedication of monks, men like Harrison helped the IRA maintain that quest.

In 1934 there was a stir among the IRA men in Shammer. It seemed as if their spartan days might be coming to an end and the years of training might soon be put to some use. A stranger bicycled down the deserted roads across the bogland and into the village. He was a handsome, vigorous man in his mid-twenties, and he spoke with an accent never before heard in that part of

Mayo. "Very finely built, very smart, very well spoken—far in advance of any of the likes of us," Harrison remembered. "He was able to speak on most any subject." His name was Bob Bradshaw, the IRA's training officer, the first Northerner that Harrison had ever met. His mission was to train the Shammer unit in the use of the IRA's most up-to-date weapon—the Thompson submachine gun.

Bradshaw was a Belfast man from Divis Street, in the lower Falls area. He joined the IRA at an early age. Though part Protestant, he used to say, "The situation in Belfast was so bad then that you had to shoot your way out." That was exactly what he did. An active career in the IRA almost came to an end when he was cornered by Northern Ireland police in a dead-end street. Bradshaw shot his way through the police cordon. In the gun battle, an officer was killed. Bradshaw fled south, where his unusual intelligence and organizing ability were recognized. His knowledge of weapons also impressed the leadership, and in 1934 he was given the task of instructing volunteers in the western units in the use of the Thompson submachine gun.

The Thompson, which was to prove the most popular weapon with the IRA until the Armalite, first came to the attention of the movement in 1921 when the guerrillas' intelligence chief, Michael Collins, wrote to John J. McGarrity about it. He requested information on "a new type of automatic weapon, the submachine gun, which is a machine gun in the form of a pistol."[1] Collins told McGarrity that he had learned that this weapon was about to become available on the market in America. McGarrity arranged the purchase of five hundred of the weapons with magazines and a supply of .45 caliber ammunition. The cost is estimated to have been nearly $100,000.[2] Collins recognized their potential in close fighting. But he never saw the shipment. It was seized by New York customs officials on June 16, 1921. The guns were impounded. In 1925, three years after the end of the civil war, they were returned to McGarrity's Clann na Gael. He did not succeed in getting them across to Ireland until several years later. By the mid-1930s they had become the basic training weapon of the IRA. They have played a vital role in every subsequent IRA campaign; somewhat more sophisticated models were used in Northern Ireland in the early 1970s. The last notable occasion on which they were employed was in the attempted assassination of a prominent Northern Ireland government minister, John Taylor, some days after Bloody Sunday in 1972.* Their importance only declined when the IRA acquired more deadly high-velocity weapons—a lot of which would come from George Harrison.

In 1934, however, such weapons were impossible even to imagine. Bradshaw stayed with Harrison and gave him the task of finding a suitable cottage in which to conduct the class on the Thompson submachine gun. Harrison found one on the outskirts of Shammer. It was a comparatively new cottage, which the owners had left to go to England. There was an old table, and the IRA men would gather round it to watch as Bradshaw took the Thompson apart, describing its features and functions. The instructions were conducted by candlelight, with an old cloth thrown over the window. Harrison recalled that Bradshaw could assemble the gun in the dark, or blindfolded. He said he was the best weapons instructor he ever met. Harrison picked up a lot of extra experience having the training officer as a house guest. Soon he graduated to guard duty, and stood watch by the cottage door as Bradshaw carried out his tasks.

After about two months, Bradshaw got on his bicycle and moved off to instruct another IRA unit. Harrison never saw him again. But he would never forget him. (Bradshaw ended up in internment camp in the 1940s. When he was released, he abandoned the IRA and became active in the Irish Labour party. However, he grew impatient with the squabbling left and lapsed from active involvement in politics. He was a good friend of Brendan Behan and other notable figures of the Irish literary renaissance of the late 1940s and early 1950s. Though close to many writers, he did not himself write much. But in 1969 he published a series of articles in *The Irish Times* recalling his childhood in Belfast. He was well known in Dublin as a vigorous and stimulating conversationalist until he suffered a severe stroke in late 1981.)

Following Bradshaw's departure there was an anticlimax. Shammer's IRA men had been prepared to put their training into use. But the chance to do so never came. There was no resurgence to be directed against the British stronghold of Northern Ireland.

*The Official IRA carried out the attack.

Instead, ideological disputes shook the movement, and it floundered in confusion trying to establish a coherent policy and program for the future. The enthusiasm of the Shammer volunteers waned as they realized there would be no immediate end to their inactivity.

Harrison left for England, where he worked for a time on farms in Yorkshire and Lincolnshire. In 1938 he returned to Ireland. But it was a brief stay. Already, six of his sisters and brothers had emigrated to America. Several of them had settled in New Hampshire, where an older brother worked as a stonecutter in the granite quarries. Harrison decided to follow their example. At the end of the year he left his mother and father and set sail from Cobh, County Cork, for America. He planned to get a job, save some money. If he succeeded, he would bring his parents over after him. He did, finally, in 1949. "Somehow I figured on not failing," he recalled. "America was a place I thought you could succeed at something. It was also a place where you could do a lot for the Irish cause."

For the first few years Harrison was too busy trying to survive to think about the Irish cause. But even if he had, there was little to be done about it during the 1940s, which were desolate years for Irish nationalism. He took jobs as a bartender and docker in New York. War came, and he joined the artillery. When he was demobilized in 1946, he returned briefly to bartending. Shortly afterward, however, he took a job as a security guard with Brinks. He held the job for thirty-six years.

In the late 1940s and early 1950s Harrison became active in several Irish-American organizations. Among those he joined was the James Connolly Club, named after the revolutionary socialist leader of the 1916 Rising. At this time Harrison's politics were turning leftward, partly because he had become an active trade unionist.

It was not a propitious time to be a socialist in America. Right-wing currents were strongly felt in Irish-American organizations. One of the most prominent had asked its members to sign a pledge against communism. But Harrison always stayed apart from the larger Irish-American groups, finding their politics generally uncongenial and conservative. Regardless of the tendencies within the Irish-American community, he stuck to his own socialist views and stayed with them for all his life.

It was while he was a member of the Connolly Club that he met Liam Cotter. Cotter, like Harrison, was an exile from the Irish struggle. Kerry-born, he had been in the IRA in the 1930s. With thousands of others, Cotter was interned in the early 1940s by the Dublin government of Eamon De Valera. In prison, Cotter became an admirer of Paddy McLogan, a prominent member of the movement who also knew Harrison. Cotter, a fluent Gaelic speaker, remained committed to the IRA cause when he came to New York in 1949. Harrison and Cotter became firm friends and remained so until the latter's death. They shared a common goal—a united Irish republic—and the same leftist politics.

Though Cotter was in America, he stayed in contact with the IRA. He became, in fact, a sort of representative for the movement in the United States. From the mid-1950s onward the IRA began to regroup. Though badly mauled by De Valera in the previous decade, the organization believed that by concentrating on Northern Ireland it could revive nationalist sentiment throughout the country and initiate a widespread movement to bring about the final withdrawal of all British troops from Ireland. A campaign against the Unionist-controlled state was planned. Arms were needed. A series of raids on military barracks in Ireland and England were partially successful in supplying the guerrillas' needs. Naturally, they also turned to America to see what could be done. Paddy McLogan was sent over to organize support and set up an arms supply. He met with Cotter and Harrison to see if they could provide the weapons necessary. The network established by McGarrity was destroyed by the war. New contacts would be required. McLogan found Harrison and Cotter ready to cooperate.

At this time, Harrison lived with his parents at 465 East Ninth Street in the Park Slope section of Brooklyn. Down the block from the Harrisons lived a family of Corsican origin, the De Meos. A young Italian kid introduced Harrison to George De Meo. They became friends. Their families frequently visited each other. De Meo told Harrison that he was "on the fringe of the Mafia," but he stayed clear of their disputes. "At family wakes," Harrison remembered, "George De Meo was always the man in charge." Harrison also quickly learned about De Meo's interest in guns. According to Harrison, he knew more about guns than any man he had ever met. And De Meo ran a gun store just outside the city.

De Meo had no real politics, in Harrison's estimation. But he once mentioned to Harrison that he thought "Ireland was a good cause." Harrison also knew that De Meo had been questioned by the police in connection with arms shipments to Cuban rebels. Before long, Harrison and De Meo forged a crucial link in the chain of the American connection. Slowly at first, but building up over the years, De Meo began supplying Harrison with arms for the IRA. During this time, only Cotter and some high-ranking IRA men knew of De Meo's existence as a supplier. So it would remain for twenty-five years.

Another important link in the chain forged in the late 1950s was the man who became the IRA's chief messenger to America. He was never arrested or named, and he remained in this role until the 1980s. Harrison called him "the Emissary"; all that was known about him was that he was a man with a long career in the republican movement, and held in high esteem by the few IRA men aware of his role. From the late 1950s onward the Emissary came to America regularly with a "shopping list" of IRA requirements. Occasionally he would bring funds from the IRA to Harrison and Cotter with which to make the necessary purchases.

Gradually the network developed. It included John Joe Martin, a former IRA man who had been active in the thirties and forties, and Tom Falvey. Falvey, a Kerry-born IRA man, had the responsibility of storing and cleaning the weapons. In later years the network would open up important contacts in Pennsylvania, Massachusetts, and other parts of the country. At no time did it number more than twelve people, four of whom eventually died violent deaths.

The Cotter-Harrison-De Meo link was the network's most vital part. At first, their contribution was small. They supplied the IRA mainly with Colt .45s and a few German submachine guns called Schmeissers, which can be used as semi- or full automatics; however, they started to acquire shipments of M-1 carbine rifles and its prototype, the Garands, the standard World War II infantry rifle. The Garand is known as a reliable and accurate sniping weapon, useful up to about five hundred yards, but it is bulky and inconvenient to conceal. The M-1, which replaced it, is an easy-to-carry semiautomatic, and one of the basic weapons of the U.S. infantry. It can fire about ten to twelve rounds per minute. They also picked up a quantity of Thompsons, and a batch of P.38s, German-made handguns. But their biggest breakthrough came in 1958 or 1959, when they got a couple of .50-caliber machine guns, powerful enough to take down a light aircraft.

One of Harrison and Cotter's main ambitions at that time was to get a rocket gun. They felt that for the border campaign to be successful, the IRA needed the kind of powerful but portable gun that could take out an armored car, or destroy the wall of a barracks with one well-aimed shot. As the 1950s campaign developed, it consisted mainly of "flying column"–style attacks on isolated police stations, with the occasional ambush. It was being fought in the border countryside, a network of narrow, twisting lanes, hedgerows, and fields. Eventually, they picked up several bazookas, which would be of use in such terrain. Cotter received training on the weapon, and when they managed to get a few of them across to Ireland, he followed to give the IRA instructions in their use. (One of his pupils was the future IRA leader Daithi O'Conaill.) However, some of the bazookas turned out to be defective, and were not used until the early 1970s.

Most of the weapons left America from the Brooklyn docks. On one occasion Harrison and Cotter arranged to send over some bazooka parts with two Irish sailors. Packing the parts in two suitcases, they went down to the dockside to meet the sailors. It was a bleak winter's night, and bitter cold. Harrison and Cotter paced up and down the dark dockside in the freezing weather until the sailors arrived, two hours late. They handed over the cases. But when the sailors set off to find their ship, they couldn't locate it in the dark. The four men were searching the dockside when a police car pulled up. A police officer rolled down his window. "What's up?" he asked, looking at the four of them as they stood there pinched white with cold. "These are my two cousins," Harrison said, pointing to the sailors, "and they're just back from a weekend on the town. You know how it is," he smiled, speaking his thickest Irish brogue. "Well, the lads are so befuddled they've misplaced the ould ship." The sailors held the suitcases full of bazooka parts and tried not to shake too much.

"What's the ship's name?" the helpful policeman asked. Harrison told him. He nodded. "It's just around here—follow me," the cop answered, and drove the car slowly in front of them until they reached the ship. Then he bade them a safe journey and drove off.

As the two young men hauled the heavy cases up the steep gangplank, Harrison watched them. One of them stopped at the top. "It's cauld!" he shouted before stepping onto the ship. "And I thought to myself," Harrison remembered, "God! How many poor devils like him have done the same thing for Ireland over the generations!" Many years later, in 1972, a bazooka was fired at a police station in Belfast. It scored a direct hit and wrecked part of the side wall. No one was injured. "That's our handiwork," one of Harrison's confederates said to him when he heard about it.

Around 1960 or so Harrison and Cotter met the poet and playwright Brendan Behan in New York. Behan was himself a former IRA man who had taken part in McGarrity and Russell's doomed bombing campaign in England in 1939. Though he had since cast a jaundiced eye on republican politics, Behan agreed to smuggle weapons to Ireland—almost certainly more for the devilment of it than for any political reason. Harrison and Cotter packed a few Thompson submachine guns, handguns, and about two thousand rounds of ammunition in Behan's trunk. Behan had the trunk sent to a fictitious address in Dublin. The IRA leadership were not kept informed of Behan's arrangements, and became angry with him. But Behan shot back. "I got the stuff over three thousand miles of water to them. If they couldn't get it another two miles—well, fuck them!" he exclaimed to a friend of Harrison's later. However, after some confusion, the shipment reached its destination safely.

Another incident from this time stuck in Harrison's mind. It involved George De Meo. De Meo had arranged for an arms pickup for Harrison on the Labor Day weekend in 1958. The plan was that De Meo would drive to Manhattan with the arms in a van, and meet Harrison and Cotter at the corner of Fifty-eighth Street and Third Avenue. The meeting was arranged for 11 P.M. Cotter and Harrison arrived on time and waited. Eventually, around midnight, one of De Meo's runners arrived. He said De Meo was on his way. Harrison noticed, however, that the young man, who had previously been involved in smuggling arms to Cuban revolutionaries, seemed restless and ill at ease. After a time, the runner said there was something wrong and they should leave. But just then the van came in sight. Harrison and Cotter were standing in the doorway of a jeweler's shop when De Meo pulled up against the curb. "It's in the back," De Meo said. De Meo's companion was a man Harrison did not recognize. He was impatient and asked Harrison and Cotter to complete the deal and hand over the cash there and then. Harrison refused, insisting on checking the guns first. As they were about to do so, a squad car came up Third Avenue and pulled over. A cop stuck his head out and asked Harrison and Cotter what they were doing. Harrison explained they were merely standing on the curb waiting for their girl-friends. The girls were late, Harrison smiled.

"You mean she stood you up," the cop answered. "I know how you feel." As he was talking to Harrison and Cotter, De Meo's van pulled away and disappeared around the corner. At the time Harrison thought little of it. But years later it took on a new significance.

Harrison and Cotter were busy on other fronts. Cotter founded the IRA's Prisoners' Aid Fund. As chairman, he raised money to send back to Ireland. It was a difficult task, and he met with indifference from most Irish Americans. But they had success with their contacts in the trade-union movement. One of their largest contributors was the Transport Workers Union. Irish-American labor leader Mike Quill was its president. According to Harrison, Quill raised over $6,000 for the Prisoners' Aid Fund. Harrison said that Quill told him, "You can use it for the Irish political prisoners—or it can go to purchase guns for the Irish Republican Army." The bulk of it might indeed have gone to the purchase of arms—but this cannot be confirmed.

Both men took part in organizing protests outside the British consulate. When two IRA men from County Tyrone were sentenced to death for killing a sergeant of the Royal Ulster Constabulary (RUC), they picketed the consulate carrying slogans demanding ENGLAND GET OUT OF IRELAND and LEGAL LYNCHING IN BELFAST. (A photograph in *The Irish Times* showed Harrison in front of the demonstrators and Cotter holding a banner.)

By 1960 the IRA's border campaign was petering out, and no amount of protest or new weapons could have saved it. A combination of factors contributed to its failure. The Unionist government introduced internment after the beginning of the campaign. The IRA might have withstood that had not the Dublin government done likewise, rounding up almost the entire leadership. "The Irish government stabbed the movement in the back," says Harrison. Added to this was the obvious indifference of Northern Ireland's Catholics to the proclaimed struggle for freedom.

Though the attacks continued for another two years, they were little more than an irritant to the authorities. Harrison and Cotter later felt that the guns they had sent over had, if anything, unnecessarily prolonged the campaign when all chance of its success had vanished. Finally, in 1962, the IRA command called a halt. Dated February 26, the announcement said, "The leadership of the Resistance Movement has ordered the termination of The Campaign Of Resistance to British occupation. . . . all arms and other materials have been dumped and all full-time active service volunteers have been withdrawn."[3] Bitterly, the IRA order referred to the indifference of the people "whose minds have been deliberately distracted from the supreme issue facing the Irish people—the unity and freedom of Ireland."[4]

The aftermath of the border campaign was a bitter one for Harrison, Cotter, and those few Irish Americans still actively supporting the nationalist cause. The IRA was torn by recriminations as the demoralized men sought to blame someone for their defeat. Harrison's close friend Paddy McLogan, by then president of Sinn Fein, was accused of undermining the campaign and working to bring it to a halt. McLogan vehemently denied this, and demanded that the IRA leadership support him. When the IRA refused to issue a supporting statement, McLogan handed in his resignation from Sinn Fein. It was to be the beginning of a period of acrimony that prefigured the IRA's final split in late 1969. McLogan would not be made the scapegoat; in his turn, he accused the IRA leadership of wanting to abandon the traditional republican policy of refusing to recognize the Dail (the Irish parliament in Dublin). He believed that powerful forces were at work within the IRA and Sinn Fein to force the movement into participation in the Dail, thus making the same compromise that De Valera had arrived at over twenty years before. McLogan was convinced that such a course would bring an end to the republican movement. Soon afterward, McLogan and several other prominent republicans were expelled from the movement.

Both Harrison and Cotter followed this controversy with great concern. Though McLogan was extremely conservative in his politics, as an undeviating republican they respected him more than any other. They were alarmed about his statements accusing the leadership of secretly wanting an accommodation with the "institutions of partition," as they would contemptuously call the Dublin and Northern Ireland parliaments. When he resigned, Harrison and Cotter informed the IRA that they too were severing their connection to the republican movement. Since that time—in 1962—Harrison was not a member of either the IRA or Sinn Fein. Because of the way McLogan was treated, Harrison refused several approaches from the leadership to come into the movement again. And he remained adamant that his friend Paddy McLogan was victimized by the IRA–Sinn Fein leadership.

However, though Harrison and Cotter were out of the movement, they retained "contacts." They also had a cache of arms that had been collected for the now defunct border campaign, but which they had not been able to get to Ireland. McLogan had been an important contact for Harrison in the shipping of arms between America and Ireland. In June 1964 Harrison became concerned that "loose talk" was creating a security risk; he wanted to get the cache, part of which was stored in the basement of an apartment building on Manhattan's West Side and part at Cotter's home in the Bronx, to Ireland as soon as possible. He contacted McLogan about the shipment. Though McLogan was no longer a member of the IRA or Sinn Fein, Harrison felt that in the turmoil shaking the movement he was the only one he could trust with the guns.

On June 30, 1964, Harrison received a coded letter from McLogan asking him to send over a "pilot lot"—that is, a few weapons as a test run. McLogan, who signed his coded letters concerning arms "Larkin," was worried that a new contact, code-named 'Jackson," was in fact working for the new IRA leadership whom he had attacked so vigorously; McLogan did not want the arms to fall into the hands of his ideological enemies. What he intended to do with them if they got safely across is not clear. Harrison believed that he merely wanted to store them in anticipation of another campaign sometime in the future. However, it will never be known, for within a month McLogan was found dead, and in circumstances that have given rise to further allegations and re-criminations.

At the beginning of July 1964 Harrison received a personal, uncoded letter from McLogan. It is chatty, good-humored, full of political gossip. President Kennedy had visited Ireland a year before and spoken in the Dail. McLogan regretted that Kennedy's speech was "framed in a manner which gave the impression that he was addressing the sovereign assembly of a free and independent Ireland." However, McLogan adds, "the sentiments to which he gave expression were worthy of his proclaimed affection for Ireland and the aspirations of the friends of her freedom." He writes to Harrison that he was expecting his wife home very soon from the hospital where she was undergoing hip surgery. In the meantime, he was alone.

On July 20, two weeks later, Paddy McLogan was found lying in the hallway of his home just outside Dublin, with a fatal bullet wound in the head. In his hand he clutched a P.38—one of the German-made pistols that Harrison had sent over several years before. His death was called a suicide. But Harrison thinks differently. He says that an investigation by some of the dead man's friends showed that McLogan had gone to the door before being shot. The trajectory of the bullet that killed him demonstrated that he had been shot from the outside, near the doorway. The idea that McLogan killed himself is, in any case, absurd to Harrison. Paddy McLogan was a strict and devout Catholic, a man who never drank and who followed the moral and social teachings of his church very scrupulously. Nor does his last letter to Harrison indicate any sign of depression or suicidal thoughts.

The death troubled Harrison, and he was bitter about those who said it was a suicide, calling them "rumor mongers." "It was a terrible tragedy," he said, twenty-one years later. "A terrible loss, personal and otherwise, of a man I had venerated so highly." As to who was responsible for that loss—if suicide is discounted, as Harrison insisted—that question has never been satisfactorily answered. Harrison suggested British intelligence agents. But he also did not discount the possibility that it was a result of the tensions within the IRA. Though expelled from the movement,

McLogan still commanded considerable support among those who opposed the leadership's trend toward recognizing the Dublin government. The debate about who had lost the border war had turned into a debate about whether or not the IRA and Sinn Fein should recognize the Dublin Parliament and fight elections. The leadership, as later events showed, was determined to follow the political road. They might have seen McLogan and his supporters as a potential barrier, whose opposition to the IRA's proposed political role could well have threatened the organization with a split. The fact that a few weeks before his death McLogan was attempting to get arms into the country could have increased such fears. The IRA leadership might have concluded he was trying to set up a breakaway group to oppose them. Harrison did not like to think so, and preferred to blame the British. But his bitterness about the affair and the IRA's role in it remained deep.

"The movement never did justice to Paddy. Some of the people who later became leaders in what are known as the Provisional IRA and the Official IRA were responsible for that climate that was set up against Paddy. There was never any proper court of inquiry into his death," Harrison asserted. "They never put his name on the role of honor—they promised to do it, but never did. The republican movement failed Paddy and failed his life. So even to this day, the ghost of McLogan stands between myself and the movement."

The ghost of McLogan would come to haunt the IRA when, five years after his death, the Northern Ireland crisis provoked a crisis within the organization. Would it continue along the political road leading to recognition of partition which McLogan fiercely opposed? Or would it revert to the gospel of "physical force" that for so long had been the basis of the IRA's existence? Though McLogan was not there in 1969 to take part in that dispute, others emerged who believed that political accommodation with partition was now impossible. The split that might have happened in the early 1960s occurred in 1969. And those whose faith lay in force knew where to turn for the means by which that faith could be made reality.

Early in 1969, the Emissary came to visit Harrison and Cotter. Northern Ireland was poised on the edge of a major conflict, as civil-rights marchers fought with extreme Protestants. The Emissary's message to them was simple: "This thing is wide open." Cotter said he thought the riots would burn themselves out. But Harrison agreed with the Emissary.

The Emissary said he was going back to Ireland and heading for Derry. The movement needed weapons. Harrison and Cotter had not forgotten the McLogan affair. But they were not going to let that get in the way of sending whatever they could to help the IRA, which they believed would have to defend the Catholics in the near future. Harrison said he agreed to turn over whatever they still had left in their dumps to the IRA. These were weapons collected in the late 1950s for the border campaign. Harrison remembered that they had some seventy "good weapons" and about sixty thousand rounds of ammunition. Among the guns were twenty carbine rifles with folding stocks—"the best we ever had," said Harrison—a few handguns, and several "grease" guns. The grease gun, so-called because of its resemblance to the grease gun used by garage mechanics, was a World War II submachine gun; according to Harrison, it was about as effective as a Thompson, but a lot more difficult to operate and maintain. They made plans to have them taken across to Ireland, but it was not until mid-1969 that they reached the North—in time to be used in the fighting that erupted that August.

The events of the summer of 1969, when British troops were sent into the streets of Derry and Belfast, convinced them of the urgency of the crisis. The Emissary was in Derry when the severe rioting broke out and the troops were sent in. He wrote to Harrison describing the seriousness of the situation, and asking for him to send any help at all. Some of the arms were already en route. Harrison and Cotter also gathered about $800 and sent it directly to the Emissary. According to Harrison, it was the first money to reach the movement in the current crisis.

Another event that galvanized Harrison that summer was the American tour of civil-rights leader and member of the British Parliament, Bernadette Devlin. Like Harrison, she was a revolutionary socialist, and her view of the developments in Northern Ireland was close to his own. "When I first saw Bernadette emerge, he remembered, "I said to myself, I don't know if I'm seeing or hearing right." He compared her with Frank Ryan, a left-wing IRA leader of the 1930s who fought on the republican side in Spain against Franco. Cotter was, as ever, more cautious. "Don't get carried away," he warned his colleague. He still believed it would "blow over."

"But what if it doesn't?" Harrison recalled asking him.

"Then we could be in for busy times," came his friend's reply. Cotter's answer proved prophetic. The deepening crisis in Northern Ireland would put all their resources to the test.

Early in 1970, Harrison and Cotter had their first contact with a leader from the reorganized IRA, which had just endured the worst split since the civil war in 1922. The Emissary had told Daithi O'Conaill that the two men were still prepared to help out. When O'Conaill came to New York at the beginning of that year, a meeting between them was arranged.

The three men met in the old Horn & Hardart automat near Columbus Circle on Manhattan's West Side, just a few blocks from Central Park. The meeting lasted two hours. O'Conaill at first outlined what he believed would happen in Northern Ireland. He called the use of the British troops as a peacekeeping force "farcical," and said that the armed struggle would have to be stepped up. Both Harrison and Cotter said they agreed with him. Then he asked them, "Well, what can you do?" The two men told O'Conaill that they wanted to stay clear of the fund-raising activities that he had been helping to set up with other contacts. Then O'Conaill asked them, "How about the armed struggle?"

"There's no problem with that," Harrison replied. That was where their expertise lay, and that was where they would be of most use to the movement. They saw a renewal of the armed struggle, and their commitment to it outweighed the bitter feelings about past disputes. "There's one thing Paddy McLogan wouldn't want and that would be for us to deny help," the two men told O'Conaill. They told O'Conaill they would do all they could.

"We kept our promise," said Harrison.

Harrison was soon in contact with the people he had worked with in the 1950s—Tom Falvey and John Joe Martin. Both were ready to build up the network again. The key man was De Meo. By this time De Meo was running a gun shop in Yonkers; he had other business connections, including a bar he owned in Mount

Vernon, and various properties around New York in which he had part interests. Harrison approached De Meo, who agreed to see what he could do.

At first the supply was small. He estimated that in the first year of their renewed efforts they could only come up with about forty weapons of different kinds, mainly handguns. In early 1971 pressure began to build up. The officer in command of the British troops in Northern Ireland declared "war" on the IRA at the beginning of February. The IRA responded by raking a British army patrol with submachine-gun fire. Several soldiers were wounded, one of whom died shortly afterward. The British army had suffered its first fatality in Ireland in almost fifty years. The Emissary let Harrison know that things had to be speeded up. If the IRA was to seriously challenge the British on the streets and in the countryside, modern weapons were needed.

"The British were not going to give up easily," said Harrison later. "They'd only give up the way we gave up in Vietnam—when it became expensive for them in terms of lives. So I knew we had to hit them hard, and increase the supply as much as we could."

Either late in 1970 or early the following year, Harrison and Cotter made their first real breakthrough in acquiring new, more modern weapons. They purchased their first AR-15s, better known as the Armalite. The Armalite was a semiautomatic version of the M-16, the standard infantry weapon of the U.S. army. Used mainly for hunting, it was light, easily broken down and concealed, and useful at ranges up to four hundred yards. It fired high-velocity rounds, and was ideal for guerrillas operating either in cities or in the open countryside. From 1971 onward supplies of the AR-15 increased, some coming through De Meo. The IRA came to rely on the Armalite as its basic weapon. "They went Armalite crazy," Harrison recalled. He said that one female IRA volunteer was nicknamed "the Armalite widow" because she had killed so many British soldiers using the gun.

Late in 1971 the arms suppliers bought their first M-16, which Harrison called "the best infantry weapon in the world." Like the AR-15 sporting version, the M-16 was light and portable, but could be used as a full automatic, with a rapid rate of fire. They paid $250 for the first M-16, but soon saw the price shoot up to $400.

The IRA also needed a reliable sniping weapon that would give them a good chance of a first-round kill at long range. Among the guns Harrison purchased at this time were some old Mausers—bolt-action rifles from the First World War, which had sighting scopes and were useful for sniping.

1971 was a confused year. "Everyone wanted to be a gunrunner," recalled Harrison. A lot of Irish Americans wanted to get involved in it—or at least talked as if they did. A few did, and there were quite a number of arrests as a result between 1972 and 1974. But none of those charged had any connections with the Harrison-Cotter network. It operated separately, kept underground, and maintained its distance from organizations like the INAC. "Security was the main consideration with us," said Harrison.

Things didn't settle down until early 1973. From then on the arms network was supplying the IRA with between two and three hundred weapons a year. By this time the number of people involved in supplying, cleaning, and storing the weapons before they were shipped was about six, which it never exceeded. This included the Emissary, De Meo, contacts in Boston and Philadelphia, and Harrison and Cotter themselves. According to Harrison, apart from himself and Cotter, only two other people involved in the operation ever met with De Meo: Paddy McLogan (in the 1950s) and Tom Falvey. The operation was kept tightly controlled (the FBI confirms this). Though Harrison occasionally helped check and clean weapons from other sources, his main supplier was De Meo. De Meo got many of his weapons from his own contacts in North Carolina. A lot of them came from a U.S. marine base there, Camp Le Jeune.

Soldiers would smuggle out ammunition or guns and sell them to local arms dealers, who in turn would sell them to De Meo. Then he usually stacked them in the trunk of his car and drove north for New York. He would sell them to Harrison and Cotter, who always carried out the purchases for the IRA. They would clean the guns and oil them, helped at times by Tom Falvey. The weapons would then be wrapped and given to Falvey, who had overall responsibility for storing them. The next stage, the transportation of the material to Ireland, was out of Harrison's hands. He never knew the methods that were used in any detail. He did not know those involved in this side of the operation. Nor did they know of him. At most, he would arrange for the weapons to be picked up and moved. When he had to move the weapons to a prearranged pickup place, he would pack them in empty flower cartons, which he obtained from a florist at the corner of his street.

Harrison and Cotter would sometimes store the weapons in their own homes. Harrison recalled one occasion in 1975 when he had one of the largest consignments he had ever purchased in a small room next to his living room in his house on East Ninth Street. It consisted of some two hundred rifles and 150,000 rounds of ammunition. The night he put the weapons there, his doorbell rang. Outside were two men who identified themselves as agents of the Bureau of Alcohol, Tobacco and Firearms. They asked if they might come in. Harrison said, "Of course." They entered the house, and made themselves comfortable in the living room. Their host, maintaining as casual a manner as possible, offered them tea. The agents gladly accepted. They informed Harrison that they were subpoenaing him to appear before a grand jury in Concord, New Hampshire. The grand jury was enquiring into illegal arms trafficking in the state. Apparently, a check made out to a New Hampshire gun store had been traced to him. Harrison did not say anything, merely that he would appear with his lawyers before the hearing. The agents finished their tea, bade their farewells, and walked out, leaving the stack of arms and ammunition in the next room untouched. Harrison later appeared before the jury and out of thirty-five questions they asked him answered two: he gave his name and address. He was not recalled and no indictments were brought against him.

The haul that was in the next room was worth $50,000. Where did Harrison, who worked as a security guard, raise the money needed for such a transaction? Harrison was adamant that none of the money he handled to buy weapons was ever raised under the auspices of the INAC. In a written statement to this author, Harrison said: "I wish to categorically state that all funds collected here to supply the wherewithal to maintain the armed struggle against the forces of British imperialism and its native quislings were raised through individual subscriptions from people who were committed to the cause of Ireland's freedom." He continued: "The allegations of the Brits and their Irish lackeys that funds raised by Irish Northern Aid were used for that purpose are a blatant falsehood and I repudiate them as a calculated fabrication designed to sow discord." The allegation was also made that the founder of the INAC, Michael Flannery, was the arms network's banker. Harrison denied this as well. The network, he claimed, had no "godfather" figure. Certain individuals were regular contributors, but their contributions never exceeded $1,000 at any one time. The Emissary would sometimes bring funds. The money raised was held by a member of the network. Harrison kept a strict account of all such funds, and also of how much he spent. He estimated that from the early 1950s until 1981, approximately $1.1 million passed through his hands for weapons and ammunitions purchases. "I was good on prices," he boasted.

The weapons sent by the Harrison-Cotter network were being put to rapid use by the IRA. Between 1970 and 1974, 285 members of the British army and Northern Ireland police force were killed, mostly by the IRA. Hundreds of civilians also died, generally in bombing attacks or by Protestant assassins, but the IRA was also responsible for killing Protestants in retaliation and for the accidental deaths of bystanders caught in the crossfire. Many of the soldiers and policemen who died were shot with the guns Harrison and Cotter had purchased. For Harrison, however, these deaths were the inevitable result of British imperialism, and caused him no doubts about the moral legitimacy of the IRA's campaign or his part in it. However, he did admit that on several occasions both he and Cotter had to question what the IRA was doing.

"I sometimes questioned their targets," Harrison said. "And I felt there was sectarianism creeping in." He said there were a couple of incidents where he thought the IRA was hitting at the wrong targets. There was a particularly gruesome instance in early 1976. A Protestant paramilitary group, the Ulster Volunteer Force (UVF), murdered five Catholics in one night. The following day, the IRA stopped a bus taking Protestant workers to their jobs; the workers were taken out of the bus and mowed down with Armalite rifles. Ten were killed. Harrison said, "We were very conscious of the fact that the UVF was openly going in for brutal sectarian murders, and you can understand the response. But we felt that the response should be directed against British soldiers." After the killings of the ten Protestants, Harrison said he and Cotter told the Emissary that it would "hurt our fund-raising here and hurt our position." On another occasion the IRA in Belfast killed several Catholics who it alleged were criminals. When Cotter heard about it he exclaimed, "I'm appalled at this!" Both he and Harrison complained to the Emissary, who promised to inquire into the incident. Later, he told them that the killings had been spontaneous" and had not been sanctioned by the IRA command.

In spite of these uncertainties, Harrison and Cotter maintained the supply of arms to the IRA. Whatever the organization's mistakes, both men felt that the course it was pursuing was the only way of defeating the British and building the socialist republic to which they aspired. And to do that, arms were essential. Some idea of the kind of pressure the network was under throughout the early and mid-1970s may be seen in the numbers of weapons that the IRA was losing to the security forces through raids and arrests. These figures come from those compiled by Northern Ireland security forces.[5]

Between July 1972 and December 1973, the British army and Northern Ireland police recovered 1,369 weapons of various kinds, including 665 rifles, 62 machine guns, 449 handguns, 169 shotguns, 10 rocket launchers, and 14 mortars. During the same period, they lifted 155,039 rounds of ammunition belonging to the IRA. In 1974 the security forces deprived the IRA of 628 weapons—289 rifles, 221 handguns, 67 shotguns, 15 mortars, and 4 rocket launchers, as well as 59,151 rounds of ammunition. That is, between July 1972 and December 1974, the IRA lost a total of 1,997 weapons and 214,190 rounds of ammunition. The following year, there was a slight decline in the numbers recovered by the army and police. Between March 1975 and March 1976, 155 rifles were retrieved, as well as 15 machine guns and 192 handguns. However, a confidential British army document shows that in the same period (March 1975–March 1976) the IRA acquired 234 rifles, 335 handguns, and 27 machine guns to offset their losses. This coincided with one of the peaks of the Harrison-Cotter network's operation. The same document gives figures for the period March 1976–March 1977, which show a swing to the security forces. During that time, according to army statistics, the IRA lost 442 weapons (rifles, handguns, and machine guns) and managed to acquire 338. The army believed that was one of the first occasions when the guerrillas were losing more guns than they were getting. It also happened to coincide with one of the most serious setbacks suffered by the arms network in the United States.

John Joe Martin died in Ireland, where he had moved in the late 1960s. He had been a part of the operation from the 1950s, providing valuable links across the U.S. border to Canada, and though not subsequently involved after his move to Ireland, he was regarded as a great loss. But in 1976 the network suffered a much greater blow.

Liam Cotter, like his close friend George Harrison, worked as a security guard. Indeed, it was Harrison who got Cotter work with the Purolator security company in 1953. The two men were together on the night of April 11, 1976. Harrison went up to Cotter's house in the Bronx to pick up five handguns that had been there for some time. They cleaned the guns together, as they had often done before. Harrison left about 11 P.M. Recalled Harrison: "Next day I got a message at work. One of the dispatchers said, 'You have a friend that works for Purolator called Cotter?' I said yes. She said, 'He's been shot dead.'" Cotter and another guard, Johnny Clark, had gone into a cinema in Times Square to pick up the returns of the week. As they were leaving with the takings, they encountered three men waiting for them in the corridor. Cotter and Clark were ordered to put their hands up. But Cotter went for his gun. He loosed two shots before one of the gunmen, whom Cotter had not seen, opened up with a shotgun from behind. Cotter's rib cage was blown in. Another gunman shot Clark through the heart. Next day Harrison and one of Cotter's brothers who lived in New York went to the morgue to identify the body.

It was the greatest loss that Harrison and the network had suffered so far. For Harrison, in personal and political terms, it was matched only by McLogan's death twelve years before. "More than anybody I know," he said of his murdered colleague, "Liam was responsible for bringing the Irish struggle into correct historical perspective—relating it to other struggles. As well as being involved in the arms struggle he was also very public; he raised funds, and also had a deep appreciation of Irish culture and its importance. He was a socialist in the tradition of James

Connolly." Like Harrison, Cotter never married. His whole life was dedicated to the Irish struggle. His body was brought back to his native County Kerry to be buried near the town of Tralee.

Four men were eventually convicted of the robbery and killings. But as with the death of McLogan, Harrison felt unsatisfied with the simplest explanations offered. "There were too many key men in the network blown away like that," he said. "When a key man goes out like that you may know who fires the bullets but you have to ask yourself who orchestrates it." Harrison's unease came partly from the fact that in the same period that saw Cotter's murder, two other men known to Harrison were also to die violently. One of them, though not linked to the network, was an important fund-raiser. Like Cotter's, their murders would be explained merely as criminal acts. The fund-raiser was a union organizer in Philadelphia. He was shot dead by gunmen in what the police described as a gangland killing. The other was Boston-based. He was gunned down in a Mafia-related dispute.

The immediate problem of finding someone to help replace Cotter was partly solved when Tom Falvey undertook some of the dead man's many responsibilities. Falvey, an ex-IRA man descended from a family whose connections with the Irish struggle went back to Fenian days, had been part of the network since 1958. He now accompanied George Harrison when arms deals were consummated with De Meo, and transported weapons to the dumps, as well as helping to clean and oil them. But there were larger problems that had to be solved concerning the IRA's campaign in Northern Ireland, then in its sixth year.

By the beginning of 1977 the IRA seemed to be losing the war against the British. Violence decreased drastically, and many guerrillas were arrested. The British changed their tactics. There were fewer foot patrols, and therefore fewer targets for IRA snipers. Soldiers more often entered the Catholic areas in armored cars, which were strengthened so as to resist the armor-piercing weapons possessed by the guerrillas. Of these, according to the confidential British report, only the Garand rifle was of use, and that was "largely ineffective." The British relied more heavily on the presence of undercover army teams. These would stake out buildings in the cities and suburbs, waiting to ambush IRA men or those they suspected of being IRA men. (Several innocent civilians were killed as a result of undercover army shootings.) In 1978 an IRA spokesman admitted to a Dublin magazine that this strategy "makes operations much more difficult than was thought conceivable a few years ago." The IRA responded by reorganizing its structure somewhat. Instead of units based in neighborhoods, the guerrillas formed cell structures made up of volunteers taken from different areas. Such "active service units," as they were called, would operate on a citywide basis and then disperse. In this way it was hoped to make it more difficult for the security forces to trace those responsible for guerrilla attacks. The IRA also required weapons to suit the new circumstances. If the opportunities to mount attacks were declining, when attacks were made they had to be sensational and effective; a powerful yet portable weapon was needed.

By 1977 the IRA had only two such weapons in its armory—the bazooka and the RPG-7 rocket. The bazookas had come from Harrison in the 1950s; some of them were defective and others were used only intermittently, since they were clumsy and difficult to carry. The RPG-7s were acquired from other sources in 1972, mainly through Europe. Easier to handle, and more devastating than the bazooka, the rocket had an effective range of almost 1,500 yards. The British army regarded it as one of the most dangerous weapons the IRA possessed, and were concerned that it would acquire more of them. (In late 1977, an arms shipment destined for the IRA was intercepted in Antwerp and found to contain thirty-six of these rockets and seven launchers.) The RPG-7 was effective against armored cars and capable of wrecking a police station. However, the British army observed in its confidential 1978 report that till then the IRA's "inadequate training has resulted in the mishandling of the RPG-7." The report added, "But this could change." However, the IRA never seemed to master the RPG-7 and it gradually dropped out of use. Instead, they found a deadly substitute in America.

In early 1972 Paul Tinnelly, a leading member of the Official IRA from South Down, received information about an arms depot in Danvers, Massachusetts. He learned that it was possible to break into it without much difficulty. He passed word on to the Official IRA leadership, but they rejected the plan as too risky; in any case, they were about to call a halt to their military activities.

Four years later, there was a raid on the depot, though police thought it had nothing to do with either wing of the IRA. A joint Irish-Italian Mafia operation cleared the depot of its weapons, which included M-60s. Soon after that, the Harrison network learned that a quantity of M-16 rifles and—more importantly— seven M-60s were on the market. The M-60 was a powerful, general-purpose machine gun, the standard machine gun of the United States army. It had a rapid rate of fire, six hundred rounds per minute, and according to the British army was capable of shooting down a helicopter, "given a suitable mounting or specially constructed fire position." It was easy to use, and in the words of the British army's secret report "does not call for complex adjustments." It needed a two-man crew to operate it. Though heavy, it was portable enough to facilitate a quick getaway. And it was usually extremely expensive. One source estimated the black-market price of an M-60 in 1978 at over $1,000. However, the Harrison network paid much less.

In July 1977 six M-60s left New York and began their journey to Ireland. (One remained behind in storage and wasn't moved until 1979.) They arrived there in September, and were eventually spirited across the border into Northern Ireland. For several months nothing was seen or heard of them, as the guerrillas began training their volunteers to use them. The M-60s' first public appearance was on January 30, 1978, in Derry, during the ceremonies commemorating the sixth anniversary of Bloody Sunday. The IRA unveiled the weapon as an accompaniment to their threat that the war against Britain was to be intensified.

Later, press photographers were allowed to take specially staged shots of an IRA volunteer wearing a green balaclava hood and dressed in a military outfit holding an M-60, with an ammunition belt and bullets like rows of shark's teeth streaming from its magazine. The volunteer posed beside a wall on which was painted the words: "'78 and still not beat!" (In Ulster speech eight" rhymes with "beat.") The IRA were using the M-60 as a prestige weapon; as proof that whatever setbacks and operational difficulties the organization faced, it was still capable of threatening the stability of the state.

Later, the M-60 had a more deadly debut. A foot patrol of British soldiers was making its way back to base in the small, fiercely nationalist village of Crossmaglen, when the back doors of a van parked in the street flew open. The M-60 inside fired one burst, raking the patrol. Three soldiers fell dead. The van doors slammed shut and the vehicle sped off to vanish in the surrounding countryside before the terrified survivors could respond. In subsequent incidents, the M-60 was used to attack armored vehicles, Land Rover patrols, and helicopters. Within a short time it claimed the lives of another five soldiers and policemen, and injured many more. But by 1985, of the original six dispatched in 1977, only one remained in the hands of the IRA. Its use was infrequent. One of the last instances to date was on May 24, 1985, when along with a .50-caliber machine gun—another weapon originating from the Harrison-Cotter network—an M-60 was used to attack an army helicopter near Crossmaglen. Though the windscreen was smashed, the helicopter landed safely.

The network was now averaging shipments of about three hundred weapons a year. But from the mid-1970s onward it was faced with increasing problems. The key man lost in Boston in 1977 was a serious blow. Further troubles came with the arrival in New York of an Irishman who claimed he had been sent over by the IRA to collect funds. He began intimidating local Irish-American bar owners, threatening them if they didn't contribute. Word reached Harrison. Inquiries revealed that the newcomer was a former IRA man who had been disowned by the movement. Harrison was worried that his actions would interfere with his own efforts and bring them into disrepute. He contacted the IRA, who dispatched a prominent member of the movement to America to deal with the troublemaker. But by the time the guerrilla chief arrived, the troublemaker had fled to San Francisco, where he handed himself over to the police for protection. This, however, proved a relatively minor matter compared with what was to follow.

Some of the problems derived from changes within the IRA itself. The 1977 reorganization had affected the movement throughout; activists from Northern Ireland were taking command and control at all levels, including the leadership of the political wing, Sinn Fein. Old stalwarts like Daithi O'Conaill were gradually edged aside. (One of the only ones to survive these changes was Joe Cahill.) While this meant that the IRA took a more leftward turn—more acceptable to Harrison's own politics—

it had what for him were unwelcome ramifications in America.

The Northerners, mainly Belfast men, wanted not only to control the movement throughout Ireland, but also to take into their hands the arms-supply network in America. The Belfast-dominated leadership wanted to see a transition to IRA control; Harrison had remained outside the movement and steadfastly refused to join because of the McLogan affair. A group of new men who had been handpicked by the IRA in Ireland began establishing new contacts, with the aim of setting up their own operation in America. George Harrison retained his old function, but his operation and that of the newcomers were linked through transportation and shipping contacts.

Said Harrison, "I was having trouble getting stuff moved." Pickups weren't being made on time, and there were too many unnecessary telephone calls. He recalled that as 1979 began, "there was something ominous in the air." Just at this time, he clinched one of the biggest arms deals so far. It was a consignment from De Meo, and consisted of over 150 weapons and 60,000 rounds of ammunition. Among the guns Harrison acquired were two more M-60 machine guns; fourteen M-16s; many mini-14s, the sporting model of an M-14, a rifle popular with the IRA; and a Soviet-made AK-47. The latter was a compact assault rifle comparable to an Armalite; this shipment contained one of the few Harrison was able to acquire.

Much of the material originated in North Carolina, in the marine base of Camp Le Jeune. After Harrison completed the deal, it was packed into a cargo vessel, which was listed as carrying industrial equipment, including paper-shredding machines. What happened next was a disaster for the IRA. One of the people involved in shipping the arms called Dublin from the States. He said "the Frigidaire was on his way." The call was bugged by security forces in Dublin. The police assumed correctly that "the Frigidaire" was the code name for an arms haul. The vessel left New York in September 1979. The cargo arrived at Dublin's north docks in late October. The arms haul was supposed to be left there until the IRA came to pick it up. When the ship docked in Dublin it was watched by a force of undercover policemen. But the IRA had been alerted that something was wrong. Though the police waited for days, no IRA men showed up to collect the precious haul. It sat on the dockside until finally the authorities decided that their entrapment had failed. Calling in a group of Irish reporters, they revealed the illegal arms cache—it was one of the largest that had ever fallen into their hands.

"That phone call was unnecessary, commented Harrison. "It should never have been made." But it proved only the first mistake. The second was even more serious. When the Irish police examined the captured arms haul they discovered that three or four of the weapons' serial numbers had not been removed. This allowed them to trace their place of origin. That led to Camp Le Jeune, North Carolina.

A massive inquiry was now launched, with the aim of using these clues to smash the IRA arms network in America. Customs inquiries traced the shipment to New York and a company called Standard Tools, a small shipping business run by a County Leitrim native called Barney McKeon from the Brooklyn dockside. McKeon was later arrested and charged with weapons smuggling. The authorities alleged that he packed the guns inside industrial-equipment parts before shipping them to Ireland. After a mistrial, he was eventually convicted.

In the meantime agents followed the trail of the Dublin arms haul to the doorstep of George De Meo. The police inquiry uncovered the arms ring based around the marine camp. Between 1973 and 1978 they estimate that about ten million rounds of ammunition went missing, one case of 840 cartridges at a time. Of these, the FBI believe that about one million went to De Meo and through De Meo to Harrison. Survivalists and right-wing groups apparently bought up much of the rest of the supply. It was easy to get material off the base. Security at Camp Le Jeune was so slack that a local TV news team was able to break into camp headquarters to demonstrate how vulnerable it was.

De Meo was arrested and convicted of smuggling arms to the IRA. He was sentenced to ten years in prison. De Meo, already in his mid-forties, could not face the prospect of such a long sentence. In August 1980 his lawyer approached the Justice Department. He had a deal to propose. A few months later De Meo, his lawyer, and federal agents met in a hotel on Manhattan's East Side. De Meo said that in return for a reduced sentence he would give the FBI the IRA's chief arms dealer in America. The authorities agreed. De Meo's sentence was reduced to five years in a minimum-security prison, and the FBI launched their most ambitious plan yet to wreck the IRA's American support network.

At the time the FBI was preparing their plan of action, George Harrison was concerned for De Meo. When he heard about the ten-year sentence, he told De Meo, "I wish I could do it for you." Harrison began to make arrangements for getting money to De Meo's wife while her husband served time. He made it clear to De Meo he would support him in whatever way he could.

"I couldn't walk away from a man like that," Harrison said.

He wasn't suspicious when De Meo arranged to meet him. De Meo said he would like to talk with him before he began his sentence. Harrison agreed at once. "I had no doubts about him," Harrison explained later. He did not realize that because of his co-conspirator's information, the FBI was making him the focus of its investigation.

According to the FBI, until De Meo named Harrison the authorities had no idea of his role in the arms-supply network; they were not even aware that he had once been subpoenaed by a New Hampshire grand jury investigating illegal arms purchases.

De Meo met Harrison three times after his arrest. Each time he was wired, and everything the two men said was recorded. They also tapped Harrison's telephone. De Meo told Harrison that he was going to introduce him to someone who would take care of business while he was inside.

"Are things available?" asked Harrison.

"Yes, and bloody good stuff, too," De Meo replied.

Harrison was in a difficult position. He felt as if the whole arms network was disintegrating around him. He sensed danger, though not from De Meo; yet he knew he could not back away from it just yet. "I had always thought of leaving the IRA plentifully supplied before I left the scene," he explained later. He was under a lot of pressure from Ireland. Late in 1980 the Emissary had visited him, along with the IRA's chief of staff and a leading member of Sinn Fein. They wanted to stabilize the network after the disaster of 1979, and get the supply moving again. The need for weapons was now greater than ever. "I said to myself, 'You can't walk away from it now.' So I went for one last big one," Harrison said. He asked De Meo what there was. De Meo arranged to meet him again with a sample. On the next occasion they met De Meo had with him a MAC-10 submachine gun, a weapon popular with guerrillas in Central America. It fired easily available .45-caliber ammunition at about twenty rounds per second. It had enough fire power to cut a person in half, according to police.

"Yes, that's great stuff," Harrison answered.

"There's a lot of them available," his longtime supplier affirmed. Harrison also enquired if De Meo could get him armor-piercing ammunition for a 20-mm cannon that he had obtained earlier. De Meo said he thought he could. He also arranged a meeting between Harrison, Falvey, and the new "contact" who was to replace him while he was in jail. In the meantime, the hunger-strike crisis was developing rapidly.

If Harrison had any uneasiness about the way things were going, it was swept aside by the events of May 1981, when Bobby Sands died. "The atmosphere was electric," Harrison recalled. He was impatient to consummate "the big deal." De Meo set up the meeting for May 17, at the site of a new two-family brick house he was building for himself in Pelham, New York. There, De Meo introduced Harrison and Falvey to a bearded, sandy-haired, blue-eyed man in his mid-thirties wearing casual clothes. De Meo said his name was John White.

"He looked like an operator," recalled Harrison. "Out to make money. I've seen them before—cool, calm. White looked the type all right." When De Meo introduced his long-time colleagues to White he said, "They're as straight as they come."

"I think we'll be able to do business together," the new man said, in what Harrison remembered as a crisp, unattributable accent; he guessed it might have been "suburban."

White produced two carbine rifles without their magazines, which he said he would obtain later. Harrison gave him $800 for the guns. They talked about what was available. White claimed he had access to 350 MAC-10 machine pistols. They were going for $250 each. Harrison said that he would take whatever he had available; he would be able to put his hand on $50,000 in a short time. They parted with White, agreeing to bring the carbine magazines around soon. Harrison took the two rifles back to his house on East Ninth Street.

One of the carbines was fitted with a bug—an electronic homing device attached to its stock. The FBI were hoping that Harrison would move the rifles to an arms dump, which they would then be able to pinpoint. But Harrison never moved them. One of them turned out to have a defective firing mechanism. By June 5 the batteries were dying and the signal was too weak to pick up.

Soon after their first meeting, White brought the two magazines to Harrison's home. Harrison offered him a glass of whiskey, which he accepted. They talked guns. White said there were forty-seven MAC-10s immediately available, as well as twelve Soviet-made AK-47s and an Uzi submachine gun. The Uzi is a highly prized, Israeli-made weapon, very compact and effective up to three hundred yards or more. "I was looking forward to going over them bit by bit," recalled Harrison. He was especially eager to get the Uzi. According to him it was one of the most deadly weapons ever developed. "Small, well put-together—whoever developed it was trained in Germany and studied the German masters; the moving parts overlap so there's no wasted space." He said it was the perfect weapon for urban guerrilla warfare, one the IRA would appreciate. (In fact, as far as is known the smaller, left-wing Irish National Liberation Army, INLA, was the first to acquire the Uzi submachine gun in Northern Ireland. It is believed they got it through Middle Eastern and European contacts in 1977.)

The conversation turned from guns to the general situation in Northern Ireland, and the turmoil caused by the hunger strikes. "It's going to mean a big political advance for the movement," Harrison said. "Some of the younger ones might want to retaliate." White listened, finished his whiskey, and left. The next time Harrison met him he had some ammunition with him—twenty-five rounds for the 20-mm cannon that the network had acquired. Unknown to Harrison, the ammunition had been rendered inert in police laboratories in Washington, D.C. White told him he was working on the shipment, promising him forty-seven MAC-10s, plus an assortment of other guns. "Soon I'll have things ready," White said.

Meanwhile, Harrison was getting ready for the big purchase. He had informed the IRA of the pending deal. The IRA sent one of their leaders, Eamon O'Doherty, to oversee it. According to police, O'Doherty was a former IRA chief of staff. In 1981 he was the IRA's "international agent," with responsibility for organizing arms shipments. Among the countries where he set up such deals was Libya. In America he was attempting also to stabilize the network after its recent disruptions and make sure that future arms purchases got to Ireland safely. During surveillance on Harrison's house, the FBI had observed O'Doherty coming and going through the spring. (O'Doherty was later arrested by police at the Port Authority Bus Station in New York and deported to Ireland.)

After June 5, the FBI increased surveillance to a twenty-hour watch.

Another leader seen at the house along with O'Doherty was Joe Cahill, who had slipped across the Canadian border that spring. As the IRA's fund-raiser, Cahill was in the States trying to drum up financial support. Both men were observed at the house together in June 1981 as they got ready to finalize the arms shipment.

On June 18, the day after White brought the ammunition for the cannon, agents listened as he called Harrison to tell him that the price of the arms haul would be $16,800—$1,800 more than expected. White arranged to make the delivery on the nineteenth. They continued listening as Harrison then made a call. The taped telephone conversation went:

Harrison: Michael.
Other man: Yes, George.
Harrison: I will see you, I would hope between eight and nine tomorrow night.
Other man: Very well, very well.
Harrison: I'll go right to the house.
Other man: Very good.
Harrison: Over the stated amount, you know, if possible because, well in other words, I'll explain later. All right, Michael?
Other man: All right, very good, George.
Harrison: Take care now.

The man at the other end of the line hung up. The FBI believed it was Michael Flannery, founding member of NORAID.

The FBI investigation drew the bureau's attention to several other Irish Americans. On several occasions, Harrison met and spoke with two brothers, Danny and Patrick Gormley. The Gormleys came from a family of twelve children in County Leitrim, the sons of a blacksmith. Danny, a Vietnam veteran, was a union organizer and worked at Avery Fisher Hall in Lincoln Center. The FBI concluded from what they observed and heard in the wire tap that Danny Gormley was the network's "banker." On one occasion agents observed Paddy Gormley and another unidentified man drive a Western Union van to the home of Tom Falvey. Falvey had mentioned previously to De Meo that somebody important was to visit his house that night; the FBI thought it might be Joe Cahill. Instead, they watched as Gormley and his helper appeared to load something from Falvey's garage into the van. The agents followed the van to Brooklyn, to the corner of Ridgewood and Grant avenues and a two-story apartment building owned by Paddy Mullins, a worker in the telephone company and an assistant grand marshal of the St. Patrick's Day parade. The van was parked near the building's garage, and though the agents had difficulty seeing what was going on, they concluded that whatever was in the van was being moved into the garage. In fact, they were weapons that were being moved to Mullins's house to make way for the expected new shipment.

Of those who were seen to be implicated by the expanding investigation, only Danny Gormley was regarded, along with Falvey, as a key part of the Harrison network. Mullins, Paddy Gormley, and Michael Flannery were all on its fringes.

In the discussions at which the delivery date was finalized, White at first asked Harrison to hire a truck and meet him at the docks, then drive to pick up the shipment. But Harrison said no; it would be best to bring the weapons to Tom Falvey's house. At that time Harrison was using Falvey's if the cache was a large one; otherwise he stored weapons in his own house in small amounts. White agreed. "You'll be bringing more people with you?" he inquired of Harrison the day before delivery. Harrison said he wouldn't. The only people there would be Tom and himself

On June 19 Harrison worked a thirteen-hour shift. Work finished, he went to the Queens home of Michael Flannery, and entered the house carrying a blue plastic bag. When he left a short time later, a white envelope was seen protruding from the bag. It contained almost $17,000. Then Harrison took the subway to 179th Street in Queens to see Falvey. Falvey met him at the subway station and drove him to his home. About half an hour after they got there, White called to say he would be arriving soon. Later that evening White's truck came down the street. "We watched him from Tom's window," Harrison remembered, "trying to back the pickup truck into the driveway. And, you know, he couldn't drive very well and took a long time to do it." At that time, that was the only complaint they had. The weapons were unloaded, checked, and stacked in Falvey's garage: forty-seven MAC-10s, a batch of twelve AK-47 rifles, and the Uzi. Harrison counted out $16,800 in hundred-dollar bills and gave them to White, plus another hundred dollars for the rent of the pickup. White said he'd be back the following Wednesday with 50,000 rounds of ammunition, which they would pay for when it was delivered. The transaction was over quickly, and White left. Harrison and Falvey went over the guns again when he'd gone. Then, shortly before 10:30 P.M. they too left. Falvey was to drop his friend off at the 179th Street subway.

It was a hot, still summer's night, Harrison remembered. They climbed into Falvey's old Buick. Harrison was carrying his plastic bag. Both men were excited, anxious, and yet satisfied: it was a good deal, and as the car left the driveway they talked about the events in Ireland: chaos loomed as the hunger strike seemed to be reaching its climax, and the IRA needed the guns as quickly as possible. Harrison recalled going over the whole haul again, item by item, thinking of how useful the machine guns would be in street ambushes, of the ammunition for the 20-mm cannon with which the IRA could knock a helicopter out of the sky.

They were nearing the corner of 179th Street and Hillside Avenue when Falvey looked to the side and saw a car pull alongside his. Its lights began to blink. There were four men inside. "They're pulling me over," Falvey said to his companion. Harrison told him to relax, not to worry. The old Buick pulled up at the curb. Suddenly the other car screeched to a halt in front of Falvey. Then behind them another car pulled up sharply. The men in the car in front leaped through the open doors and ran toward the Buick; each had a hand in his pocket. "Out!" they screamed at Harrison and Falvey. "Out. Keep your hands up!" The two men obeyed; as they did so one of the men from the front car pulled a gun and pointed it at them. He took Harrison's bag.

"Hand it over," he shouted. Slowly, Harrison obeyed, moving closer to the man with the gun. "Not so close," he was told. He backed off a little, and reached out with the bag. The gunman took it and ordered Harrison and Falvey to get over against a railing that ran along the street. They obeyed, and the man stuck his hand into the bag. He pulled out two cans of Schaefer beer. He smiled and looked at Harrison. "Where's your gun, George?" he asked. Harrison did not reply.

"We had planned to follow George to see if he met anyone after I had done the deal," said John White, a.k.a. John Winslow, undercover agent for the FBI. "But then he came out with his bag full of something. The MAC-10s are only about nine inches long. And the bag was obviously weighted. The agents thought he might have had one of the machine guns. We couldn't let him get away with it, so they arrested him." It would have been very embarrassing, Winslow explained, if they lost track of one of the guns and it had found its way back to Northern Ireland and been used to kill someone. The FBI had already prepared for this eventuality. They realized that if they did have to move against Harrison and Falvey earlier than expected, word might leak out to the others involved in the arms deal and the haul might be moved; to forestall this, search warrants for Falvey's garage, that of Mullins on Ridgewood Avenue, and the home of Harrison were prepared in advance. Shortly after the arrests, agents swooped down on all three buildings.

According to Harrison, some seventy officers from the Joint Terrorist Task Force surrounded his home, while a helicopter hovered above its roof. He said between fifteen and twenty police agents burst in, accompanied by a sniffer dog. In the house were Harrison's eighty-two-year-old sister and his niece. The policemen searched the house from around midnight until 8 A.M. the next morning. When they left they took with them the two carbines Winslow had sold him a month before. They also carried off twenty cartons of evidence, including nine boxes of papers and several thousand dollars. Among this material were the records he had kept of over thirty years of arms dealings for the IRA. Most of these papers remained in the hands of the FBI, as did the money, which Harrison claimed should be returned. "I have no hesitation," he said, angry that it has not been given back, "in calling

Reagan and his henchmen thieves as well as thugs." Police also found Joe Cahill's passport. But once again the man himself had slipped through their hands. Meanwhile, raids on Falvey's garage retrieved the arms just "sold." The following day, a search of Mullins's garage by customs officers uncovered, according to agent Winslow, fourteen M-16s, the 20-mm cannon, a flame thrower, and a lot of ammunition—including the cannon rounds "White" had sold Harrison. The flame thrower was a particularly dangerous weapon. It fired a gelatinous substance that would stick to the target until it burns through the flesh. It had an effective range of 150 feet. The M-16s were leftovers from the Danvers, Massachusetts, raid. Since the arrest of Barney McKeon, the network had been having a problem in moving the stuff to Ireland.

Agent Winslow said that there was some regret that they were panicked by Harrison's bag into springing the trap before they had planned. But he affirmed: "We were happy to recover the guns in Paddy Mullins's basement and bleed their treasury dry." He smiled. "I could have charged them more for the van and maybe gotten a better price for the guns.

During the whole time of his arrest, Harrison said nothing. While he and Falvey were being held in Federal Plaza that night, an FBI agent called Louis Stevens came in to speak to them. According to Harrison, he said, "We know what you are. We respect you for your patriotism. But this has got to stop. Is there anything you have to say?" Harrison, hardly acknowledging Stevens, uttered his name and address. Then he added, "You're wasting your time with an interrogation. Whatever I am I am, and that's it."

And what kind of man was it that the police had entrapped?

Even the police had to agree that neither Harrison, nor Falvey, nor the other three later arrested and charged, fitted the portrait so often painted of the "international terrorist." "The situation in Ireland is different," agent Winslow said, when asked what he thought of the IRA and its American connections. "Most of the people involved have been nationalists for years and years." Winslow, who has Irish blood in him, said of Harrison, "He reminded me of my father and his friends."

Danny Gormley, Paddy Mullins, and Michael Flannery were arrested later—Mullins within hours, Flannery after he returned from a trip to Ireland in September, and Gormley not until April 1982. The manner of Flannery's arrest was the cause of some bitterness in the Irish-American community. He was lifted by agents as he left church near his home on September 22, 1981. The agents handcuffed him and marched him down his street in full view of his neighbors. His home was ransacked. Flannery was regarded by many Irish Americans as a father figure, one of the most respected men in the community. "The administration was trying to say, look, this is how much we care for you and your Irish-American leaders," said Harrison. "They tried to diminish the stature of a man whose shoelaces they are not fit to tie. But their schemes backfired."

The trial began in the fall of 1982, and ended with Judge Joseph McLaughlin's verdict on November 5. The defense had turned what seemed like an open-and-shut case of arms smuggling into a complex and contentious argument about the role of the CIA in the illegal arms network. In a daring and aggressive strategy, the defense lawyers—Michael Dowd, Frank Durkan, Michael Kennedy, William Mogulescu, Lawrence Vogelman, and Barry Scheck—set out to show that George De Meo worked for the CIA. Since the CIA knew about the arms shipments, which, they argued, were carried out with the agency's approval, it could not have been illegal for the five men to send the arms to the IRA. The accused had never intended to break the law, the lawyers said, because all along they operated on the assumption that they had the government's approval because of the De Meo connection.

The defense team's defiant approach was based on a piece of information that had been dug up about De Meo. In 1969 De Meo and a confederate, a gun-store owner called Earl Redick, had been indicted for smuggling arms to Haiti. Redick, who was then based in Fayetteville, North Carolina, had been a former U.S. army intelligence officer; he was an excellent gunsmith, and De Meo had been one of his steadiest customers. When the 1969 indictments came before the court, the charges were suddenly and mysteriously dismissed. In news reports of the nontrial it was alleged that the CIA had engineered the dismissal of all charges against De Meo because he was one of their operatives. Michael Dowd and David Lewis traced Redick to Paraguay. He agreed to speak with them and they visited him for six days. By the time they left, Redick and his lawyer Carl Barrington, Jr., had agreed to appear as defense witnesses for the five men.

Though De Meo had been given immunity by the government, which promised he would not have to appear as a prosecution witness, that could not prevent him from being subpoenaed by the defense. The day he was due to appear, the atmosphere of the court, which was packed with NORAID supporters, was very tense. Harrison remembered it vividly. The judge turned to the prosecutor, David Kirby, and said: "We're ready now for Mr. De Meo."

"I happened to glance up toward the witness box," said Harrison. "And there he was in front of me. I looked him right in the eye. He turned away. I must admit I felt sympathy for him— and regret. But I'll tell you this—I was happy I was George Harrison and not George De Meo."

De Meo was scowling with anger. The defense realized that they were running a risk in bringing him to court; what he might say could be damaging to their clients. But they held to their aggressive plan and interrogated him on CIA arms-selling plots involving Cubans, Haitians, and Guatemalans, as well as Irish republicans. De Meo invoked the Fifth Amendment over eighty times. But when they asked him directly of his role as a CIA agent, he denied straightforwardly that he had ever had such a role.

The defense questions were framed in a complex of double negatives that wove a web of insinuation around the hostile witness. "If you were a CIA agent, sir—and I know, of course, you are not—would you have to say you weren't?" a lawyer asked De Meo at one point. They asked him if he had ever worked for the Alcohol, Tobacco and Firearms Agency. He took the Fifth. They asked him if he ever worked for the FBI. He took the Fifth. They asked him if he ever worked for the U.S. customs service. He took the Fifth. Then they asked him if he ever worked for the CIA. He simply said no. But the defense, by creating an atmosphere of doubt and doublethink, made De Meo's very denials sound like confirmations of their contention that he was a CIA operative.

De Meo refused to answer any questions about the 1969 incidents and aborted trial. This in itself created suspicions. These were dramatically confirmed when, the day after De Meo was on the stand, the defense produced Earl Redick, his former confederate, in the Brooklyn courtroom. Redick presented a no-nonsense, soldierly appearance. He gave the details about his background and his connection with De Meo in a manner befitting his demeanor. He testified that De Meo had frequently boasted about his CIA connections. On one occasion, when he bought some .38 carbines and submachine guns from Redick, De Meo told him that he was selling these to the IRA "on behalf of" the CIA.

According to Redick, De Meo told him, "The Company was paying the bill," and that "agents would safely see [the weapons] on board ship to Ireland." Tension and curiosity increased when Redick came to tell the story of the 1969 trial. After their arrest, Redick said, De Meo had appeared nonchalant about it and assured Redick that the case would not come to trial. He boasted that "the Company" would take care of them. After all, De Meo claimed, it was a CIA shipment. When the trial began, Redick's attorney, Carl Barrington, noticed three strangers in blue suits in the courtroom. They looked as if they belonged to some agency or other. Then the district attorney asked the judge if they could have a private conference in chambers. The judge agreed, and retired behind closed doors with Barrington and the district attorney. According to Redick, the prosecutor told Barrington and the judge that the government didn't want this trial to proceed "all that bad." The judge asked why. "National-security reasons," he was told. Then, said Redick, his lawyer asked the prosecuting attorney who the three men in the dark blue suits were. "CIA," he was told. Though the government did not want the trial to go ahead, it also did not want to be seen to move for a dismissal of the charges. The prosecutor suggested to the judge that the defense should ask for a motion of dismissal to be granted. The defense of course agreed, as did the judge that he would grant it. They returned to the courtroom and the trial proceeded along the lines suggested. The defense asked for dismissal and the judge granted it immediately. Redick and De Meo walked free, leaving behind them a trail of provocative suggestions concerning a CIA connection.

For a day the prosecution cross-examined Redick but couldn't shake him. Redick insisted forcefully that one of the reasons he had operated with De Meo was because of his assurances that it was being done under the protective wing of the CIA, and the

1969 acquittals confirmed that for him. When Kirby challenged Redick's testimony about the 1969 trial as being without substance, since Carl Barrington, his lawyer at that trial, was unable to confirm what he had just been saying, Redick contradicted the prosecutor by pointing out that Barrington was actually sitting in the courtroom and would no doubt be delighted to testify. Kirby was stunned and caught off balance. Though Barrington was there listening, the government did not call him to the stand.

This was the core of the defense strategy. But it called other witnesses to reinforce its contention that it was plausible for the CIA to operate a clandestine arms network supplying the IRA. One of them was Ralph McGehee, a former CIA case officer who testified that by the very nature of things "you can't go on getting weapons for twenty-five years without the CIA knowing about it." As to the logic behind this, McGehee's explanation was stark in its simplicity. He said: "If the CIA did not control weapons, some other country would." The defense also produced former attorney general Ramsay Clark to place the CIA's denials that De Meo was an operative in their proper context.* "It was a uniform practice for the CIA to deny any domestic activity . . . but we were always skeptical," he told the court.

Mick Flannery was the only defendant to take the stand. It was necessary for one of them to testify that he had known of De Meo's alleged CIA connection. In traditional Irish-republican fashion, Flannery turned the trial into an attack on Britain's policy in Ireland. Pointing a long bony finger at the prosecutor, the eighty-year-old militant exclaimed, "The real prosecutor in this case is the one we've known all our lives—the British government." Flannery then treated the judge and jury to a history of the Irish struggle against Britain and his role in it. He described his first action as an IRA volunteer—an attack on a police station— and his first encounter with the most feared unit of the British army, the Black and Tans. The prosecutor's objections to this testimony were overruled, and the history lesson lasted the whole morning.

---

*Something of the nature of George Harrison's politics can be gleaned from the two character witnesses who appeared on his behalf: David Ndaba, then secretary of the African National Congress's mission to the United Nations, and Bernadette McAliskey (née Devlin).

The court resumed after lunch. Michael Kennedy, Flannery's lawyer, asked the stenographer to read back the last question he'd asked before recess. The judge intervened and told him that wouldn't be necessary, "We had just arrived at the Battle of the Boyne," he said with a grin. (The Battle of the Boyne, fought in 1690, is one of the landmark events in Irish history.)

Flannery testified about his financial contributions for the purchase of weapons. He said he had given money whenever Harrison had asked him. The NORAID money was kept strictly separate. He insisted that he would not have become involved in the gun-purchasing scheme with Harrison had he not known that De Meo had "government connections."

"Because you did not intend to violate the law?" his lawyer asked him.

"Correct," the old man replied at once.

The defense had forced the government onto the defensive, and obliged it to prove that the CIA was not involved. To do so, the prosecutor called Launie Ziebel, general counsel for the CIA. He produced three documents that certified that the CIA had no record of any link with De Meo. The court had earlier been shown a heavily edited FBI memo in which De Meo's name was listed. The memo said that the FBI had been informed by the CIA that De Meo was not working for them. Ironically, the latter had been adduced by the defense as proof that in the totally duplicitous world of undercover agencies, such denials must always be seen as affirmations. In this context, the CIA's own documentation was given little weight, or interpreted to mean the opposite of what it actually said. By the trial's end, the defense had spun an entangling web of double meaning and innuendos, using the CIA's own reputation for chronic deceitfulness to substantiate the allegation of a CIA connection and so tie up the prosecution's case. In his summation, Kirby tried to cut through it to what he saw as the real matter at issue. He said: "There's no CIA involvement in this at all. It's a fabrication. They don't have any other defense. Each of these defendants was caught red-handed. They didn't have anywhere else to turn." To which Michael Kennedy replied for the defense in his summation: "It is up to the government to prove that the CIA was not involved with the defendants, not our burden to prove that it was.

For two and a half days the jury considered its verdict, before finding all five men not guilty.

It was a stunning upset for the government. Special agent John Winslow, the chief prosecution witness, was outraged at the finding. He referred to the allegations about the CIA as "Preposterous. De Meo had no connection whatsoever with the CIA." Asked about the 1969 aborted trial of Redick and De Meo, which was a key factor in the defense argument, Winslow said: "The charges were dropped against De Meo—it was alleged that it was a CIA request that it be dropped. It had nothing to do with the CIA. It is an aspect of the case I can't go into—it was more to do with protecting sources that were active." All that Winslow would say was that it involved not the CIA but the U.S. Marshals Service.

It would seem clear, then, that De Meo had some link to government agencies. When these allegations were being made, Harrison remembered the night in September 1958 when he and Cotter had to scuttle a planned arms deal with De Meo on Third Avenue and Fifty-eighth Street. It occurred to Harrison that the suspicious circumstances of that evening could have been explained by the possibility that De Meo was at that time attempting to set up him and Cotter. The arrival of a New York City cop on the scene forced them to abandon their plan. But as far as Harrison was concerned, this was just surmise. De Meo proved unreachable after the trial and was in no mind to discuss the allegations made against him.

What is known, however, is the fact that the CIA had on other occasions become involved in arms trafficking. Three years after the trial, the *New York Times* ran a series of articles on illegal arms traffic in which several agents and prosecutors told the paper that they knew of arms-smuggling cases having to be abandoned because it was learned that there was a CIA or government connection. One Florida prosecutor told the *Times:* "The Government has ways of making cases disappear. . . . We'd open arms trafficking cases and then the agent would call back later and say the case no longer exists. . . . The file has been removed, and we'd get word later that the intelligence people were permitting the arms deal to go on or were conducting it themselves."[6] A man whom the *Times* described as a "major" East Coast arms dealer—one who sometimes sold on the black market—said of other arms dealers: "The ones that are smart and are making it, work with the government. All of them work with the CIA, the FBI, the Defense Intelligence Agency, or somebody else. I've always worked with the Government . . . as long as they know what's going on, they don't stop you." He said that such dealers may sell arms to groups or nations of the Soviet bloc or the Irish Republican Army.[7] But most of the cases with CIA links that the *Times* story referred to involved pro-U.S. Central Americans. When this story was presented to the FBI, agent Winslow vehemently denied that the De Meo case was another example of such covert government operations. He claimed that he had never come across such a connection. And he knew nothing of any previous attempt by De Meo to set up Harrison and Cotter, as Harrison says might have been the case in 1958.

During the trial, the world the defense team portrayed of covert CIA operations was like that of Orwell's novel *1984*. It is a place where the state controls even its opponents, who, unknown to themselves, survive only as long as the hidden puppetmasters holding the strings desire them to. No greater contrast could be found to the world of George Harrison, where right and wrong were clearly etched and the enemy was obvious. It is the greatest irony of all that Harrison's career as an arms dealer, inspired as it was by simple moral fervor, should have come to an end in a murk of alleged government amorality, where all distinctions between friends and foes were blurred. There might well be doubts about the accuracy of this portrayal of De Meo's role as painted by the defense. But there can be no doubt that with the arrest of Harrison, his gunrunning career ended and the IRA's most vital source of weapons was blocked.

Harrison, however, remained committed to the armed struggle and was candid about his willingness to resume his former role if the chance ever arose. He made no attempt to exaggerate his contribution to the guerrilla campaign. But the importance of Harrison's network to the IRA can be gauged by the problems the guerrillas had in getting arms from other sources. Attempts to establish supply lines from Europe proved extremely difficult. An early effort in September 1971 ended disastrously in Amsterdam when the police interrupted an IRA shipment. Another haul destined for the IRA was intercepted in Antwerp in November 1977.

Similar setbacks have occurred in Europe in 1982, 1985, and 1986, with large quantities of weapons falling into the hands of the authorities.

The IRA had other sources. One was Libya. But there, too, it had had severe logistical problems. In March 1973, the Irish police halted a fishing vessel, the *Claudia,* off the Irish coast, and found Joe Cahill on board with five tons of Libyan arms. He was sentenced to three years' penal servitude, but was released before his sentence was completed due to ill health. But the IRA did not always have such ill luck when running guns from Libya. Before the *Claudia* mishap, a freelance arms dealer flew a haul of arms from Libya to Ireland. He landed his plane on a small, isolated airfield, where the guns were unloaded. However, there was a tragic aftermath. Against the advice of his confederates, the pilot took off, intending to continue on to America. His plane vanished over the Atlantic. It is presumed that he ran out of fuel and crashed.

After Harrison's arrest, the IRA had little success in getting weapons from America, once its most productive source. In 1982 the FBI succeeded in breaking up another arms network based in New York. The wiretap on Harrison's telephone had led the authorities to a Belfast man, Gabriel Megahey. A former seaman with the Cunard Line, Megahey had been expelled from the English port of Southampton in the early 1970s because the police suspected him of smuggling arms. (One route the IRA had for its arms traffic led from the Southampton docks, where IRA volunteers would pick up the guns when they came in on board ships.) Megahey later came over to the United States. When the FBI became suspicious of him they put a tap on his telephone. Soon they had the names of four other men—Eamon Meehan and his brother Paul, Paddy McParland, and Andy Duggan—all of whom were implicated in illegal trafficking. Duggan led them in turn to another Belfast man, Brendan Doherty, who was trying to purchase electronic components for making bombs. An undercover agent was introduced to Duggan, who brought two young Belfast men to him. They were looking for surface-to-air missiles for the IRA. This deal fell through. In the meantime, however, the undercover agent had met with Megahey in a midtown-Manhattan hotel to set up another arms deal. The FBI later followed the Meehan brothers as they drove a rented truck loaded with twelve boxes to the garment district, where they were observed transferring the boxes, plus others, onto a container truck. The truck was followed to Newark docks in New Jersey, where it was searched by customs officers. They found fifty weapons, a stack of ammunition, and blasting caps for bombs. As a result of this investigation, the Meehan brothers, Andy Duggan, and Gabriel Megahey were arrested; Paddy McParland eluded the police for a time, but was eventually arrested and charged. Though McParland was acquitted, the others went to prison on arms-smuggling charges.

Though not as serious a setback as the Harrison arrest, the loss of this potential source of supply was a bad blow to the IRA. Another was suffered in September 1984 when a Boston-registered vessel, the *Marita Ann,* was halted by Irish authorities off the west coast of Ireland. They discovered a huge arms haul, which had originated in the United States. The Irish had been informed of the shipment by U.S. officials. For a long time the police did not release details about the *Marita Ann* haul. Harrison saw this as proof that it was a setup from the beginning. He surmised that the arms found on the ship might be the same as those used to set up him and his confederates, and that they might be used in the future as bait for other would-be IRA arms smugglers.*

After the breakup of the Harrison network, there was a real decline in IRA violence in Northern Ireland. In 1985 there were fewer fatalities than at any time since 1970. While other factors undoubtedly influenced IRA policy—such as the increased emphasis on Sinn Fein's political activity—the loss of the guerrillas' most reliable weapons source was bound to have serious consequences for their ability to maintain an aggressive

---

*Seven indictments were eventually handed down on April 16, 1986, involving six Massachusetts men, and a former marine who is an Irish citizen already serving ten years in Ireland on a gunrunning charge. Only one of the men was in custody in the U.S. at the time. Another was reported to have been murdered by the IRA, who suspected him of collaborating with the police. The details released about the arms shipment said that it consisted of ninety-one rifles, eight submachine guns, thirteen shotguns, fifty-one handguns, hand grenades, 70,000 rounds of ammunition, and several bullet-proof vests. The Alcohol, Tobacco and Firearms Agency said that the weapons were either stolen or purchased.

campaign. What indications there were from repeated attempts to reestablish that network suggest that they were not successful, and that the IRA could no longer look to America for the arms it needed. One attempt had to be aborted in 1985 when an IRA operative discovered that a so-called arms source was offering a 20-mm cannon for sale—the same one that the FBI had lifted from Mullins's garage in 1981. Obviously another entrapment had been planned. For the IRA, the American black market for arms became so riddled with undercover agents and informers as to put in jeopardy any effort to acquire weapons there.

Harrison was not aware of any major shipments of arms that had successfully reached the IRA from the U.S. since the late 1970s; that is, before his network's destruction. Yet he remained hopeful that in the future the supply could be resumed. But whether or not the IRA would ever reestablish its capacity to procure the means of war in America remained to be seen.

For Harrison, there was only the struggle. And in the struggle there was continuity. The soldiers and policemen who died at the hands of the IRA using his weapons in Northern Ireland were the political descendants of those who fell against the IRA in the 1919–21 war of independence. The struggle receded into the endless past as it ran forward into the future. And in his mind, it linked Ireland with the struggling forces of the third world.

"The struggle in Ireland," he said, "is part of the anti-imperialist and anticolonial struggle which is going on all over the world, as is the struggle against fascism, which is the offspring of imperialism." He was as much at home picketing the South African consulate on Park Avenue as he was outside the British consulate on Third. He could as often be heard speaking out at a meeting denouncing General Pinochet's Chile as he was raising his voice to condemn Margaret Thatcher's policies in Northern Ireland. He remained a committed supporter of Puerto Rican independence all his life, and was active in support of the Sandinista government in Nicaragua. His moral certainty bestowed on him a simplicity and a clarity that was as startling as it was relentless in its capacity for commitment. Yet Harrison defied the stereotypical views commonly held of Irish-American IRA supporters. There was not a trace of sentimentality in the man, either about Ireland or anything else. He had not set foot in his native country in almost fifty years. Nor did he want to go back very much. He said he would rather pay a visit to Nicaragua, or Cuba, perhaps. Harrison greatly respected Fidel Castro, particularly for his statement in support of the hunger strikers in 1981. And he was an ardent student of Che Guevara, who Harrison proudly said was of Irish extraction.

He estimated—conservatively—that in his time he had sent between 2,000 and 2,500 weapons to Ireland and about a million or more rounds of ammunition. "I think we did better than even Joe McGarrity," he said, speaking of his great forerunner in the arms-smuggling business. But like those sent by McGarrity, they did not bring the dream of a republic any closer. George Harrison was not dismayed by this. At seventy-one, he believed there was time yet, if not for him, then for the forces of Irish republicanism. Defeat had made them patient.

Postscript

The week of October 12, 1985, was a busy one, as usual, for George Harrison. On Friday the eleventh he attended an antiapartheid function. The following day he took part in a demonstration outside a branch of Citibank in Manhattan to protest overseas investment in South Africa. At around 4 P.M. he walked over to the British consulate on Third Avenue to do picket duty for a while. Then he had a bite to eat and set off for the subway station at Forty-second Street and Fifth Avenue. He was going to an event he looked forward to—to celebrate the coming together of different guerrilla groups fighting against the regime in El Salvador. It was about 6:30, and dusk was gathering. He had gone down the first flight of steps into the subway when he noticed someone approach him from the left rear. He was white, about 5 feet 8 inches tall, in his late forties, well dressed in a tweed jacket, and husky. He snarled at Harrison, who turned around in time to see that the stranger was carrying a gun in his hand. The gun was equipped with a silencer. Harrison knew when he saw the silencer that he was not dealing with an ordinary mugger. Suddenly the gunman raised his weapon, and when Harrison went to defend himself, smashed it down on his head.

Harrison staggered backward. The gun came down with a crash again, followed by another, and yet another blow. Harrison lunged for him and was within grappling distance when his assailant turned and ran off down the steps into the subway. He might have seen the approach of the young man who came to Harrison's assistance. By then Harrison was covered in blood. He is convinced that the man had followed him some distance before striking in the subway. At the El Salvador meeting a nurse bandaged him up and arranged for him to get home.

Harrison did not report the attack to the police, whom he regards as his enemies. As far as he was concerned, the attack fitted into a pattern. His friend Paddy McLogan died in mysterious circumstances in Ireland. His friend Liam Cotter was killed two blocks from where Harrison himself was attacked. Two other men vital to the network died in what he also regarded as mysterious circumstances in the late 1970s. So it did not seem surprising to George Harrison that powerful forces, dismayed at his escaping jail, were now determined to see him dead.

4
CONGRESSIONAL CONSCIENCE

Between the arcadian dreams of an Ireland lost and the utopian hopes of an Ireland yet to be won stands the firm and complex reality of the Irish-American politician. Both arcadians and utopians are usually by the nature of things outsiders. The politician by nature is an insider, concerned with pragmatics, with what can and can't be done. He inhabits a world of concessions, not sacrifices. His concern for ideological purity is subordinated to his desire to run the political machine as best he can. It is not surprising, then, that the Irish Americans who built one of the most efficient political machines of all—that of the Democratic Party—should show a capacity for political pragmatism that in the end will probably have a greater impact on Ireland's future than the endeavors of arcadian and utopian conspirators. This sobering acquaintance with the reality of power has, paradoxically, led them to appreciate the difficulties of involving the U.S. at a high level in the Irish problem: Before Clinton, only two presidents in the twentieth century have made public statements about the Irish conflict. The first was Jimmy Carter and the second was Ronald Reagan.

It was probably the only occasion in his life that President Ronald Reagan quoted his White House predecessor Jimmy Carter favorably, and one of the few that witnessed a conjunction with another ideological enemy, House Speaker Thomas "Tip"

O'Neill. The occasion was November 15, 1985, the same day the Anglo-Irish Agreement between the British and Irish governments was signed at Hillsborough in Northern Ireland. The agreement gave the Irish government a recognized role in the running of Northern Ireland for the first time. At the time of the signing, President Reagan and Tip O'Neill met in the Oval Room. Their purpose was to declare American support for the agreement, which was almost universally welcomed as a breakthrough in the long-running Northern Ireland conflict, and to pledge a generous aid package—a sort of mini-Marshall Plan—to help bolster Northern Ireland's weak economy.

The event in Northern Ireland represented the end of a long-drawn-out series of negotiations between the governments of Irish Prime Minister Garret Fitzgerald and British Prime Minister Margaret Thatcher. But the event in the Oval Room marked the beginning of the end of an even longer quest, one that began long before there was any talk or even hope of an innovative plan to solve the Northern Ireland problem.

It began in the days of Jimmy Carter, whom President Reagan was moved to quote: "It is entirely fitting," said Reagan, "that the United States and other governments join this important endeavor. As President Carter said on August 30, 1977, 'In the event of a settlement, the U.S. government would be prepared to join with others to see how additional job-creating investment could be encouraged, to the benefit of all the people of Ireland.'"

Reagan's quotation of Carter as Tip O'Neill smiled with approval is more than just another example of how in America the Irish question so often defies the usual ideological borders and makes allies out of enemies. It was the American connection in its most powerful guise, representing links forged between Ireland and Washington's Irish-American political elite throughout the 1970s, when the Irish government and its diplomatic service struggled to outmaneuver what it regarded as dangerous pro-IRA influences in the nation's capital. These were embodied in the unlikely form of Mario Biaggi, a Democratic congressman from the Bronx, a highly decorated former New York cop with a reputation as a law-and-order conservative, whose only previous connection with Ireland was his friendship with an Irish-American colleague on the police force. This feat had to be accomplished at the same time that the Irish government tried to undermine support for the IRA's American sympathizers. To recount that struggle, and its final outcome, is to follow the often devious course that the Irish question has taken as it has wound its way through the corridors of power in Washington.

For the Irish government, the stakes were high: the powerful influence of the United States. While it has always been taken for granted at a sentimental level that the U.S. has strong ties with Ireland, it was a different and more difficult matter to turn that connection into a diplomatic lever with which to move Britain toward finding some solution to the Northern Ireland impasse. The Irish government began from a weak position and with little precedent for a hopeful outcome to its goals. In spite of the many links between Ireland and America, no United States government in this century had shown any willingness to involve itself directly in the dispute with Britain. Two world wars and a host of common global interests have fastened the Anglo-American partnership with stronger bonds than most Irish or Irish Americans care to admit. However, it is probably true that the Irish diplomats who undertook the task of involving the United States government had fewer illusions about what they might achieve than those Irish Americans, often with IRA sympathies, who believed that Ireland's struggle for national unity had a prior claim on Washington's support. But at first, things seemed to be going in the latter's favor.

In the early 1970s, powerful political figures like Senator Edward Kennedy and Representative Hugh Carey—later governor of New York—were quick to fire off condemnations of Britain's Northern Ireland policies. They did so without consultation with that other concerned party to the strife, the Dublin government. When Carey, after returning from Belfast in 1971, denounced the British army as "thugs," Dublin winced. When Senator Kennedy at the same time called for an immediate withdrawal of British troops from Northern Ireland and the establishment of a United Ireland," the Irish prime minister was moved to respond by saying that the senator from Massachusetts did not know what he was talking about. As far as Dublin was concerned, it was worthy of Kennedy to be angered by what he saw in the aftermath of internment, but it was also important that his wrath should be

diplomatically focused. Such condemnations of Britain could easily be interpreted as lending moral support to the IRA, which the
Irish government viewed as more of a problem than British policy, however brutal that was at times. For successive Dublin governments it was a question of harnessing legitimate Irish-American
political concern about Northern Ireland to a credible program
of reform that would be clearly seen as a real alternative to the
IRA. Thus, it was hoped, Washington might be brought to bear
on London.

The question became a crucial one in the mid-1970s for a variety of reasons. For the Irish authorities, 1974–1976 were years of
disaster and disappointment. The most daring initiative of the
decade, the Sunningdale Agreement, which involved the Irish and
British governments, as well as Unionist and Catholic politicians,
came to nothing. The government that evolved from it and that
had included Catholics for the first time in the history of Northern
Ireland collapsed under loyalist paramilitary pressure. In the wake
of the collapse, Britain opened up secret talks with the IRA leadership. Dublin was sidelined, and the moderate constitutional nationalist party of Northern Ireland, the Social Democratic and
Labour party (SDLP), which had formed part of the power-sharing
government, was left wandering in the political wasteland.

To add to Dublin's unease, in Washington there emerged an
active pro-IRA lobbying group, the Irish National Caucus (INC),
dominated by a Northern Ireland-born Redemptorist priest, the
Reverend Sean McManus. Though the Caucus's beginnings are a
matter of dispute, even among its own members, it seems to have
become active in 1974 with the aim of lobbying on behalf of Irish
unity. Among those involved in its formation were Mick Flannery,
the founding father of the Irish Northern Aid Committee; Jack
Keane, then president of the Ancient Order of Hibernians (AOH),
the largest Irish-American organization; and Teddy Gleason, the
powerful trade-union leader. When the Reverend McManus came
to the fore, along with a close friend, Fred Burns O'Brien, the
Caucus developed a series of goals. The most immediate ones were
to lift the visa restrictions preventing IRA and Sinn Fein spokesmen from coming into the United States, and try to persuade
Congress to hold open hearings on Northern Ireland. (Hearings
on the situation had been heard before the Subcommittee on

Europe of the Committee on Foreign Affairs on February 28 and March 1, 1972. But no republican spokesmen were allowed to present their case.) The makeup and the aims of the Caucus were the cause of Irish government concern; it was shortly justified by the clearly pro-IRA statements the group began to issue. They appeared in *The Irish People*, the weekly newspaper strongly identified with NORAID and the IRA. *The Irish People* hailed the Caucus as a "recently formed pro-Provo Irish American pressure group."[1] It had already started publishing Caucus statements such as that which described leading members of the IRA and Sinn Fein, Daithi O'Conaill, Ruairi O'Bradaigh, Seamus Loughran, and Seamus Twomey—the last two were Belfast men whom the police considered high-ranking IRA members—as the equivalents of Thomas Jefferson and George Washington.[2]

By 1975 the Caucus had branches in Boston, New York, and New Jersey, where small groups of activists lobbied their local representatives. They also had the attention of Representative Mario Biaggi.

At first Biaggi, who came to Congress in 1968 denouncing black rioters as "insurrectionist" and "subversive," might not have seemed a likely candidate to become embroiled in Northern Ireland. In his twenty-three years as a New York cop, Biaggi shot fifteen people, two of whom died, and was wounded ten times himself. As a holder of the New York City Police Department's "Revolver Award for Devotion to Law and Order," Mario Biaggi certainly had the keystone for his reputation as a conservative spokesman for right-wing anxieties. His constituency, the Tenth Congressional District, which straddles the Bronx and Queens, was a heavily Italian-American middle-class neighborhood, where crime was a major concern; he had a small Irish-American population, about 10 percent, far from enough to make Ireland a burning issue. As he repeatedly said when accused by critics of playing for the "green vote": "The Irish-American vote is nonexistent in my constituency." In 1972 he polled 129,539 votes against his liberal opponent's 8,360. The margin remained fairly constant afterwards. Clearly, Biaggi was not a politician in need of a marginal vote. His appeal was so strong that in 1972 people began to think of him as a prospect for mayor. Mayoral elections were due the following year, and Biaggi seemed to have all the credentials.

1972 was a big year for all things Italian, thanks to the success of the movie *The Godfather.* Biaggi's very Italian good looks and geniality seemed like a winning combination with his "hero cop" record. But along came the first of two major controversies in his career. Biaggi had been questioned by a grand jury investigating the sponsorship of private immigration bills in Congress in 1971. There were allegations that some lawmakers were being bribed. As Biaggi's campaign for mayor got under way, rumors were circulating that he had taken the Fifth Amendment, refusing to answer questions about his finances. The press hounded him and other stories surfaced concerning alleged links with the Mafia. Biaggi tried to shrug it off: "I expect it," he said wistfully, "I'm Italian. All I ask is a straight shot. No rumors. Facts. And I'd like to see the same treatment given to other people who want to be mayor. He categorically denied taking the Fifth. Finally, the judge released the details of the investigation, which showed clearly that Mario Biaggi had misled people rather drastically. He had indeed taken the Fifth. His campaign for mayor went to pieces.

"I made a mistake," he said, smiling. "I paid for it. It cost me the election." Two years later, when the Reverend Sean McManus walked into Biaggi's office, it is unlikely that the congressman realized that he was on his way toward the second major controversy of his career—but one of international proportions. For his part, the Reverend McManus did not know that Biaggi already had something of a history of interest in the Northern Ireland crisis.

"A big Irish cop called Pat McMahon of the 24th precinct told me all about it in 1942 or '43," said Biaggi, explaining his earliest connection with Northern Ireland. "But it wasn't until the thirteen young folks were killed—murdered—in Derry that I got deeply involved." A few days after Bloody Sunday, Biaggi dispatched his daughter Jackie to "observe" what was happening. She was there at the massive demonstration to protest the Bloody Sunday killings. What she told her father made him speak out on several occasions in Congress against British policy. But with the arrival of Sean McManus and the Caucus, Biaggi was persuaded to take a much more active role. Soon after their first meeting, he was convinced to visit Ireland on a trip organized and sponsored by McManus's group. Among those whom McManus arranged for the congressman to meet were high-ranking members of the IRA and Sinn Fein.

The visit was perfectly timed for the IRA's purposes. Throughout the spring of 1975, while secret talks went on with the British, the guerrillas maintained a truce with the British army. There were rumors that the Labour Party government of Harold Wilson had arrived at an understanding with the IRA prior to a British withdrawal. The IRA was anxious to bolster its image in America and establish itself as a serious and credible political force—one that was on the verge of a major breakthrough. Biaggi's visit was an opportunity for it to do so. The congressman came to Dublin with the Caucus's director of information, Fred Burns O'Brien.

On April 30, the congressman co-chaired a press conference with the Sinn Fein president, Ruairi O'Bradaigh, and another leading party member, Maire Drumm, from Belfast. Drumm had a reputation as one of the most fiery and outspoken advocates of IRA violence. The year of Biaggi's visit she had spoken of "pulling down Belfast stone by stone," and a British government minister had called her a "Madame Defarge sitting by the guillotine." Eighteen months after she met Biaggi, she was gunned down by loyalist assassins in a Belfast hospital where she had gone for treatment. Also at the conference were two IRA men from Belfast—the ubiquitous Joe Cahill, not long out of jail after serving time for arms smuggling—and Seamus Loughran. Loughran was thought by police to be chief of the Belfast IRA.

Biaggi committed himself to working to change the United States visa policy that had kept IRA spokesmen out of America for several years. He said he would press for open hearings in Congress. And he ended up praising the IRA because "it had focused attention on the problem in the six counties" of Northern Ireland. In other words, the congressman more or less identified himself with the policies of the Irish National Caucus, and pledged to work on their behalf. Though Biaggi met with a wide range of other political representatives, including British government officials in Belfast and the moderate SDLP, his adventure with the IRA drew most attention. The Dublin government was appalled that an American politician should lend credence to the IRA's campaign. According to Dublin's views, the IRA did not focus attention on the problem—the IRA was the problem.

Biaggi, meanwhile, seems to have remained unaware of the controversy gathering around him. Of the meetings with the IRA he spoke nonchalantly. "I was gathering facts. If anyone thinks that a member of the Congress of the United States of America condones violence, he is very foolish." The congressman continued to lobby in Congress for the Caucus's aims, which he saw as an extension of his own civil-rights concerns. These included a campaign on behalf of the rights of enlisted men, and legislation to help refugees from the Cyprus civil war. Biaggi was also prominently identified with attempts to improve conditions in hospitals for retarded children. According to Biaggi, his efforts in regard to Northern Ireland were merely part of his overall humanitarian concerns.

Civil rights were becoming a very topical issue with the sudden rise of Jimmy Carter on the political scene. The former governor of Georgia made civil rights a central part of his 1976 campaign for the presidency of the United States. Six days before the election he met with the Irish National Caucus. He issued a statement afterward calling for "an international commission on human rights in Northern Ireland," and said that the Democratic Party was committed to Ireland's reunification and that the United States should adopt a more active role on the Northern Ireland issue. The Caucus claimed that Carter had agreed to make these commitments in return for its support.

The gloom that prevailed in Dublin government circles turned to alarm. For an American congressman to fall under the influence of a pro-IRA lobbying group was embarrassing. But for an American president to do so would be a diplomatic disaster of frightening proportions. At the time, the foreign minister of the Irish government was Garret Fitzgerald—the future architect of the Anglo-Irish Agreement. With his support, the Foreign Affairs Department launched a counteroffensive to try to regain the initiative in America.

Two key figures in this attempt were professional diplomats: Sean Donlon, former consul general in Boston and head of the Anglo-Irish section of the Foreign Affairs Department, and Michael Lillis, a press officer in the New York consulate who was promoted to the Washington embassy in 1976. They evolved an ambitious strategy with two broad aims. The first was to counteract the growing pro-IRA influence in Washington and undermine general support for the organization in America. The second was to use Washington to persuade the British government to adopt a more vigorous program in Northern Ireland, one that would embody concessions to moderate Catholic nationalists and reaffirm the commitment to power-sharing. Since it seemed impossible to persuade the British directly, it was thought that perhaps if leading figures in America were to express their concerns, the London government would be more willing to take note of them. At least that was how the Irish reasoned—and, ironically, they were led to think it might work partly by the very success of the Irish National Caucus.

However, there was another powerful factor in the government's estimations. This was John Hume, leader of the SDLP, the party of Northern Ireland's moderate nationalists. Hume had begun his political career as a civil-rights activist in Derry. He became a member of the local Northern Ireland parliament in 1969, and went on to found the party of which he has remained the principal spokesman. He was deeply involved in negotiating the Sunningdale Agreement, and in 1974, at age thirty-seven, became head of the Commerce Department of the first Northern Ireland government to include Catholics. Power-sharing, though quickly doomed, became Hume's fundamental answer to the Northern Ireland crisis—the only one that he believed could offer the war-torn state a chance of survival. When Hume was a student at Maynooth College near Dublin he had come to know Sean Donlon. The two remained friends and became firm political allies during the Sunningdale talks, in which Donlon played a key role. In 1976 Hume was in America, where he struck up a friendship with Senator Edward Kennedy. Kennedy was impressed with Hume's arguments in support of power-sharing. Hume formed an important link in the American connection, which joined the Irish government to one of the most prominent political figures in Washington. That link was reinforced by the tenacious lobbying of Michael Lillis when he arrived in Washington in the fall of 1976. Lillis won the confidence and respect of Tip O'Neill, who was quick to appreciate the concern of the Irish government over the rise of the Caucus and its connections with the incoming president.

O'Neill, a bluff, hearty Boston Irishman with a grandfatherly mop of white hair, looked right at home in front of a plate of boiled beef and cabbage and a mug of beer. But his geniality masked an extremely able and pragmatic politician. Since 1936, when he was elected to the Massachusetts legislature, O'Neill's life had been absorbed in politics, based on the belief that government should be directly involved in maintaining the welfare of the citizen. When forty years later he became House Speaker, and so occupied one of the most powerful positions in Washington, he was determined to apply that belief to the problems that still bedeviled the land of his ancestors. To begin with, he was ready to do what he could to redress the balance in favor of Irish government influence in Washington. Lillis persuaded O'Neill to get together with Senator Kennedy, Hugh Carey (governor of New York since 1974), and Daniel Patrick Moynihan, just elected Democratic senator for New York. Carey, the former representative, was a rather lugubrious-looking individual with an acerbic tongue, often politically unpredictable, and given to bitter outbursts against opponents. Moynihan, a former Harvard professor, had the reputation of being an intellectual, was a former U.S. ambassador to the United Nations, and had worked in the administration of President Kennedy. His bow tie, tweed hat, and supercilious air gave the impression of a man for whom politics was more of an intellectual exercise than anything else. (In any other country than the United States it would be impossible to imagine O'Neill and Moynihan in the same party.) Lillis welded the four of them—dubbed "The Big Four"—into a club with which to beat NORAID and Caucus supporters. The blows fell regularly, beginning on St. Patrick's Day, 1977, when they issued their first joint statement.

The first statement was brief. It expressed concern over the "continuing tragedy" in Northern Ireland, and said that "continued violence cannot assist the achievement" of a just and peaceful settlement but can only "exacerbate the wounds that divide" the people. It went on: "We appeal to all those organizations engaged in violence to renounce their campaigns of death and destruction. . . . We appeal as well to our fellow Americans to embrace the goal of peace and to renounce any action that promotes the current violence or provides support or encouragement for organizations engaged in violence. We make this appeal on St. Patrick's Day, 1977, a day on which Irish peoples of all traditions everywhere should feel proud to rejoice in our common heritage, and a year in which peace should come at last to Northern Ireland."

Though the statement spoke of the "underlying injustices at the heart of the Northern Ireland tragedy," its emphasis clearly fell on those connected with the violence. This roused much indignation among NORAID and Caucus supporters, who demanded to know why the "Big Four" had not condemned British atrocities and injustices. However, these militant nationalists were not the only ones to be disturbed by the statement's focus. Veteran civil-rights activist Paul O'Dwyer, who was then in his last year as president of the New York City Council, lamented that the statement had turned attention away from where it should be concentrated, on British government policy, and instead seemed to blame Irish Americans—at least by implication—for the intractable crisis. "The fact that this notion was projected by four Irish-American leaders gives it a measure of authenticity," he said at the time.

The Big Four's statement was coy in that though it condemned violence it did not name any specific organizations. One month later, on a visit to Ireland, Hugh Carey was less coy. Speaking before the Royal College of Surgeons in Dublin, Carey lashed out bitterly at the IRA—"those fascinated by death as a political weapon." He called them "sick," and asked scathingly, "Is the assassin the best hope for positive political change? . . . Is it human rights that flows from the barrel of a gun? Just what is this mad fascination with killing and maiming and burning?" The majority of Irish Americans, he claimed, supported their St. Patrick's Day statement. "It is our view," he said, "that the day is gone when those on either side who call for 'ourselves alone' will be listened to—for now we in America hear new voices, we are taken with men of new courage." "Ourselves alone" is the English translation of Sinn Fein. The men of new courage, though not named, were understood to be John Hume and his party. Later, Carey was more explicit when he denounced the IRA as "killers" and "Marxists." The speech was a typical Carey performance, swinging between the overwrought and acerbic to the maudlin and sentimental. And it caused an uproar both in Ireland and in New York. New York

Daily News columnist Pete Hamill berated the governor as an overprivileged denizen of New York night spots remote from the realities of Northern Ireland, and lavished as much praise on the IRA as Carey had heaped abuse. It is hard to say which outdid the other in sentimental hyperbole.

Back in New York, Carey was subject to heckling from angry Irish-American militants. Typical was the eighty-five-year-old gentleman who told Carey: "I have just returned from a vacation in Belfast, where I go every summer. I would like to remind the governor of some words he used a while ago about the IRA: 'killers' and 'Marxists.'" His voice rising tremulously, the objector went on: "I stayed at the home of a Belfast IRA man. And he and his wife got up every morning to go to Mass and receive Holy Communion!"

However, in spite of the evident outrage they were causing in some quarters, the Big Four were bent on their course. A month after Carey's attack on the IRA, Senator Kennedy followed suit, appealing to the IRA and the Protestant Ulster Defense Association—the major loyalist paramilitary group—to halt their campaigns. And, he said, "Let no American have it on his conscience that his efforts or his dollars helped to make the violence worse. While he condemned the paramilitaries, he praised John Hume as a man of extraordinary courage and wisdom and understanding," calling him "one of the finest and most creative political leaders of our generation." Carey had wound up his speech with a line from Yeats. Kennedy gave his audience half a verse:

> I shall have some peace here, for peace comes dropping
>   slow,
> Dropping from the veils of the morning to where the
>   crickets sing.

(In fact, the senator mildly misquoted the poet's lines, leaving out the "And" in the first line and making "cricket" plural.) "Perhaps . . . the morning of which the poet spoke is about to reveal its light," concluded Kennedy.

The hope that the Massachusetts senator referred to so poetically had more pragmatic underpinnings than the lyricism of his remarks might have indicated. By May 1977 O'Neill had approached President Carter and brought up the subject of Northern Ireland. Neither the president nor his aides knew very much about it, though Carter was reminded of his Pittsburgh commitment in late 1976, in which he'd pledged to work for human rights. A further meeting was arranged for June. The Big Four met with Carter's secretary of state, Cyrus Vance, who promised to work with them in producing some sort of presidential "initiative" on Northern Ireland.

Normally, the State Department, which tends to be anglophilic, would have resisted such an endeavor. But in 1977 it was, as one Irish diplomat put it, "running scared of Carter." He came into Washington as an outsider, threatening change, and proclaiming his determination to take a personal interest in foreign policy, of which his concern for human rights was to be the foundation stone. The proposed initiative took shape under the influence of the Irish embassy. The president would make a statement about Northern Ireland. Throughout the early summer of 1977 there was more speculation about what it would contain. The British were uneasy when it was learned that there would be a promise of American aid but that it would be linked to finding a satisfactory solution. The British embassy, having at first tried to discourage any initiative at all, then tried to detach the promise of aid from the search for an acceptable solution. But on this the Irish and their Irish-American supporters—four of the most prominent politicians in the country—would not budge. Against such a lineup, there was little the London government could do. (Apart from everything else, at the time the British could not afford to go against the House Speaker because they needed to win his support on the controversy over the Concorde supersonic jet. A vocal environmentalist lobby was opposing its use of Washington's airport. With Carey, they faced the same dilemma. They required his backing so the Concorde could use JFK airport in New York.)

However, the British embassy persisted in subtle attempts to win its case. One week before Carter made his speech, a story was leaked to British newspapers that the initiative would contain a promise of aid with no strings attached. Diplomats involved in the negotiations saw it as a last-ditch effort to draw the initiative in the direction indicated by the story. Though it proved embarrassing to the Americans, it did not succeed. On August 30, President Carter made his statement on Northern Ireland, and the long-awaited initiative was revealed. It was all of seven short paragraphs. The president said:

> Throughout our history Americans have rightly recalled the contributions men and women from many countries have made to the development of the United States. Among the greatest contributions have been those of the British and Irish people, Protestant and Catholic alike. We have close ties of friendship with both parts of Ireland, and with Great Britain.
>
> It is natural that Americans are deeply concerned about the continuing conflict and violence in Northern Ireland. We know the overwhelming majority of the people there reject the bomb and the bullet. The United States wholeheartedly supports peaceful means for finding a just solution that involves both parts of the community of Northern Ireland, protects human rights and guarantees freedom from discrimination—a solution that the people of Northern Ireland, as well as the Governments of Great Britain and Ireland can support. Violence cannot resolve Northern Ireland's problems; it only increases them, and solves nothing.
>
> I hope that all those engaged in violence will renounce the course and commit themselves to peaceful pursuit of legitimate goals. The path of reconciliation, cooperation and peace is the only course that can end the human suffering and lead to a better future for all the people of Northern Ireland. I ask all Americans to refrain from supporting, with financial or other aid, organizations whose involvement, direct or indirect, in this violence, delays the day when the people of Northern Ireland can live and work together in harmony, free from fear. Federal law enforcement agencies will continue to apprehend and prosecute any who violate the United States law in this regard.
>
> United States Government policy on the Northern Ireland issue has long been one of impartiality, and that is how it will remain. We support the establishment of a form of Government in Northern Ireland which will command widespread acceptance throughout both parts of the community. However, we have no intention of telling the parties how this might be achieved. The only solution will come from the people who live there. There are no solutions that outsiders can impose.

At the same time, the people of Northern Ireland should know that they have our complete support in their quest for a peaceful and just society. It is a tribute to Northern Ireland's hardworking people that the area has continued to attract investment despite the violence committed by a small minority. This is to be welcomed, since investment and other programs to create jobs will assist in ensuring a healthy economy and combating unemployment.

It is still true that a peaceful settlement would contribute immeasurably to stability in Northern Ireland and so enhance the prospects for increased investment. In the event of such a settlement, the United States Government would be prepared to join with others to see how additional job-creating investment could be encouraged, to the benefit of all the people of Northern Ireland.

I admire the many true friends of Northern Ireland in this country who speak out for peace. Emotions run high on this subject and the easiest course is not to stand up for conciliation. I place myself firmly on the side of those who seek peace and reject violence in Northern Ireland.

To many, it seemed a very modest exercise, too well padded with cautious and diplomatic language to appear as a threat to the Northern Ireland status quo. Indeed, compared to other Carter foreign-policy initiatives, such as Camp David, it was on a very small scale. But diplomatic geiger counters in both London and Dublin were measuring a high degree of activity where casual observers could detect none. The statement was important as far as the Irish government was concerned—in fact, for them it was something of a triumph.

However cautious and prudent it proved to be, the principle of America's nonintervention was broken. The Irish had successfully controlled the content of the statement to suit their designs, so that it had all the elements they sought in their broad strategy in America. IRA sympathizers had been soundly condemned, the British had been given notice that American aid would be forthcoming only if there was a peaceful settlement in the form of a "Government . . . which will command widespread acceptance throughout both parts of the community," a veiled reference to power-sharing, which the Irish could thus say had received the seal of approval at the highest levels in Washington. Undoubtedly, the key paragraph was that promising aid "in the event of such a settlement," suggesting as it did that the current inertia was not welcome. Over eight years later, President Reagan would resurrect this paragraph to provide the foundation for the ambitious aid program offered in the wake of the Anglo-Irish Agreement.

After the Carter statement the Irish diplomatic mission in Washington could not conceal its delight or its growing confidence. One of Speaker O'Neill's aides gave them what the Irish saw as the ultimate compliment when he said, "The Irish diplomatic mission is second only to that of the Israelis."

However, in spite of this breakthrough, the Irish government derived little immediate satisfaction in its efforts to prod Britain toward reaching a settlement in Northern Ireland. The British Labour government was led by James Callaghan—a man with considerable experience in Northern Ireland's affairs. (He was in government in 1969 when the decision was made to send in British troops.) Though he gave the Carter initiative a cautious welcome, he was unable to take advantage of the offer of economic aid in return for a political solution. His government was holding on to power by a slender margin, and had come to rely increasingly on the support of the eleven Unionist MPs sitting in Westminster. Their support, naturally, had its price. The Labour government had to promise the Unionists that it would increase Northern Ireland's representation in Parliament from the twelve seats of which it had consisted since partition to seventeen. The Unionists, and Callaghan, knew that the bulk of the extra seats would fall to Unionists, increasing their strength even more (and thus, ironically, putting them in a stronger bargaining position in any future hung parliament). Callaghan also knew that as long as his government depended on Unionist votes, there was no question of any attempt to make power-sharing a central part of British policy in Northern Ireland.

While the Irish diplomatic offensive was blocked on this front, it moved aggressively ahead on the other, aimed at discrediting pro-IRA groups in Washington. All Caucus attempts to renew its earlier contact with Carter were turned back.

The Caucus had sent accounts of the torture of Irish prisoners in Northern Ireland jails to the State Department. In 1976 Carter had promised to make such violations an issue. But the material submitted to the administration was simply ignored. When the State Department published its annual overview of the human-rights situation worldwide, Northern Ireland was not even mentioned.

Frustrated, the lobbyists turned to Mario Biaggi. A short time after the Carter speech, Jack Keane, President of the Ancient Order of Hibernians and founding member of the Caucus, met with the congressman from the Bronx and suggested that he set up a committee on Irish affairs that would press Congress to hold open hearings on Northern Ireland. The hearings would focus on human-rights violations that reputable sources were documenting in the British-controlled state. Biaggi agreed at once, saying he was "flattered" to be asked. In the fall of 1977 he began to enlist congressional support for his Ad Hoc Committee for Irish Affairs. By late October he had signed up seventy-nine members. A few months later, the list had increased to ninety-three. It encompassed the entire ideological spectrum, from Illinois Republican Henry Hyde, on the right, to Stephen Solarz, the New York Democrat, on the left. The committee, with Biaggi as its chairman, wanted to hold hearings as soon as possible. Both the Irish mission and House Speaker O'Neill were watching the development closely. The Irish made it clear to O'Neill that he should do all in his power to make sure hearings were not held.

O'Neill quietly informed the head of the Foreign Relations Committee in Congress, which would have to approve of the Biaggi motion, that this would be an inappropriate time to stir up trouble over Irish rights. O'Neill did this in spite of the fact that world bodies like Amnesty International were registering their alarm at the increasing number of convictions obtained in Northern Ireland's non jury courts on the basis of confessions alone. It was evident that the police were forcing confessions from prisoners in order to obtain convictions. In 1976, for instance, of 1,200 prosecutions under emergency legislation more than 900 resulted in convictions. Of these, nearly 80 percent were obtained on the basis of confessions. A report published by Amnesty in 1978 documented a host of torture cases, and condemned the British for allowing such practices to continue. However, as far as the Irish government and its diplomatic mission were concerned, open hearings dealing with these allegations would have played into the hands of the IRA and its American supporters. To the Irish authorities it was more important that the IRA be given no opportunity to enhance its credibility than that the British be criticized for their violations of human rights.

"There is no question that the Irish government has been a substantial force in resisting any request for hearings," said Biaggi. "There is no question that the Irish government's representatives in Washington have been very close to Speaker O'Neill and as a result we have not been able to have hearings. The chairman of the Foreign Relations Committee has told me he'd be glad to give me hearings—but the Speaker prohibited him. And the situation still applies."

Having checkmated Biaggi's congressional moves, the Irish mission pursued a more risky course to discredit the congressman. Early in 1978 they saw what they thought was an opportunity to do so. The Irish prime minister, Fianna Fail leader Jack Lynch (in power since June 1977), had previously given an interview on Irish radio which was widely interpreted as a call for British withdrawal from Northern Ireland. He had said that the British should "indicate in a general way" that it would like to see a united Ireland. He also attacked Britain's continued support of the Protestants as a "steel wall against which intransigent Unionists can put their backs—and nothing will shift them." Thus, the prime minister argued, the road to reconciliation was blocked. The interview created a controversy in Britain and Northern Ireland, with Unionists and British spokesmen rushing to condemn it as "playing into the hands of the IRA."

On January 24, 1978, Biaggi wrote to Prime Minister Lynch on behalf of the Ad Hoc Committee. "I wish to commend you," said the letter, "on your recent call for a declaration of intent from Great Britain to withdraw her troops from Ireland." Biaggi hailed it as "an important initiative" and said, "The Ad Hoc Committee is most interested in seeing that this declaration of intent becomes a reality." He concluded, "I would be most grateful for your comments on the overall prospects for peace in Ireland, as well as your assessment of the efforts which the Ad Hoc Committee might undertake to contribute to the goal of peace."

Biaggi's letter was a naïve attempt to ingratiate the Ad Hoc Committee with the prime minister. He obviously had a lot to learn about Irish politics if he imagined that an Irish prime minister could possibly allow anything he said to be identified with someone supported by the pro-IRA Irish National Caucus. When the Irish mission learned of Biaggi's letter, they persuaded Lynch that here was an opportunity to administer a stinging rebuke to the meddling congressman and his Ad Hoc Committee. In Dublin, Sean Donlon, who was being groomed for the post of Irish ambassador to the U.S., supported Lillis in urging Jack Lynch to draft a strongly worded reply to Biaggi which could then be made public. That it was an extremely unusual course to adopt—it was, after all, an attempt to discredit a member of the United States Congress—did not restrain the Irish diplomats, still confident as they were from their recent successes with Jimmy Carter. Lynch agreed. He wrote to Biaggi accusing him of supporting the IRA. Lynch's letter noted that the Irish National Caucus which had been "closely associated with the cause of violence in Northern Ireland," welcomed the setting up of his committee as a "victory for itself." The prime minister observed that Biaggi had visited Ireland at "the request of the Caucus."

The prime minister continued, "We in Ireland have also noted your public identification when here with supporters of violence who have no democratic mandate from our people." He concluded by telling Biaggi that Irish government policy had been seriously misrepresented in Congress and "in view of the extent of this confusion and of the seriousness with which I must view it, I am issuing copies of our correspondence to members of your Ad Hoc Committee and other congressional leaders. I would hope that in doing so, the existing confusion will be removed and the cause of peace and political progress in Ireland advanced."

The letter quickly found its way into the hands of the press. Editorial after editorial poured scorn and derision on the Bronx politician for thinking that he knew anything about Northern Ireland. He was generally held up to ridicule as a dupe of clever pro-IRA manipulators or abused as a cynical politician playing for the Irish-American vote. But Biaggi had never received such national attention before: he was the first U.S. congressman to have been publicly attacked by the head of a friendly government.

Compared to this the controversy over the Fifth Amendment when he was running for Mayor of New York was a local row.

"It was less than I would have expected from a man in his position," said Biaggi with statesmanlike detachment. "It was designed to destroy the Ad Hoc Committee. We had heard about it beforehand . . . something was going to happen that would destroy the committee." He said that the Irish mission was "all a-twitter about it" for some days before Lynch's letter was released. According to the congressman, however, things did not go as planned.

"It was the best thing that ever happened to us because . . . what the prime minister did with that single thrust was he made us international. People in the European Parliament, in the Italian government, English representatives, were asking 'What about this Biaggi? What kind of man is he?' And they were told—'He's a fine man.'" Biaggi also claims that not only did his name become more internationally known, but his committee actually increased its membership from 93 to 125. As far as is known, the controversy led to the resignation of only one member—Paul McCloskey, Jr., a California Republican.

The Lynch letter had adverse affects in the Irish-American community. It was significant that the only reputable newspaper to defend Biaggi was *The Irish Echo,* a politically moderate weekly with the largest circulation of any Irish-American paper. Its editor, John Thornton, defended Biaggi's trip to Ireland as an attempt to get "the whole story" of what was happening.

Another sign that the Irish-American community was not in agreement with the Dublin attack on Biaggi came when Jack Keane, president of the AOH, threatened to cancel his organization's upcoming convention in Killarney. An estimated seven thousand members and their families were scheduled to make the trip; it would have represented a considerable loss to the area. (The organization was divided over Keane's threat. In the end, the trip went ahead as scheduled.)

The controversy over the Lynch letter definitely soured relations between leading Irish Americans and the Irish diplomatic mission. Lillis in particular was bitter about Biaggi's defenders. On more than one occasion he expressed anger and annoyance at the *Echo* for its editorial line. (At a private reception attended by both Thornton and Lillis, tempers became so frayed that the two men had to be separated physically.)

Relationships between the mission and concerned Irish Americans deteriorated further with the arrival in Washington of Sean Donlon, the new Irish ambassador to the U.S., in 1978. Donlon, at thirty-eight the youngest man ever to be appointed ambassador from Ireland, was as tenacious a lobbyist as Lillis. When Lillis left for Ireland that same year, Donlon determined to keep up the pressure on those the Irish government regarded as impediments to its policies. On March 17, 1978, the Big Four were joined in their statement by Senators Gary Hart, the future presidential hopeful, Thomas Eagleton, George McGovern, Joseph Biden, and Patrick Leahy. Once more they concentrated their fire on Irish Americans who supported the IRA. But this time they had critical words for the British too, and appealed to them for more "effective leadership." And they asked for a genuine commitment from the Protestants to find a "settlement that is fair to Protestants and Catholics alike."

The statement reflected the frustration at Britain's continuing inertia felt by both the Big Four and the Irish government. Strains began to appear among the Big Four. Governor Carey, once more proving something of a maverick, refused to attend a dinner in New York honoring James Callaghan, the British prime minister. His press secretary issued a statement saying that he did not attend as "he did not want to share the dais with the Prime Minister of Great Britain because of the situation in Northern Ireland." Carey was up for reelection and was hoping to placate the Irish-American vote after his outspoken attack on the IRA the previous year. (He was subsequently reelected for another term.) The British government, however, regardless of growing impatience in America, went ahead and gave the Unionists their extra seats at Westminster. This was their only "initiative" on Northern Ireland and it was not one that would give either Washington or Dublin grounds for optimism about Britain's future intentions.

When the time came in 1979 for the now ritual St. Patrick's Day statement, its content showed a clear shift of emphasis in Dublin's attitude and that of its political allies in Washington. It hit hard at London. "The time is long past for the British government to reappraise its failing policies in Northern Ireland and to initiate a more effective effort to end the violent impasse. But this cannot happen absent the political will within Britain that it should happen. In this respect we are all dismayed by the lack of priority given by the two major British political parties to the subject of Northern Ireland at their recent party conferences." (Not only is it difficult to get British politicians to address the issue at their party conferences; it is hard to persuade them to debate the problem in Parliament itself. On one occasion, what was heralded as a major debate on Northern Ireland in Westminster was attended by 80 M.P.s out of a possible 600. Before the debate was halfway finished, 31 had left.)

The statement then departed from its perennial calls for power-sharing and said that "Britain must be prepared for bolder alternatives." They suggested a confederation between Northern Ireland and the Irish Republic, or some other "constitutional arrangement" linking Northern Ireland with the Republic of Ireland. If such a step were taken, they said, "It would be a logical outgrowth of President Carter's statement in 1977 for the United States to join with Britain and the European community to provide financial or other assistance."

At the time it was mere whistling to the wind. Britain had no intention of undertaking any major initiative. The Labour government was faced with a general election and a rejuvenated Conservative party under the abrasive leadership of Margaret Thatcher. In these circumstances the reference to the Carter initiative seemed completely irrelevant, a piece of nostalgia about more optimistic times. By 1979, power-sharing was a dead letter; Britain was concentrating on Northern Ireland as a law-and-order problem, and there was nothing the Big Four or Dublin could do to persuade them differently.

That did not prevent Ireland's ambassador from pursuing the other goal of his country's broad strategy, the discrediting of those identified with the IRA. Though the Caucus was successfully isolated from the highest circles of power, it had close ties to Biaggi's committee, which was still active, and Donlon was determined to counter it. Breaking with usual diplomatic protocol, the ambassador lobbied individual congressmen. His constant message was that the Ad Hoc Committee was a puppet of IRA supporters. He occasionally approached congressmen identified with the Biaggi committee. Representative Hamilton Fish, a Republican from New York and one of the most active committee members, became involved in a case concerning six Irishmen who many said had been wrongly convicted of a bombing atrocity in England. One of those who contacted Fish was Father Raymond Murray, a Northern Ireland priest well known for his work in drawing attention to alleged injustices committed by the British and Northern Ireland authorities. (Along with another priest, Father Denis Faul, Murray has been the most assiduous chronicler of security-force violations of human rights.) He outlined the case of the six men and the evidence that gave serious grounds for questioning the fairness of their trial and the means of their conviction. Fish tried to enlist the support of Congress in persuading the British to reopen their cases. When Donlon learned of this he wrote to Fish questioning Father Murray's motives. In the letter, Donlon quoted a prominent loyalist politician's attack on Murray as someone who constantly undermined the work of the security forces. When the letter was revealed some six years later in 1985, the leader of the AOH called for Donlon's resignation. But by then Donlon, as head of the Foreign Affairs department, was on the verge of one of the most important achievements in his career—the signing of the Anglo-Irish Agreement. The government rallied to his defense.

Outside Washington, whenever Donlon addressed Irish-American groups, he was so relentless in his attacks upon the IRA, NORAID, and the Caucus that some regarded his behavior as obsessive. On one occasion, at a meeting in Westchester with prominent local Irish Americans, he had to be escorted from the room after several people present began to hurl abuse at him following his speech.

It did not appear that the Irish were having any more success in dissuading politicians from joining Biaggi's committee than they were in persuading the British to break the impasse in Northern Ireland. Indeed, at the height of their anti-Biaggi campaign, the Ad Hoc Committee recruited Senator Dennis DeConcini of Arizona, a prominent Democrat, although at first, according to a DeConcini aide, the senator was uncertain about joining because "the good guys and the bad guys are difficult to identify in Northern Ireland." Using this disarmingly (if not alarmingly) simple yardstick the senator obviously decided that Biaggi was on the side of the "good guys," for he became one of the more active members of the Ad Hoc Committee.

The Caucus and the committee were still working hand in hand, regardless of the Irish government's campaign. The Caucus sponsored two committee members, Congressmen Hamilton Fish and Joshua Eilberg, on a trip to Ireland to inquire into the United States visa policies restricting IRA and Sinn Fein spokesmen from visiting America. Denials are most often issued under Section 212(a)(28)(F) of the Immigration and Nationality Act, which bars from entering the U.S. people who belong to an organization advocating the overthrow of government by force. Eilberg was chairman of the Subcommittee on Immigration, Citizenship and International Law, of which Fish was also a prominent member. During their trip Fred Burns O'Brien, the director of information for the Caucus, acted as the "unofficial adviser."

The two congressmen were to draw up a report for the Immigration subcommittee. During their eight-day visit they met with a wide variety of organizations and individuals, including representatives of the IRA, Sinn Fein, the Protestant UDA, and the left-wing Irish Republican Socialist Party (IRSP). They questioned officials in the American consulate in Belfast, then headed by Charles Stout, and spoke with the British. Stout admitted to them that the consulate made its decisions as to who should receive a visa and who should not on information from British and Irish government sources. They also found that "Presumption of participation in terrorist groups and activities in some cases were made on the basis of political affiliation." That is, someone associated with Irish republican views was automatically branded a "terrorist" and denied a visa. Often records of detention without trial were used as justification for denial, even though the applicant had no criminal record.

An anomaly the congressmen uncovered was the different treatment that the Protestant paramilitary received. Stout told them that membership of the UDA did not constitute grounds for visa denial. "This is the Department [of State's] determination, as I understand it," he said. "As I see it, the UDA is a different type of organization. Its aims are different. It does not try to overthrow the government in Northern Ireland, or kill police.

To my knowledge this is a political question." He said that although he had instructions that in any case of suspected IRA
membership the person's visa application was to be sent for review to the State Department, he had no such instruction regarding the Protestant paramilitary groups. He did not seem to
be aware of the UDA's involvement in the collapse of the power-
sharing government in 1974, or its key role in the bloodiest sectarian murder campaign in recent Irish history. As a result,
prominent members of the UDA, including its chairman, Andy
Tyrie, and Andy Robinson, one of its most important military organizers, were allowed to visit the U.S. in 1975 and 1979, while republicans were generally kept out. Members of another
Protestant extremist group, the illegal Ulster Volunteer Force, a
quasifascist organization that has been involved in some of the
most vicious murders ever to take place in Northern Ireland,
were also given visas.

In their report, Fish and Eilberg wrote: "The delegation failed
to understand the rationale of labeling only the individuals in the
Provisional IRA as terrorists and exonerating individuals in Loyalist paramilitary organizations. This practice is reflected in the is-
suance of visas to well-known members of these Protestant
paramilitary organizations, and the denial of U.S. visas to alleged
members of the IRA." Their report concluded that "the State
Department may have acted unfairly and unjustifiably in denying
or revoking non-immigrant visas to certain Irish nationals desir-
ous of visiting the United States." After 1980, the State Department applied its policy of visa restrictions more evenhandedly,
denying applications from well-known loyalist paramilitary as well
as republican leaders.

The restrictions were maintained largely at the insistence of
the Irish government. This was in spite of the fact that the government was on record as saying that it had no objection to elected representatives or their nominees—except "spokesmen for
violence with no mandate from the people"—visiting the U.S.
After 1978, Sinn Fein had many representatives elected, including its president, Gerry Adams, who won a seat in Westminster in
1983. Yet for years, when Adams applied for a visa to come to the
U.S., his application, too, was squashed. In truth, Sinn Fein's electoral successes make their representatives even less welcome in

America as far as Dublin was concerned, because it gave them more credibility.

Biaggi's committee was active on other fronts, and in the summer of 1979 scored one of its best publicized successes. The Congressman was informed that the Northern Ireland police, the Royal Ulster Constabulary (RUC), had ordered a consignment of three thousand handguns from a U.S. weapons factory. Inquiries showed that since the beginning of the Northern Ireland crisis, ten thousand guns had been shipped to the RUC from America. (This is about four times the number George Harrison claimed to have sent to the IRA.) Biaggi thought this was incompatible with the U.S.'s claim to be "impartial" in the Irish conflict—a claim the State Department had reiterated in 1979. He also believed it to be in violation of United States law. Clause 502(b) of the Foreign Assistance Act prohibits the sale of weapons to groups that have violated human rights. In 1976, 1978, and 1979, the RUC had been found by various world bodies, including the Strasbourg Commission on Human Rights and Amnesty International, to have violated prisoners' human rights through different forms of torture and physical abuse. Assembling this information, and supported by other members of the Ad Hoc Committee, Biaggi proposed an amendment to a State Department appropriations bill that came to the floor of the House on July 12, halting weapons sales to the RUC. It could not have been more provocatively timed: July 12 is the day of Ireland's major Protestant celebration, commemorating the defeat in 1690 of the Catholic pretender to the English throne. But in 1979 it was loyalist forces that suffered a setback on that date, when, after a forty-five-minute debate, Biaggi's amendment passed.

On this occasion Tip O'Neill did not intervene. As Speaker of the House, he controlled the flow of legislation on the House floor, and could have squashed the amendment as he had Biaggi's other Irish initiatives. However, in 1979, O'Neill, along with Kennedy, Carey, and Moynihan, had his own deep frustrations with Britain's Northern Ireland policy. Their St. Patrick's Day statement that year was particularly outspoken about British inertia, and Governor Carey had been moved to call for economic sanctions against Britain to force it to withdraw from

Northern Ireland. (A British Conservative party spokesman responded testily: "I am afraid these Irish Americans are a menace. All they do is encourage the IRA.") O'Neill allowed the amendment to go through as a warning to the British. A few days later, the U.S. government announced that all arms sales to the RUC were being suspended pending an improvement in the force's human-rights record. News of the ban was greeted with predictable outrage by Northern loyalists, the British, and the *New York Times* (twice in one year the *Times* editorialized against the decision). The new conservative administration under Margaret Thatcher made several overtures to the U.S. to have the ban removed. When the ideologically sympathetic administration of Ronald Reagan took over in 1981, Thatcher tried again, but Reagan turned her down. Said Biaggi, "We don't mind them lifting the ban if we can be assured that they no longer engage in unlawful human-rights violations."

Biaggi was not so successful, however, in his other major Irish scheme of that year. It was probably one of the most harebrained and grandiose he ever undertook. Inspired by President Carter's Camp David initiative, the congressman thought he could do the same for Northern Ireland. His plan was simply to bring together the paramilitary groups, both Protestant and IRA, have them call a ceasefire, hold a conference, talk out their differences, and reach a permanent agreement on peace and cooperation. Biaggi would act as the peace-conference coordinator. The Reverend Sean McManus, the chairman of the Irish National Caucus, seems to have been the main instigator of this unlikely effort. Originally planned for the spring, it did not take place until the fall, when Biaggi and McManus went to Belfast. They set up headquarters in the Europa Hotel near the city center. Preliminary contacts ensured that at least most of the participants would show up; but to what purpose was never made clear, since the IRA regarded the whole affair very warily. It was plain to them there was no use talking peace if the British government was not directly involved. The UDA, however, was more enthusiastic. They told Biaggi they were fed up with being used by Unionist politicians and had decided to start thinking politically for themselves.

The IRA sent along observers—Daithi O'Conaill and Ruiari O'Bradaigh. Gerry Adams, the Belfast leader, also attended. At one time O'Bradaigh and O'Conaill might have had the influence to persuade the IRA to take Biaggi and McManus's schemes more seriously. But by 1979 younger, more left-wing activists like Adams were gaining control of the movement. And they were not sympathetic to the peace proposals.

Biaggi recalled Adams: "He was sitting in the back with a small group. I sensed his presence as a pall." Biaggi asked for a temporary truce. He practiced "shuttle diplomacy" between suites, going from loyalist to republican, trying to get them to agree. Unfortunately, Biaggi was no Henry Kissinger. "We talked for over four hours. The IRA said the truce wasn't on their agenda." The conference dissolved. There was going to be no Camp David-style settlement for Northern Ireland.

For the Caucus, however, the peace efforts had more serious consequences. The IRA later condemned the whole initiative, saying that since it left out the British it fostered the idea that the Northern Ireland problem was a purely sectarian one that could be resolved by Protestants and Catholics talking to each other. It accused McManus of playing into the hands of the British government.

The IRA were not the only ones upset about the conference. Other members of the Caucus agreed with the republicans. Strains that were already showing because of unhappiness with McManus's leadership increased, and by late 1979 the Caucus was badly split, with units in New Jersey, Illinois, and Pennsylvania breaking away to form their own organization. When McManus tried to reorganize the dissident chapters by replacing the leadership with his own supporters, he was told that he had no legal right to do so. Each chapter was a state-incorporated body; the Reverend McManus's organization's jurisdiction ended at the boundaries of Washington, D.C.

McManus was in trouble in another quarter. The Irish Northern Aid Committee was unhappy with the Caucus's activities and accused McManus of trying to poach its supporters. Flannery, NORAID's founder and one of the founding members of the Caucus, attacked McManus, saying he was trying to infringe on NORAID's areas by organizing fund-raising dinners. "The Caucus was founded as a political movement. It was not supposed to be a fund-raiser," Flannery said. The Caucus's finances were supposed to come from private subscriptions. *The Irish People,* which had once published McManus and Fred Burns O'Brien's statements, now denounced them. It reported: "Flannery objects to these people raising money on the back of the suffering people in Ireland whilst not sending a penny to relieve it." "McManus," the paper continued, "has publicly pledged that no money he raised would be sent to Ireland." It said that the Caucus, through its Peace Forum, had attempted to portray "the war of national liberation as a sectarian battle between two communities in the north," and quoted Flannery as saying that McManus's influence with U.S. congressmen was "mostly mere publicity."[3] McManus dismissed NORAID's objections as silly. But more serious accusations were being made. In Ireland, the IRA issued a statement saying that the Caucus's director of information was persona non grata with the movement, and that he should stay out of the country. There were hints that O'Brien, a lawyer with the Customs Service, was an agent for the U.S. government. Flannery actually accused O'Brien of being an agent. O'Brien denied being in the CIA, though Flannery had not mentioned that particular body. After that, relations between the two groups were bitter. The Caucus adopted a much softer line on Northern Ireland, distancing itself from the IRA. "I did for many years support publicly the IRA," McManus admitted. "But we are now a nonviolent organization. Our job is to make Ireland an issue with the American people. It's irrelevant what any group thinks of us."

The Caucus maintained its links to Biaggi's committee. But beyond that, its real influence seemed to be mainly with Irish newspapers, which often gave prominence to McManus's statements. Typical of the publicity given to him was an incident that occurred during the 1981 hunger strike. A Belfast Catholic newspaper ran a front-page story claiming that Reagan was going to intervene with Thatcher over Northern Ireland. The story was based on a statement McManus made saying that he had approached the president and been given assurances that there would be action to stop the fast. In fact, the Caucus had been unable to gain access to the White House since early 1977. Reagan had no intention of intervening, even when the Irish prime minister made an appeal to him. Four years later, when a U.S. aid package was announced in support of the agreement, McManus tried to maintain that the package was his work, much to the chagrin of the Irish government and House Speaker Tip O'Neill. For the aid was the culmination of many years of hard work on the part of the Irish government and O'Neill, begun with the Carter statement in 1977. Though that statement had not resulted in any immediate progress as far as influencing the British was concerned, the initiative it contained was not allowed to die.

From his arrival in Washington in 1978, it had been one of Sean Donlon's principal tasks to keep that initiative alive. In their 1979 St. Patrick's Day statement, O'Neill, Kennedy, Moynihan, and Carey—with the backing of other senators and governors in a loose grouping that two years later became known as the Friends of Ireland—referred to the possibility of American aid if a satisfactory settlement were reached. The initiative surfaced in the Democratic party election platform in 1980. When that party went down to defeat at Ronald Reagan's hands, Donlon was quick to gain access to the new powers in the White House.

Donlon built on a personal relationship he had with Judge William Clark, a political intimate of President Reagan's since his days as governor of California. (Clark's grandfather had had connections with the Donlon family in Ireland many years before.) Clark became national security adviser in 1981, and through Donlon became an important link between the White House and the Irish prime minister's office in Dublin. Between 1981 and 1985 Clark visited Ireland five times to discuss prospects for a Northern Ireland settlement with Donlon. He kept the White House apprised of all developments on the issue. Any time Thatcher was due to meet Reagan, Donlon set up a meeting with Clark to discuss Northern Ireland and how the administration might let Thatcher know of its continuing concern about the situation. Other Reagan intimates with whom Donlon was on close terms were Ed Meese, who later became attorney general, and James Baker, Reagan's chief of staff at the White House. Reagan himself had a sentimental interest in his "roots," which he quickly demonstrated by making a visit to the Irish embassy on St. Patrick's Day 1981.

Said one Irish diplomat, "Reagan has been sneered at for being a one-day-in-the-year Irishman. But we've had a lot of presidents who were never Irish on any day."

The Friends of Ireland came to regard Donlon as indispensable to their own efforts in maintaining interest in the Northern Ireland issue. So much so that when Charles Haughey, leader of the Fianna Fail party, became prime minister, and told Donlon that he was being shifted to the United Nations, both Kennedy and O'Neill informed Haughey that if he wanted them to continue their work in Congress as Irish government allies, Donlon would have to stay in Washington. The Irish prime minister backed down and left Donlon at his post.

In 1981, at the height of the hunger-strike crisis, Garret Fitzgerald became prime minister. Fitzgerald was a close friend of both Lillis and Donlon. He appointed Donlon to head the Foreign Affairs Department in Dublin. This was a powerful posting, more to his liking than the U.N. But although Donlon returned to Ireland, he maintained strong personal links to Washington with both the Friends of Ireland and Clark. Regardless of which envoy Ireland sent to Washington, Donlon, 2,500 miles away, was regarded as the real U.S. link. By the time he took up his post as head of Foreign Affairs, events had already begun that would start a chain reaction leading to the Anglo-Irish Agreement and an opportunity for Donlon's influence to finally bear fruit.

The 1981 hunger strike helped propel Sinn Fein to electoral success. The moderate constitutional nationalist party of John Hume, the SDLP, found itself in an ever-weakening position as the prospect of British initiatives to solve the crisis remained remote. In 1983 the SDLP and the main political parties in the Irish Republic—Fianna Fail, Fine Gael, and the Labour party—established the New Ireland Forum. It would review the political problems of Northern Ireland and take advice and expert opinion from all political groups, excluding those that supported violence—which meant that Sinn Fein was not asked to participate. Though the Unionists boycotted it, the Forum, after a year's hearings, produced a report outlining three alternatives for ensuring a settlement of the long-running crisis: a unitary state, a federal-confederal state, and a system of joint authority.

Late in 1984, Garret Fitzgerald, Ireland's prime minister, met with Margaret Thatcher to discuss the Forum's conclusions. In a press conference afterward Thatcher brusquely dismissed each of the Forum's suggestions with her famous "Out, out, out," remarks. They seemed to deliver a death blow to the relations between Dublin and London, and to have seriously damaged the SDLP's hopes for progress based on the Forum's findings.

However, the American connection saved the Irish prime minister from humiliation. Donlon telephoned Washington and spoke with O'Neill. He told him that if the process started by the Forum were to survive, Thatcher had to be brought to heel through American influence. O'Neill contacted Reagan and insisted that when the president next spoke with Thatcher he make plain the administration's unhappiness with continued British refusal to consider any movement on Northern Ireland. Reagan had already proved to be one of the busiest presidents in regard to Ireland, at least on a symbolic level. After his 1981 St. Patrick's Day visit to the embassy, he had the Irish prime minister as a guest of the White House. On St. Patrick's Day, 1983, Reagan was once more at the Irish embassy. The following St. Patrick's Day Garret Fitzgerald was again Reagan's guest. 1984 also saw Reagan off to Ireland on a much-publicized visit. So when O'Neill came to Reagan late in 1984, concerned at the Thatcher reaction to the Forum proposals, he found the president ready to go beyond the mere symbolic gesture. Reagan had also been approached by Mario Biaggi in the wake of Thatcher's brutal dismissal of the Forum findings. Biaggi wrote to the president on behalf of the Ad Hoc Committee and expressed Congress's "deep concern" over Thatcher's action.

On December 22, 1984, Mrs. Thatcher arrived in Washington to meet with Reagan. The media's attention was devoted to her support for Reagan's Strategic Defense Initiative, and there was no reference to any talks on Northern Ireland that the two leaders might have had. However, Reagan did bring up the issue. In a letter in reply to Biaggi's the congressman was informed that "The President stressed the need for progress and the need for all parties concerned to take steps which will contribute to a peaceful resolution of the existing problems of Northern Ireland." The reply also claimed that the British prime minister had expressed a strong desire for progress to be made.

Thatcher was due back in Washington in February to address a joint meeting of both Houses. O'Neill sent a message to Sir Oliver Wright, the British ambassador, in which he stressed that Congress would appreciate it if Thatcher addressed the Northern Ireland issue in her speech. When the British prime minister arrived to give the speech, O'Neill met with her and reiterated his concerns.

Thatcher's subsequent address demonstrated that the woman who had earned the sobriquet of "Iron Lady" could also be very flexible when occasion called for it. Her remarks on Ireland were models of conciliation—a startling contrast to her staccato dismissals of a few months before. "Garret Fitzgerald and I and our respective governments are united in condemning terrorism," she began. Then, in what sounded like a direct quote from the New Ireland Forum report, she continued, "We recognize the differing traditions and identities of the two parts of the community in Northern Ireland, the Nationalist and the Unionist. We seek a political way forward acceptable to them both and which respects them both." She concluded by saying that Garret Fitzgerald and she would continue to consult together in "the quest for peace and stability in Northern Ireland," and hoped the U.S. would continue to support them.

Her remarks on Ireland were greeted silently by Congress. Conciliatory or not, she was given to understand that Congress and the administration were united in their desire that her government should do more than espouse cooperation with Dublin. Patience was running out. For Tip O'Neill there was a very personal motive for his desire to see progress in Northern Ireland. The 1985 session marked the beginning of the end of his active political life. He was due to resign his seat from Boston's Eighth Congressional District at the end of 1986, a seat he had held since it was vacated by John F. Kennedy. Before he gave up his political position, O'Neill was determined that the long struggle—begun when Carter was president—to persuade the British to reach settlement would show results. In the end, he was not disappointed.

1985 proved to be one of the most active in the history of Anglo-Irish relations. Five years before, the Irish and British prime ministers had agreed on a series of regular meetings to monitor the Northern Ireland situation and other delicate matters affecting both their countries. Contacts between the two governments, particularly between the offices of the prime ministers, were stepped up. By spring of 1985 there were rumors that the two governments were at last hammering out a new initiative on Northern Ireland. Among the key figures on the Irish side, besides Sean Donlon, there was Michael Lillis, who had joined the Foreign Affairs team in 1983.

The negotiations were secret, but Washington was kept up to date on their progress. As the months went by with no concrete results, the rumors increased. Had the British agreed to joint authority with Dublin over Northern Ireland? Was Thatcher preparing to reform the Northern Ireland police force and abolish the Ulster Defense Regiment—the locally recruited militia with a long record of anti-Catholic hostility? Were the talks aimed at bringing about the return of a power-sharing government? By late summer speculation had reached fever pitch. Northern Ireland's Unionists, worried that the British were about to abandon them to Dublin, issued dire threats of the consequences of any such "sellout." In September, William Clark went to Ireland and met with Donlon and Garret Fitzgerald. He was told that the two governments were close to a settlement. He returned to the White House and told his successor on the National Security Council, Robert McFarlane, who also shared Clark's keen interest in Ireland, that the administration should begin to put together an aid package.

Details of the settlement only emerged on November 15 as Fitzgerald and Thatcher met in Hillsborough, outside Belfast, to put their governments' signatures to it. Among its most controversial and innovative proposals was one giving the Dublin government a recognized role in Northern Ireland for the first time in the history of the partitioned state. An Anglo-Irish intergovernmental council was set up, with ministers from the Dublin and London governments meeting regularly to discuss such matters as policing, the judiciary, and the situation in the prisons—all areas of concern for Northern Ireland's Catholics. To support the work of the Intergovernmental Council, an Anglo-Irish secretariat was established near Belfast. Its head: Michael Lillis.

In return for recognizing Dublin's role, the agreement contained the Irish government's acceptance of the right of the Protestant majority to remain within the United Kingdom. There had long been a de facto recognition by Dublin of the Unionist position and the border. Indeed, since the Irish government has never had the capacity, or the will, to force or persuade the Unionists otherwise, there has been little alternative for Dublin except to live with the reality of partition. But for the first time, the Anglo-Irish Agreement gave that de facto recognition a de jure status. This troubled many nationalists, just as Dublin's new role provoked intense Unionist opposition to the agreement. The IRA condemned it, and the Unionists immediately commenced a campaign of escalating resistance to attempt to bring it down, as they had done with the power-sharing initiative eleven years before.

However, this did not prevent the Reagan administration, nor the Friends of Ireland, from finding in the agreement the "peaceful settlement" that will "command widespread acceptance throughout both parts of the community," which President Carter established as a precondition before the promise of American aid could become a reality. When Reagan and O'Neill joined together in the Oval Office the day the agreement was signed to promise that the aid would now be forthcoming, it was not immediately clear what form it would take. Both merely said that they would work closely together and with Congress to see that their commitment would be swiftly implemented. The administration drafted a bill that offered $250 million over five years to resuscitate the industrial and economic life of those areas north and south most affected by the long-running crisis.

However, even the highest of aspirations become entangled in the political web of give-and-take. Throughout the winter and early spring of 1986, there were indications that the aid was being used for ends other than those for which it was originally intended. First, it was suggested by Senator Lugar, chairman of the Foreign Relations Committee, that its approval by the Senate would depend on whether or not the Senate ratified the extradition treaty between the U.S. and the U.K. that would facilitate the extradition of IRA fugitives from America. No treaty, no aid. Then the White House threatened that aid for Ireland would become mixed up with its struggle to get aid for the Contras fighting against Nicaragua. (The Democrats in Congress were resisting a Reagan bill that would have given $100 million to assist the anti-Sandinista forces.)

Senator Kennedy, on behalf of the Friends of Ireland, approached Donald Regan, the White House chief of staff, to discuss changes in the administration's Irish bill. As the administration's bill stood, the aid was to be given mostly in the form of loans and guarantees, with only 40 percent cash. Kennedy was asking (with the support of both the British and Irish governments) for 80 percent to be administered in cash payments, with the remainder in guarantees and loans. Regan told him there would be no changes until the Democrats in Congress proved more cooperative on Nicaragua.

Congress drafted its own bill and O'Neill shepherded it through the House just before St. Patrick's Day, 1986. The House bill guaranteed five yearly payments of about $50 million in cash to the shattered economy of Northern Ireland and the areas in the Irish Republic most affected by the violence, plus other aid in loans and guarantees. The aid was approved in time for Garret Fitzgerald's visit to the capital for the St. Patrick's Day festivities. However, both the House bill and that of the administration remained stuck in the Senate Foreign Relations Committee, with Senator Lugar favoring the administration's but wanting it tied to approval of the extradition treaty. Other senators opposed this. The conflict was eventually resolved.*

The Speaker's old adversary on the Irish question in Congress, Mario Biaggi, was not going to be left out of this, the most widely publicized and heralded development in the last ten years of Ireland's troubled history. Biaggi and thirty-four other Ad Hoc Committee members had earlier written to Reagan asking that whatever aid was given be administered fairly, with no money going to industries that discriminated against Catholics in their hiring practices.

Biaggi, then serving his ninth consecutive term in Congress, had parted company with the Reverend McManus and the Caucus on the question of the Anglo-Irish Agreement. The Caucus had vociferously condemned it, and Biaggi had given it support.

---

*At the beginning of July 1986, the Senate agreed on a $50-billion aid package for one year, which became law that summer. The U.S. authorized further contributions over a five-year period, committing a total of $250 billion in aid.

(Later, McManus seems to have changed his course somewhat by supporting the aid to Ireland that came as a result of the agreement.) But Biaggi's expression of support was qualified in such a way as to allow the pro-IRA paper, *The Irish People*, to headline a story BIAGGI LEADS HOUSE IN OPPOSING ACCORD. A story on the same topic in *The Irish Echo* reported that Biaggi supported the agreement. After eighteen years in Congress, Mario Biaggi is an old hand at phrasing things in a manner that enables people on opposite sides of any argument to think he supports them.

Perhaps this is what helped his political career glide through two major controversies and withstand the hostile maneuvers of successive Irish governments and their diplomatic mandarins. He became something of a venerable figure; he told of how House freshmen would seek him out for picture-taking sessions, the results of which were displayed on district-office walls. His Italian geniality was obvious. He held no grudges and regretted the passing from the House of Tip O'Neill. "I don't see anyone on the scene with his warmth or charm or with his ability," he said as he contemplated the future. Nor did he see any realistic hope of his long-sought-for congressional hearings ever being granted, whoever replaces O'Neill as Speaker.

Mario Biaggi, in keeping with his image of gray-haired venerability, accepted this with statesmanlike calm, but he could not resist the occasional swagger. Musing in his office in the Bronx, surrounded by over one hundred plaques and awards from almost every ethnic group in America, as well as a wide variety of mementos—a visitor would at one time have found a harp carved by IRA prisoners propping up a photograph of Biaggi and Muhammad Ali—the congressman obviously enjoyed the notoriety the Irish question had brought him. "Any time the Brits come over to talk about the Irish issue," he recalled, "I'm invited by the chairman of the Foreign Relations Committee to attend. I always walk into the meeting a little late. You can see all the heads—they're turning—they're saying, 'That's him—the devil incarnate, that's him, that's him.' Renowned!" And Biaggi, the former cop, smiled: "The fact that a Mario Biaggi was the chairman of the Committee on Irish Affairs was humorous initially, but it has its advantages."

For well over a century, Irish Americans had been trying to involve the nation of their adoption in the dispute between Ireland and Britain. The U.S. economic support of the Anglo-Irish Agreement marked the first time that an American government had become directly involved with an Irish-British settlement at any level. The U.S. now had an immediate interest in seeing the agreement survive. In the coming years, this would prove an important factor with the British government in influencing its determination to make the agreement work against whatever opposition the Protestants could muster to oppose it. For the Irish government, American involvement represented its greatest diplomatic triumph—the one that underpinned its major success in persuading the British to reach a settlement. The ramifications for the government's struggle to persuade Irish Americans not to support groups like NORAID and the Caucus would be significant. Already, the Anglo-Irish Agreement had affected support for Sinn Fein in Northern Ireland, causing a decline in its vote in a provincewide election, with more Catholics turning again to the moderate SDLP, whose leader, John Hume, was one of the architects of the agreement. In America, a similar decline could be predicted in support for the IRA's sympathizers. NORAID had depended on British atrocities to provoke Irish-American anger and keep the dollars flowing. With the agreement in force, monitored by interested parties in the U.S. and Dublin, and the Irish government officials close at hand in Northern Ireland itself to represent Catholic grievances, Britain would have to show more sensitivity in its dealings with the nationalist community, leaving NORAID with fewer opportunities to appeal to Irish-American outrage.

Whatever the impact of the Ango-Irish Agreement, no one dared claim that the Northern Ireland crisis was over. But by 1986 it was clear that it had moved onto a different level, one more acceptable to the new tripartite alliance of Dublin, London, and Washington. Unless Protestant violence got out of hand, politicians could view the next few years as a time of opportunity for them to undermine—perhaps significantly—the IRA's base of support in both Ireland and America by pressing reforms in Northern Ireland. That they were in a position to do so was due in large measure to the power and influence of the American connection and the success with which Irish diplomats utilized it.

5
NORTHERN IRELAND ON TRIAL: EXTRADITION AND THE U.S. COURTS

In the mid-1880s, what would now be called "international terrorism" was a matter for great consternation among the governments of Europe and the United States. Between 1883 and 1885 Irish bombers set off a series of dynamite explosions in English cities. The campaign was organized from the United States. On May 3, 1886, in Chicago, a vibrant center of anarchism, a workers' demonstration was attacked by a police unit. Shots were exchanged and a bomb was thrown. Seven policemen were killed in the explosion, and over twenty workers died in police gunfire. Anarchism and dynamite—only recently invented—were on everybody's lips. In the summer of 1886, the British and United States governments drew up a new extradition treaty that would ease the return of Irish rebel fugitives—what the *New York Times* called "dynamite miscreants"—to England to stand trial. The Irish-American community reacted violently. The old Fenian and Indian Wars correspondent, John Finerty, directed a broadside from the columns of *The Citizen* at the new treaty, which was then before the Senate Foreign Relations Committee. "Of course the object of this treaty is plain upon its face, the English are the cowards of a bad conscience, and they want to control the movements of the 'extreme' enemies of their empire, resident in the United States."

"We are liable to look after our own dynamiters—we don't go around asking other people to save us from them—but England knows she cannot take care of hers without assistance from her subsidiary Government at Washington."

Finerty with great indignation pointed out that England—"the favorite haunt and refuge of all the extremists of Europe who plotted the assassination of Kings and Emperors"—had refused to extradite bombers and would-be assassins on the grounds that they were "political prisoners" and not criminals in the ordinary sense of the word. But she was applying a different standard when it came to Irishmen wanted for dynamiting attacks in London and Birmingham. The proposed treaty had listed such attacks as extraditable offenses, which would not be regarded as "political." Finerty wrote: "If dynamite has ever been used in London it was evidently not for the purpose of murder or of wanton destruction, but to produce a political effect. . . . Now, if dynamite should at any time be used for political purposes in England how are the persons who use it, and who may escape to the United States, to be regarded?"

One hundred years later, Finerty's question was still a matter of great controversy. In America, Irish fugitives from the Northern Ireland crisis were no longer sought for dynamite offenses. Dynamite had been replaced by more sophisticated weapons of guerrilla warfare. But those who were accused of committing crimes connected with Northern Ireland's unrest still claimed that those acts were political and should be regarded as such. They appealed to the political-offense exception clause in the 1972 treaty between the United States and the United Kingdom—a clause standard to the nearly ninety treaties in force between the U.S. and other nations. It read: "Extradition shall not be granted if: the offense for which extradition is requested is regarded by the requested Party as one of a political character; or the person proves that the request for his extradition has in fact been made with a view to try and punish him for an offense of a political character."

After the late 1970s this clause and its interpretation by the U.S. courts in cases concerning wanted IRA men was the cause of a bitter controversy, at times conducted with little regard to legal fact. As in 1886, Britain, in its attempts to extradite Irish rebel fugitives, insisted that their acts were those of mere criminals. The American administration joined them in pressing this case as vigorously as it could. As far as Reagan was concerned, the extradition struggle in the U.S. courts was one battle in the general war against "international terrorism." That is why, although there were only three cases after 1978 in which IRA men successfully appealed to the political-exception clause, the administration regarded it as a matter of utmost importance that such decisions be made impossible in the future.

The political-offense exception, although not then denominated as such, evolved in the late eighteenth century, with the establishment in Europe and America of democratic republics. It was a mechanism for giving shelter to fugitives from repressive monarchies and conservative regimes. Early on in America it was established that the judiciary, not the executive branch of government, should have the power to hear extradition cases. This way hearings would not be decided in terms of political expediency—as might be the case if the president or his secretary of state were faced with an extradition request from a valued ally. However, one of the anomalies of extradition proceedings is that the power to hear them is not given to the courts as such but to individual judicial officers—magistrates or federal judges—said to be "sitting in chambers." The judge or magistrate reviews the case and determines whether or not certain legal prerequisites are satisfied. If they are, the case is forwarded to the secretary of state with a recommendation in favor of or against extradition. The secretary of state exercises discretionary power and can refuse to extradite. What the judicial officer decides is binding only for that particular proceeding. Another anomaly of extradition law is that it is *sui generis:* each case is treated as unique, and from proceeding to proceeding each must be heard and judged on its own set of facts. Out of these anomalies grew the tradition that made the judge or magistrate's finding unappealable. If the decision goes against the requesting country, its only recourse is to file another extradition request and begin the proceedings all over again before a different judge or magistrate.

One of the factors the judicial officer might have to weigh in his or her consideration of a case before deciding whether or not to forward it to the secretary of state is the existence of an objective political dimension to the offense. Throughout the nineteenth century, American and British jurisprudence developed the idea of a political-offense exception. Though it was not explicitly formulated in extradition treaties until later, it was acknowledged in practice. None of the Fenian revolutionaries who fled from their failed rebellions in Ireland was ever extradited to Britain. Because of their political background, acts normally regarded as "common crimes—such as murder—perpetrated in connection with those uprisings came to be recognized as relative political offenses (as distinct from "pure" political offenses, which include treason and sedition), and in practice were nonextraditable.

In the wake of the 1883–85 dynamite attacks, the British tried to persuade the Cleveland administration to reverse that tradition and include among extraditable crimes those involving dynamite attacks on property. The British ambassador in Washington, Lord Sackville, won the support of Republicans in the Senate for the proposed new treaty. When it went before the Senate Foreign Relations Committee on July 8, 1886, the *New York Times* reported confidently, ". . . there is practically no opposition to any of its clauses." The paper predicted that "the treaty will undoubtedly be ratified some time before the adjournment of Congress. Ten days after the ratification the treaty will go into effect." It noted, "The clause relating to the extradition of malicious destroyers of property by whom life is endangered will attract the most attention as it is aimed directly at the dynamiters who are alleged to be plotting in the United States against the English Government." As it turned out, this was the only one of the *Times* predictions that proved accurate; the attention the treaty attracted among Irish Americans gave rise to outrage and anger. The treaty became embroiled in the political struggles between the Democratic and Republican parties to win Irish-American support in the 1888 presidential election. Some leading Irish Americans, such as the former Fenian leader John Devoy and Patrick Ford, editor of *The Irish World*—the most popular Irish-American newspaper ever published—accused the Democrats of favoring the new treaty and urged Irish Americans to vote Republican.* Other Irish Americans replied that the Republicans had conspired with Lord Sackville, who had promised his government's support of their candidate if they voted for the ratification of the treaty. The Irish-American congressman Patrick Collins said of the Republicans, "They dearly love a lord." In the end, the treaty proved so controversial that the Senate postponed consideration of it for six months, and it was eventually dropped. When a new treaty was drafted in 1890 it contained a clause barring extradition for political offenses and did not include the use of dynamite in attacks on property as an extraditable crime.

Throughout the late nineteenth century the ferment about extradition continued. A fiery Irish-American activist and priest, Father McGlynn, denounced a proposed extradition treaty with Czarist Russia by arguing, "Killing for political purposes is to be considered as something totally different from the crime of murder." He spoke at a meeting of nihilists, anarchists, and other radicals—including women and blacks—in New York's Cooper Union. Russia, Prussia, Austria, and the Kingdom of Naples had been among those regimes in Europe that refused to recognize the political-offense exception in their legal practice. At the time McGlynn spoke, revolutions had swept away many of them—but Czarist Russia still stood.

The extradition laws evolved in keeping with the changes sweeping Europe. In 1891 a landmark case in England established guidelines for determining when a fugitive can claim the political-offense exception. Angelo Castioni had been accused of killing a member of the administration of a local canton in Switzerland during the course of a political upheaval. He fled to England, where the courts refused to extradite him on the grounds his

*The enthusiasm the Irish had for the Republican party was partly dispelled by the Rev. Samuel Buchard, a Presbyterian clergyman. Speaking in support of the 1888 Republican candidate James Blame, he described the Democratic party as the party of "Rum, Romanism and Rebellion." This the Irish interpreted as an attack on their drinking habits, their religion, and their politics.

offense was political. The ruling found that before such grounds can be established, the fugitive must show that the act was committed during the course of a political rising, or a dispute between two parties in the state over which should control the government; it also had to be demonstrated that the act was incidental to that dispute or uprising.

These guidelines have to a large extent remained in place ever since. Judge Denman, who formulated them, kept their wording deliberately vague. He said it was not "necessary or desirable to put into language in the shape of an exhaustive definition exactly the whole states of things, or every state of things which might bring a particular case within the description of an offense of a political nature." This was strictly in keeping with the *sui generis* nature of extradition proceedings. It was at the same time a recognition of the fact that to define a political offense might result in depriving legitimate political offenders of its protection. The next occasion on which Britain's attempts to extradite Irish fugitives caused a commotion in America was not until 1903. James Lynchehaun had been convicted and imprisoned for a vicious assault on a local landowner during disturbances in 1894. Lynchehaun argued that he was a member of an uprising group taking part in a political disturbance, and that the attack took place in connection with that disturbance. The judicial officer who heard the case accepted these arguments and held that Lynchehaun's crime fell within the political-exception clause. The British warrant was rejected.

The Irish Americans who had formed the Lynchehaun Defense Committee published a pamphlet entitled "An Irish American Victory Over Great Britain," which claimed: "England cannot demand Irish fugitives and have them extradited without a full enquiry into the original facts out of which the crime grew and if those facts establish according to American notions of liberty, that the crime was political, extradition will not be granted."*

*Quoted in Michael Farrell's *Sheltering the Fugitive: The Extradition of Irish Political Offenders*, Mercier Press, Cork, 1985. Farrell points out that Lynchehaun had just been fired from his job by the woman he later assaulted, and had a reputation as a violent man. He surmises that Lynchehaun's attack on her had a personal, not political, motive.

The British apparently agreed with the sentiments of the Defense Committee. The Lynchehaun case signaled the last attempt the British would make for seventy-five years to extradite from America someone wanted for acts connected to the Irish troubles. Though many Irish rebels and guerrilla leaders fled to American after the 1916 Rising and the War of Independence, the British made no attempt to institute extradition proceedings against them. This was in itself a testimony to the strength of the political-exception clause and the Irish-American community, considering the fact that those years were some of the most violent in Irish history.

British unwillingness to lodge extradition requests for IRA fugitives in America persisted throughout the 1930s. In the 1950s some of the leaders of the IRA's ill-fated border campaign against Northern Ireland fled to the United States and remained there without threat from Britain. It was not until 1978 that Britain felt able to initiate extradition proceedings against a wanted IRA man in the hope that the request might be successful. What had changed?

The British obviously felt that the base of support for the IRA in America was so small as not to represent a significant political lobby. In the late 1970s, the statements of the Kennedy-O'Neill-Moynihan-Carey group and its supporters indicated that the major Irish-American political power bloc was in fact anti-IRA. In Northern Ireland, the British policy of criminalization—refusing to treat IRA prisoners as political—seemed to be having an impact, and the IRA was losing support. Certainly, political developments appeared to be in Britain's favor, giving it confidence that there would be little problem in extraditing wanted IRA men from America. But when the British issued their first extradition warrant in seventy-five years against a fugitive from the Irish crisis, they could not have foreseen the legal controversy that they were about to unleash. Ironically, the man against whom it was issued, Peter Gabriel McMullen, was as much a fugitive from the IRA as he was from the British government. The IRA had accused their former member of being a "gangster." McMullen had been a British paratrooper, but joined the IRA in the early 1970s. He was wanted by the British for planting a bomb in a British army barracks in Yorkshire. The IRA meanwhile accused him of trying to intimidate bar owners into giving him money and using the name of the IRA to do so.

McMullen actually handed himself over to the police in San Francisco in May 1978. An extradition warrant was issued soon thereafter. Because of his reputation, Irish-American activists did not want to become involved in his case. But civil-rights activist and lawyer Paul O'Dwyer realized its importance. If McMullen was returned to the United Kingdom, it would break over a century of legal tradition and set a precedent for future extradition proceedings involving the IRA. In conjunction with San Francisco lawyer Bill Goodman, his office undertook McMullen's defense. The case was heard before magistrate Frederick Woelfien. The defense charged that McMullen could not be extradited because his offenses fell within the scope of the political-exception clause of the 1972 treaty between the two governments. On May 11 of the following year the magistrate handed down his decision. "This has been a unique extradition proceeding," he observed, before going on to outline the political-offense exception standards that had to be met. "One, the act must have occurred during an uprising and the accused must be a member of the group participating in the uprising. Second, the accused must be a person engaged in acts of political violence with a political end. . . . Even though the offense be deplorable and heinous the criminal actor will be excluded from deportation if the crime is committed under these prerequisites." McMullen's defense complied with these standards. ". . . we find that Peter Gabriel John McMullen is therefore not extraditable under the provisions of the Extradition Treaty in force between the United States of America and the United Kingdom as of 1974."[1]

Woelfien's decision was almost casual in its argumentation. The two prerequisites were applied loosely to include what the magistrate admitted would be regarded as "heinous" crimes. Over the next few years, however, the courts would adopt far more rigorous and searching criteria before granting the political-offense exception. In doing so they would subject that exception to the greatest scrutiny it has ever received in the history of extradition law.*

The McMullen case attracted little attention. But by the time the next Irish extradition case came to be heard, circumstances had changed. In Northern Ireland Bobby Sands had commenced a hunger strike to the death in his demand for political status. In America Ronald Reagan was in the White House, and a crusade against "international terrorism" had begun.

In October 1980 a twenty-five-year-old Belfast man, Dessie Mackin, was arrested in New York. The British lodged an extradition request for him, alleging he had shot and wounded a plain-clothes British soldier during a fracas in Belfast over two years before. Mackin and another man, Bobby Gamble, had also received wounds during the fight. Both were arrested and charged. Mackin, when let out on bail, fled to the Irish Republic and then to the United States. Gamble's case went to trial in Belfast. Though he was convicted, the decision was later overturned on appeal. By this time, Mackin was in the Manhattan Correctional Center awaiting extradition proceedings. They would prove much more contentious than those involving McMullen. The Reagan and British governments were determined that the case of Dessie Mackin would mark a victory in the war against international terrorism.

The State Department began a strategy that it was to follow for the next two years. Acting on behalf of the British government, the American authorities argued that the role of the judge or magistrate in extradition cases was restricted to passing judgment on probable cause—that is, weighing the evidence presented by the requesting party to decide if it is sufficient for the individual's extradition. The government said that the judiciary had not the competence or authority to decide whether or not a crime was "political"; that should be left to the executive authority. In the course of its arguments, the Reagan administration voiced its clear concern that if left to the judiciary, determinations of what

---

*McMullen applied for political asylum in the U.S., claiming that if he were returned to Ireland the IRA would assassinate him. In April 1986, his request was rejected by the Ninth Circuit Court of Appeals on the grounds that his terrorist background made him unacceptable.

constitutes a political offense could be politically embarrassing to United States foreign policy. This anxiety—often stridently expressed—has been reiterated ever since in every extradition case involving the political-exception defense. The administration blatantly wanted the ideological needs of its current foreign-policy goals to override all other concerns.

The British were also prepared for the Mackin case. They sent over three witnesses for the hearing: Brian Garret, a Belfast lawyer; Superintendent Kenneth Masterson of the Royal Ulster Constabulary (RUC), the Northern Ireland police force; and Vincent Lynagh, the RUC's legal adviser. Also appearing on behalf of the British was Frank Perez, an officer in the U.S. State Department and deputy director of the Office for Combating Terrorism.

Frank Durkan, a lawyer with the O'Dwyer office, marshaled a group of experts—historians, journalists, and lawyers—on the Northern Ireland question. For several days magistrate Naomi Buchwald's courtroom resounded to the echoes of ancient and current Irish historical disputes. The objective of the prosecution was to demonstrate that the IRA was not a politically motivated organization and that Northern Ireland's violent upheavals were a matter of mere criminality. The objective of Mackin's defense was to establish the political roots of the crisis and the IRA's role in it, as well as showing that their client, an IRA man, was engaged in that political struggle. Mackin's history of IRA involvement had begun in 1971. He came from a family with connections to the IRA going back to the 1920s.

The objective facts of history were clearly in the defense's favor. It was relatively easy to establish that there was a political dispute going on in Northern Ireland—the actions and words of successive British governments had only to be described and quoted to prove it. (For example, the British had defended their use of internment without trial before the European Court of Human Rights by arguing that there was a "public emergency threatening the life of the nation," and that therefore extraordinary legal procedures were needed to quell it.) But it had to be established that Mackin's alleged crime, the shooting of a soldier, was part of the continuing political crisis.

Magistrate Buchwald spent six months working on her opinion.

When it was issued, on August 13, 1981, it was over one hundred pages long: in comparison, the McMullen opinion of two years before had been a mere six. What Buchwald produced was a detailed examination of the history of the political-offense exception, and a review of Irish history up to the contemporary situation in Northern Ireland.

To begin with, Buchwald dismissed the Reagan government's arguments for granting jurisdiction for deciding the political-exception defense to the executive rather than the judiciary. "There is simply no precedent," she wrote, "for adopting the Government's narrow reading . . . limiting the court's jurisdiction to a determination of 'criminality' or probable cause only. Rather, all precedent is to the contrary. Throughout more than eighty years of jurisprudential history in every case in which the political offense exception has been squarely presented . . . the courts have never declined to receive evidence on and consider the applicability of the political exception defense." She argued that this was necessary because, apart from everything else, for the State Department or president to have the power to decide such cases would make the government vulnerable to political or economic sanctions imposed by nations angered over unfavorable decisions. The use of the judiciary, with its detached and objective procedures, keeps the lid on that diplomatic Pandora's box firmly shut.

There was also no doubt in Buchwald's mind as to the nature of both the Northern Ireland crisis and the IRA. The whole legislative apparatus imposed by the British clearly indicated that in Northern Ireland they were dealing with a political uprising. She dismissed comparisons between the IRA and the Red Brigades made by the State Department's "terrorism" expert, Frank Perez; to refute them all she had to do was to quote the British army's own description of the IRA as a disciplined, highly organized guerrilla army dedicated to the traditional aims of Irish nationalism—one that commanded at least the tacit support of a section of the population. (The description referred to came from a secret British army document that had been made public three years before.) Evaluating Mackin's alleged crime in this context, Buchwald found it was "free from personal motive and substantially linked to the traditional goal and strategy of the IRA. . . ."

She was aware that some violent political acts had not been given the protection of the political-offense exception. These were usually anarchistic crimes aimed at the social rather than the political fabric of the nation. Buchwald judged Mackin's alleged attack on the plainclothes soldier quite different from those crimes. "In conclusion . . . the court holds . . . respondent Mackin has satisfied the requirements of the political offense exception. Accordingly, the United Kingdom's request for extradition of Desmond Mackin is denied. . . ."

A few weeks after Buchwald's decision, the last of the ten hunger strikers died, as the British government refused to recognize his claims to be a political prisoner. It was poignant and ironic that at the same time in a federal court in New York those claims were upheld.

There was general outrage expressed in the press both in Britain and in America at Buchwald's findings. As became customary in these cases, the anger was directed at the decision, while the evidence supporting it was ignored. She was denounced for making America a "terrorist haven" and for "legalizing terrorism." Buchwald had simply taken existing criteria and applied them to the Mackin case, though from the way the Reagan and Thatcher governments reacted it might have been concluded she had done something totally unprecedented in legal history.

However, the Reagan administration was far from giving up. It now adopted a two-pronged approach. With the aid of the State Department, the conservative Republican senator Strom Thurmond drafted a bill to "modernize" extradition proceedings. The government argued that the bill was necessary to change extradition law, particularly on the matter of rights of appeal, which it said were not clearly defined. Traditionally, appeals from unfavorable findings were not allowed. The requesting party had to file another extradition request if the first was rejected. The respondent's only recourse if the proceedings went against him was to file a writ of habeas corpus. The bill's most significant feature was that it would have given both parties to the extradition request the power of appeal of an unfavorable finding.

At the same time that the government was trying to get Congress to give it the power to appeal the Mackin decision, it argued before the Second Circuit Court of Appeals that it already possessed that power. This duplicitous approach was noted by the Second Circuit. Writing for the court, Judge Friendly complained: ". . . the executive branch did not tell Congress that the law was uncertain and would benefit from clarification. It said flatly that the law needed to be changed. Beyond this, and apart from the massive authority we have cited, what the Government told Congress was right and what it argues to us is wrong."[2] Friendly dismissed the government's appeal for "lack of jurisdiction." He also rejected its arguments in favor of giving the executive branch the power to determine the political nature of an offense. Friendly quoted the 1848 finding of Supreme Court Justice Catron on this issue. Justice Catron had written: "Extradition without an unbiased hearing before an independent judiciary . . . is highly dangerous to liberty, and ought never to be allowed in this country."

Friendly's opinion is regarded as decisive for several aspects of the controversy over the political-exception defense. It clearly and unambiguously set out the legal framework for the authority of the judge or magistrate in dealing with that defense. It refuted the administration's claims to executive and appellate jurisdiction, exposing the disingenuousness of its arguments and its tactics. The Friendly opinion was issued on December 23, 1981. Within a week, Mackin was on a plane bound for Ireland.

The same year that Mackin's case went before the courts, that of a young Palestinian was also heard. Its findings would have a bearing on future Irish cases. Ziad Abu Eam was an admitted member of the PLO who was arrested in the U.S. in 1979. Israel asked for his extradition to face charges of having planted a bomb in a market square in Tiberias during a youth rally in May 1979. The bomb killed two schoolboys. Abu Eam pleaded the political-exception defense. The Reagan administration followed the course it had adopted in Mackin's case, urging that the court did not have jurisdiction to decide what was political and what was not. Though the court rejected these arguments, it found the "definition of 'political disturbance,' with its focus on organized forms of aggression such as war, rebellion or revolution, is aimed at acts that disrupt the political structure of the State and not the social structure. . . . The exception does not make a random bombing intended to result in the cold-blooded murder of civilians incidental to a purpose of toppling a government, absent a direct link between the perpetrator, a political organization's political goals, and the specific act . . ."* The court rejected Abu Eam's defense and he was extradited to Israel on December 12, 1981—a few weeks before Mackin was deported to Ireland.

The finding in the Abu Eam case narrowed the application of the political-exception defense to exclude attacks on civilians, regardless of the political objective underlying them. By the time it was concluded, another proceeding involving the defense had commenced. This time the subject of the request was William Quinn, an Irish American from San Francisco whom the British sought for killing a London constable and for conspiring to cause explosions in England in the mid-1970s.

The thirty-three-year-old native of California was apprehended in Daly City in September 1981. He was the first American citizen to be faced with an extradition warrant for alleged IRA activities. The British said that between 1974 and February 26, 1975, Quinn was involved in an IRA unit that had sent letter and parcel bombs to a crown court judge, a Catholic bishop attached to the British army, and Sir Max Aitken, the chairman of Beaverbrook Newspapers, which owns one of Britain's most popular conservative dailies, the *Daily Express*. He was also accused of shooting dead Constable Stephen Tibble on February 26, 1975, while escaping from the police in London. The British said they had evidence to link Quinn to a group that had planted bombs in a railway station, a hamburger restaurant, and a pub. The IRA men involved were accused by the police of some forty-nine bombings, attempted bombings, and shooting attacks, which claimed eleven lives and injured scores of people between October 1974 and late 1975. The authorities claimed that the bombings were generally without warning and that if warning had been given it was given too late.

"The evidence will show," the British deposition said, "that the victims were almost all civilians: housewives, clerks, labourers,

---

*Quoted in Michael Farrell's *Sheltering the Fugitive*. According to Farrell, Abu Eam was sentenced to life imprisonment after a trial in which "major discrepancies" were shown in the prosecution's case. In May 1985 Abu Eam was one of 1,150 Palestinian prisoners exchanged for three Israeli soldiers held in Lebanon.

executives and other innocent persons. The evidence will also show that the victims were not all British."

As for Quinn himself, he had become interested in the Irish problem through attending Irish cultural events in San Francisco. He attended Irish-language classes, studied the history of the conflict with Britain, and eventually fell in with an IRA contact. This man was reported in a Dublin newspaper as saying of Quinn, "I never had to recruit him. He recruited himself." In September 1971, Quinn quit his job in the post office and flew to Ireland.

In the early 1970s Quinn was based in Donegal, near the border with Northern Ireland. He took part in IRA political fundraising events, sold newspapers, and collected money for the movement. Then, in 1974, Quinn was allegedly dispatched to London as part of an IRA operation designed to force the British government to negotiate with the guerrillas. The plan was simple: by striking in England, the IRA could convince the British to come to the conference table in Northern Ireland. The strategy, masterminded by Daithi O'Conaill, was meant to make the British agree to a withdrawal of their troops.

In the two Irish cases that had preceded Quinn's, the crimes alleged concerned attacks on military installations or personnel. It was relatively simple to connect such attacks with the political disturbances going on in Northern Ireland, thus satisfying the significant and rigorous threshold criteria, which require that an offense be incidental to an objective uprising before it can come under the political-exception defense. But Quinn's situation was different and more difficult. When the proceedings were heard before magistrate Steele Langford in San Francisco in March 1982, the brief against Quinn argued that the decisive precedents were the findings in the Abu Eam case and that of an earlier nineteenth-century trial in which an anarchist, Theodore Meunier, had been extradited from Britain for bombing a Paris cafe. Indeed, the government argued that Quinn's acts were even more extraditable than Abu Eam's, because the latter's bombing "tended directly toward implementation of the PLO's political goals," whereas "Quinn's crimes appeared to be unconnected to the political goals he seeks to achieve." The government said that the "IRA randomly and indiscriminately" bombed and terrorized the English in order that they would pressure their government into evacuating British troops from Northern Ireland. This it described as a "fanciful scenario." In response, the defense, led by William Goodman, who had been part of McMullen's defense team three years earlier, tried to show that Quinn's acts were part of a specific IRA strategy, intended to force the British to negotiate.*

It was a painstaking effort. But it did not convince the federal magistrate. After six months of deliberation he ordered Quinn's extradition. He did so on the grounds that Quinn had not demonstrated that he was a member of the IRA at the time of the alleged acts. Membership in the uprising group was essential, according to his finding, before the political-exception defense could be claimed. Quinn's lawyers petitioned for a writ of habeas corpus, and the case went to the United States district court.

In October 1983 Judge Roger P. Aguilar overturned the magistrate's ruling. He found that the bombings were intended to force the British to the negotiating table and that the killing of the London constable was also substantially linked to the IRA's aims, since it was meant to prevent Quinn's arrest, which might have led to the disclosure of IRA "safe houses" and bomb factories in the area. Aguilar also dismissed the magistrate's membership requirements. He argued that such requirements would be extremely difficult to prove: ". . . certainly the political exception cannot be denied to those political uprisings that are loosely organized or dispersed. Not much more can be said of the early American revolutionary movement against the crown." Anyway, he pointed out, if membership had to be proved it might lead to self-incrimination, and the waiving of the accused's Fifth Amendment privileges.

Calling Steele Langford's findings "clearly erroneous," Judge Aguilar granted the writ of habeas corpus and ordered Quinn's release. However, lawyers for the government blocked the order. One told the *New York Times:* "We're going to pursue every appellate remedy very vigorously. We regard this case as very significant in principle and in particular."[3] Judge Aguilar's granting of

---

*For a fuller treatment of IRA strategy at this time, see my book *Too Long a Sacrifice: Life and Death in Northern Ireland Since 1969* (Dodd Mead, 1981; Penguin, 1982).

the writ was appealed to the Ninth Circuit. By this time, Quinn had been incarcerated for just over two years. As is typical in extradition hearings involving the political-exception defense, bail was denied.

The Aguilar ruling was a sharp setback for the administration's efforts to portray the IRA as just another part of the "international terrorist conspiracy" against which the United States was said to be at war. They argued that it declared IRA activists to be political rebels even when they operated on the streets of London against individuals only indirectly—if at all—connected to the Northern Ireland struggle. This troubled many, including even some who accepted the principle of the political-exception defense; they reasoned that if the defense were to survive the administration's mounting hostility to it, then it had to be refined to include only acts directly relatable to the uprising or rebellion, and involving only the participants. The weakness of the Quinn case, they thought, lay in the remoteness from the upheavals in Ireland of those he was accused of attacking or conspiring to attack.

The Ninth Circuit heard the government's appeal on July 11, 1984. It took another nineteen months for it to reach a judgment. On February, 18, 1986—by which time Quinn was nearing his fifth year of imprisonment—the court overruled Aguilar and ordered the defendant to be extradited on the charge of murdering Constable Tibble. But the three judges who deliberated on the case had different interpretations to offer. Judge Stephen Reinhardt, who wrote the majority decision, held that the political-exception defense did not apply to Quinn because his alleged crimes took place in England. While there was an uprising in Northern Ireland, according to Reinhardt, "we cannot coclude however that the uprising extended to England." He argued that the political-exception defense ". . . does not cover terrorism or other criminal conduct exported to other locations. Nor can the existence of an uprising be based on violence committed by persons who do not reside in the country or territory in which the violence occurs. . . ." Because "an uprising is both temporarily and spatially limited," the IRA's campaign in England could not qualify for the defense. Reinhardt wrote of "Northern Ireland nationals" who "exported their struggle for political change across the seas to a separate geographical entity" in what was the most aberrant decision so far. This seemed to ignore the fact that rebellions or uprising are directed not against "geographical entities" as such but against legally constituted nation states. The IRA's campaign was aimed at the legal-political structure known as the United Kingdon of Great Britian and Northern Ireland, of which the territory of England, along with that of Northern Ireland, is a constituent part.

However, the decision was written against the background of terrorist attacks like that in Rome's airport in December 1985, when Arabs machine-gunned people lined up near the El Al check-in counter. Reinhardt was clearly trying to guard against the political-exception defense being used to cover violent assaults by organizations operating in locations far removed from places of the uprising in which they are purported to be taking part. But it was a clumsy means of doing so, overriding basic legal, political, and geographical realities.

The opinions of the other judges differed from Reinhardt's in several ways. Judge Betty Fletcher disagreed with his conclusion that the acts alleged against Quinn could not be part of the uprising in Northern Ireland because they had taken place in England. She was more concerned about Quinn's nationality—a factor never previously considered—and whether or not he had deep enough ties to Northern Ireland to qualify for treatment as an Irish national whose acts might be covered by the political-exception defense. For his part, the third judge, Ben C. Duniway, while agreeing that Quinn should be extradited to England, disagreed with Reinhardt's opinion that an uprising can only occur within the country or territory where the people taking part in the rebellion reside. He raised the more substantive issue of whether or not the political-offense exception should be allowed to cover the kinds of acts for which Quinn was wanted—that is, involving attacks on civilians and people only remotely linked to the Northern Ireland crisis.

The Quinn decision entailed further complications concerning the statute of limitations on the conspiracy charges. Reinhardt ordered that the case be referred back to the district court, where it should be decided if those limitations had expired. By March 1986, it was not known whether the British intended to seek

Quinn's immediate extradition or await the outcome of court proceedings on the conspiracy charges. Meanwhile, Quinn's attorney filed a petition for rehearing the case before the entire Ninth Circuit. He complained that some of the points the three judges had raised in their opinions were not even addressed in the arguments. The petition was denied.

The Quinn case was anomalous in many respects and produced three singular opinions. But though two of them went against Quinn, they did not infringe upon the central validity of the political-offense exception as it related to armed insurrection by an organized force against government authority within Northern Ireland.

While the Quinn case was being heard through its various stages, a fourth case came before the courts. On June 18, 1983, Joseph Doherty, a twenty-eight-year-old IRA man from Belfast, was arrested in an Irish bar on Manhattan's East Side. He was served with an extradition warrant to be returned to Belfast to serve a life sentence with a thirty-year minimum for the murder of a British army captain in 1980, and to stand trial on a charge of having escaped from the Crumlin Road prison in June 1981, where he had been held since his arrest on the first charge. In the Doherty case, the government exerted the maximum effort to close what a *New York Times* editorial had called the "terrorist fox hole" of the political-exception defense.

With Doherty, however, they were confronted with telling difficulties. Like Mackin, Doherty came from a republican family. His grandfather had served in the Irish Citizens Army (ICA), the revolutionary socialist organization founded by James Connolly, one of the leaders of the Easter Rebellion. He had known Connolly personally when the latter was organizing trade unionists in Belfast in 1911. Doherty had grown up in North Belfast, in one of the archipelago of small Catholic ghettos that lie scattered in that predominantly loyalist region of the city. During the internment operation of August 1971, Doherty's house was raided, his mother was abused, and he and his father arrested. Doherty was held on the Maidstone Prison Ship anchored in Belfast Lough, which was used at the time for an internment holding center. On his release, Joe Doherty joined the IRA.*

His life as an IRA volunteer was spent mostly in jail, however. He was not long out of internment when he was stopped on St. Patrick's night in 1973 by a British patrol who searched him and found a gun. He was charged with possession and sentenced to a year in jail. He was released on Christmas the same year. He had not long been free when he was made quartermaster of "C" company of the Belfast Brigade's third battalion, which covers the North Belfast area. His job was to store weapons, look after arms dumps, and see that the weapons were properly cleaned and distributed when necessary.

On February 1, 1974, Doherty was ordered to carry explosives to west Belfast, where another IRA battalion, the first, was short of them. He took a car with eighty pounds of explosives in the trunk and drove across town. His luck was out again, however, and he was stopped by the British army. A search of the car revealed the explosives, and Doherty found himself once more on the way to jail. This time he was sentenced to ten years.

Doherty was released around Christmas 1979. Within a week he was back in an IRA active-service unit. By this time the IRA had undergone some changes. It was now based not so much on local battalion-company structures as on active-service units that pooled men from different units to come together for particular operations. It also had new and more deadly equipment, including the M-60 general-purpose machine gun. In May 1980 Doherty was a member of a four-man active-service unit that took over a house at a road junction in North Belfast with the intention of ambushing an expected British army convoy. One of the weapons they brought into the house was an M-60 (one of the six that had come from the Harrison network in 1977). It was placed in an upstairs room near a window overlooking the road junction where the IRA hoped traffic lights would stop the convoy and give them an opportunity to rake it with machine-gun fire. The other three men involved were Paul "Dingus" Magee, the unit's driver; Angelo Fusco, a member of a well-known Belfast Italian family with

---

*Doherty's testimony to the court gives a fascinating view of the Belfast IRA in the early 1970s—its methods of induction and training.

IRA connections; and Robert Campbell, who was the operations officer and the man in charge of the M-60. Doherty was with Campbell in the second-floor bedroom, armed with a Heckler-Koch rifle. Fusco was in another room on the same floor, while Magee was downstairs keeping those family members present confined to an out-of-the-way room.

They waited for about two hours, but no army convoy appeared. Instead, Fusco came into the bedroom where Doherty and Campbell were waiting and warned that a suspicious car had pulled up a short distance from the house. When Doherty checked, he saw a group of men wearing orange armbands rush from the car. One was carrying a machine gun and another a sledgehammer. The IRA men recognized them as members of the Special Air Services (SAS), an elite undercover antiterrorist unit of the British army which had been stationed in Northern Ireland since early 1976 and had been involved in many ambushes on guerrillas. The plainclothes officers raced toward the house. It took only a few seconds for the guerrillas to react. Said Doherty later, "They weren't exactly coming in to give us a subpoena. They were coming in on a kill mission." It is not certain who fired the first shot, but soon guns were blazing on both sides. The SAS opened up with short bursts from one of their small-caliber machine guns, and the IRA replied with M-60 and rifle fire. As the SAS made for the wall and hedge near the house, one of them was cut down. He was Captain Westmacott, the officer in command of the unit. The IRA tried to escape through the back of the house but found they were surrounded by British troops on all sides. They went back, stationed themselves at different points, and waited for an all-out attack. But it never came. The police arrived, and when the priest the men had requested arrived shortly thereafter, Doherty and his three comrades surrendered.

Almost a year later the men were tried. By then Northern Ireland was in the grip of the hunger strike and Bobby Sands was close to death. Sands died during the trial, as did three other of the hunger strikers. The morale of the republicans was very low. However, events were soon to lift it. An escape plan had been approved in December 1980, but due to negotiations that had been going on between the IRA and the British to try to prevent the hunger strikers' dying, the plan had been temporarily suspended.

By June it was clear that Thatcher was not about to give in to the hunger strikers' demands, and the plan went ahead. It involved Doherty, the three others who had been arrested with him, and another four IRA men. Two guns—only one of which worked— were smuggled into the jail, and the preparations were completed. Two days before the judge was scheduled to reach a decision, Doherty, along with seven others, broke out of the high-security prison and escaped successfully. When the court was recalled, on June 12, the judge passed sentence before an empty stand. All around the Belfast Catholic neighborhoods bonfires were burning to celebrate the daring of Doherty and his fellow escapees. The IRA men got across the border into the Irish Republic. Doherty made his way to New York, arriving in February 1982. His longest period of liberty since 1971 came to an end sixteen months later, when immigration and FBI agents arrested him.

Even before the case was heard, the Reagan administration made it known that it regarded with alarm the prospect of a successful appeal to the political-exception defense. A spokesman for the State Department said, "The application of the political-offense doctrine to deny extradition could cause damages in relations between Great Britain and the United States." It would mean, according to the government, that the war against "international terrorism would suffer a setback."[4] This kind of statement helped create an atmosphere in which international terrorism became the 1980s equivalent of the McCarthyite hysteria over communism. It was certainly not a set of circumstances conducive to the objective evaluation of evidence. Yet in March 1984 it was against this background that United States District Court Judge John E. Sprizzo had to hear the arguments for and against extradition of Joe Doherty.

The now familiar scenario was enacted again. A group of distinguished defense witnesses, expert on the Northern Ireland situation, testified to its political nature. A counterset of police, lawyers, and government officials tried to convince the judge of the essentially "criminal" nature of the IRA and the offenses for which the respondent was sought.

Among those appearing for the defense were Bernadette McAliskey (née Devlin), the former civil-rights leader and member of parliament, and Sean MacBride, the son of one of the leaders of 1916, former chief of staff of the IRA, founding member of Amnesty International, and Nobel Peace Prize recipient. The British sent over a prominent Unionist lawyer, Robert McCartney; a Home Office official; and an assistant chief constable of the RUC, the Northern Ireland police, who was one of the most senior men on the force and a member of a very small group responsible for formulating police policy.

The hearings lasted eight days and produced 1,300 pages of transcripts. For nine months the judge deliberated. On December 12, 1984, he issued his opinion. It was a brief thirteen pages in length, as compared with the more than one hundred pages of the Buchwald decision on the Mackin case three years before. But Sprizzo was able to build on Buchwald's meticulous work, and in effect, to narrow down the application of the political-offense exception. After a pithy review of recent Irish history, Judge Sprizzo wrote:[5]

> Were the Court persuaded that all that need be shown to sustain the political offense exception is that there be a political conflict and that the offense be committed during the course of an and in furtherance of that struggle, the respondent would clearly be entitled to the benefits of that exception. However, that conclusion is but the beginning and not the end of the analysis that must be made to determine whether in fact Doherty may be properly extradited.

In other words, Sprizzo was intending to go beyond the traditional criteria that the McMullen and, with more thoroughness, the Mackin decision had relied on so strongly. Judge Sprizzo argued that reliance solely on these traditional criteria is "hardly consistent with either the realities of the modern world, or the need to interpret the political defense exception in the light of the lessons of recent history." He suggested that "not every act committed for a political purpose or during a political disturbance may or should properly be regarded as a political offense." He gave atrocities against civilians or against prisoners as examples of what should not come within the scope of that defense. "The Court concludes, therefore, that a proper construction of the Treaty in accordance with the law and policy of this nation, requires that no act be regarded as political where the nature of the act is such as to be violative of international law, and inconsistent with international standards of civilized conduct. Surely an act which would be properly punishable even in the context of a declared war or in the heat of open military conflict cannot and should not receive recognition under the political exception to the Treaty." But Sprizzo held that within these boundaries it is proper to consider political struggles carried out with other than conventional military means, such as insurrections and guerrilla wars. For the political exception to apply it might not even be necessary (a priori) that the rebels claim widespread political support for their acts. (In a footnote he noted: "Given the nature of [American] history it would be anomalous for an American court to conclude that the absence of a political consensus for armed resistance in itself deprives such resistance of its political character," as the U.K. witnesses had argued was the case with the IRA's campaign. Sprizzo observed that many colonists regarded the American revolutionaries as traitors.)

He rejected firmly the government's contention that the use of violence in itself disqualified the fugitive from claiming the defense. Rather, "The Court must assess the nature of the act, the context in which it is committed, the status of the party committing the act, the nature of the organizations on whose behalf it is committed, and the particularized circumstances of the place where the act takes place." Sprizzo's scrupulousness centered on defining and protecting the right of those engaged in armed rebellion (as distinct from terrorist acts) to claim the political-exception defense, which the government in the Doherty case had been trying to deny by compounding them with terrorists engaged in random attacks.

Sprizzo then proceeded to distinguish the Doherty case from one in which a bomb had been placed in a public area (as in the Abu Eam case), which was in Sprizzo's interpretation "well beyond the parameters of what can and should properly be regarded as encompassed by the political-offense exception." Nor was Doherty as complex and difficult as the case of someone wanting to effect change in Northern Ireland by committing offenses in England (as with Quinn). Finally, with Doherty, there was no evidence that showed that any civilian was treated in violation of the Geneva Convention. "Instead," Sprizzo wrote, "the facts of this case present the assertion of the political offense exception in its most classic form."

Given the government's attempts to create an atmosphere of antiterrorist hysteria, Judge Sprizzo could not but be mindful of the controversial nature of his findings. He quickly acknowledged that it was important to be clear about excluding "every fanatic group or individual with loosely defined political objectives who commits acts of violence in the name of those objectives" from availing themselves of the defense. But in making these distinctions he gave neither the British nor the U.S. governments much to be happy about in the Doherty case, for, as far as the judge was concerned, the IRA was clearly not to be compared with organizations like the Red Brigades or the Black Liberation Army. Sprizzo emphasized that the IRA had an organization, discipline, and a command structure that set it apart from other "amorphous" groups. That discipline even extended into the prisons—for, as Doherty's testimony made clear, he had only escaped under the direction of the IRA high command.*

"In sum," Judge Sprizzo concluded, "the Court finds for the reasons given that respondent's participation in the military ambush which resulted in Captain Westcott's death was an offense political in character. The Court further concludes that his escape from Crumlin Road prison, organized and planned as the evidence established that it was . . . was also political. . . . That conduct and all of the various and sundry charges which are connected therewith and for which extradition is sought are not extraditable offenses under Article V (1) (c) of the Treaty. The request for extradition is therefore denied."

Judge Sprizzo's decision provoked a deluge of outraged condemnations both from the Reagan administration and in the popular press. It had come at a time when the administration was

---

*Just how strict this discipline has been at times can be seen in the case of a group of IRA men who escaped from the Curragh Internment Camp in the south of Ireland. They were later disciplined and expelled for escaping without authorization. In the 1940s, the IRA command in the Curragh maintained a prison within the prison for its own men, for whom it took responsibility for punishing—a rather bizarre, almost Beckett-like circumstance.

trying to present a united front against "international terrorism," and the idea that a U.S. judicial officer, for the fourth time in five years (the Aguilar decision in the Quinn case not having been reversed yet), should distinguish between some politically motivated violent acts and others was obviously outrageous. Stephen Trott, head of the Justice Department's criminal division, said he was "outraged" at Sprizzo's finding. In a manner typical of the level of eloquence with which Reagan-administration officials often expressed themselves, Trott told the *New York Times:* "A guy can kill somebody, hide in another country and it's a political offense? Give me a break." Trott went on, "We've got to get rid of the 'political offense' nonsense among free, friendly nations. We're going to have to attack this treaty by treaty and redo the extradition language."

What was conveniently ignored, in the torrents of near-hysterical abuse directed at the judge, was the careful and conservative nature of his decision. It represented a limiting of the scope of the political-offense exception to actually exclude most of the kinds of crimes that the Reagan government and the popular press were accusing it of glorifying or excusing. The angry reaction had another aspect. In future, any judge or magistrate contemplating finding in favor of the political-exception defense could not help being intimidated by the prospect of the denunciations and controversy that the finding would be bound to produce.

Following the Doherty decision in December 1984 the administration proved more tenacious than ever in its pursuit of a satisfactory outcome to these troublesome cases. The Friendly opinion in the Mackin case had made it clear that the requesting party had no right of appeal if the hearing went against it. Judge Friendly had unambiguously reaffirmed that in such an outcome the requesting party had only one recourse: to file another extradition request and commence the proceedings over again. But the administration, acting on the British government's behalf, feared that Sprizzo's tightly worded and considered opinion would lead to another ignominious defeat.

It adopted a two-track approach. While continuing to fight the decision in the courts, it was at the same time quietly drafting a new extradition treaty with the British that would effectively eviscerate the political-exception clause.

In the courts, the administration named Joseph Doherty the defendant in a civil action demanding a declaratory judgment overturning Judge Sprizzo's decision. Such a demand was common enough in situations where the plaintiff needed a declaration of rights not already determined and to effect an early adjudication on those rights rather than waiting for his adversary to begin the suit. But in the context of an extradition hearing it was unheard of and extraordinary.

The administration went before a U.S. district court, calling the Sprizzo finding "fundamentally flawed" because in it "murder and assault are effectively sanctioned as a form of political activity in a democracy."[6] The route the administration sought to pursue by this means was never in doubt: once the request for a declaratory judgment was denied, the administration would then appeal that denial and so obtain the review of the Doherty decision to which it was not properly entitled under the rules governing extradition proceedings.

Doherty's lawyers called it "litigation by deception and jurisdiction by ruse." They said "It should not be permitted. . . . Despite the melange of jurisdictional bases recited in the complaint, this Court is utterly without jurisdiction in this matter and the complaint must be dismissed."[7]

The demand for a declaratory judgment was filed on February 4, 1985. Four months later the United States district court responded. Judge Charles Haight, Jr., concurred with Doherty's lawyers. "Declaratory judgment has no legitimate office to perform in extradition proceedings and, in any event, is not available to a foreign government whose extradition request has been denied." (This and the quotes following are from Haight's Memorandum Opinion and Order.)

Judge Haight reminded the government that in 1981 it had asked Congress to pass the Thurmond bill, which proposed to revise extradition statutes to allow direct appeal from a judge or magistrate's finding. On that occasion it had represented to the Congress that "the only option available to the United States, on behalf of a requesting country, is to refile the extradition complaint. . . . If in fact the Declaratory Judgment Act permitted the foreign government to obtain a prompt collateral review from a district court in respect of unfavorable extradition ruling by the extradition magistrate, it is surprising that neither the Department of State nor the Department of justice advised the Congress of that alternative vehicle for review when urging the 1981 statute upon the Congress." There was no doubt, that is, that the government was proceeding deviously (as Judge Friendly had complained in 1981) by telling Congress one thing and the Court the opposite. Haight dismissed the administration's case.

It was clear from a memorandum of law submitted by the government that it was more concerned with the diplomatic and political ramifications of the political-offense exception than it was about any genuine legal or procedural problems. Much of the memorandum was devoted to a political diatribe against the IRA as "ideological enemies of the United States," quoting Secretary of State Shultz, who also described the guerrillas as "Marxists."[8]

"Recent developments underscore the sound public policy that Provo killers should not find a haven from extradition in the United States," the Motion to Dismiss declared. The note of animus was pronounced. In theory, the U.S. is there merely to facilitate the U.K.'s extradition requests. But the Reagan administration adopted an adversary role and became for all intents and purposes a party to the proceedings.

As expected, following the Haight dismissal of its motion for declaratory judgment, the administration appealed. The appeal went before the United States Court of Appeals for Second Circuit, where it was heard by Judges Friendly, Cardamone, and Winter on December 4, 1985. The Second Circuit opinion, written by Judge Friendly—the author of the late-1981 Mackin appeal opinion—was issued on March 13, 1986. It affirmed Haight's dismissal. Discussing the government's claim to a declaratory judgment, Friendly said, "The Government's position that the denial of a certificate by an extradition magistrate is subject to review by an action for a declaratory judgment is somewhat startling," and pointed to the well-established principle that holds that only through filing a new request can the requesting party seek redress if a decision goes against it. "The Government has not cited," his opinion pointed out, "and we have not been able to find, a single case in which a declaratory judgment was used in a manner resembling that which the Government proposes here." Judge Friendly said that it was clear that what the Government really sought was not a review of Sprizzo's decision—which he called "a careful analysis of the political offense exception"—but a declaration that will bind another extradition judge in a proceeding not yet commenced."[9] That is, the government was hoping that a favorable decision on its request for overturning Sprizzo's decision would make it impossible for a magistrate or judge in a subsequent hearing to deny the extradition request. As in his decision in the Mackin case, Friendly pointed out the glaring inconsistencies in the government's approach, and the deviousness with which it was conducting the case.* With this door shut firmly in its face, the government was left with four options: to refile and begin a fresh extradition proceeding, to petition the Second Circuit for a rehearing of the appeal, to drop the extradition case altogether and proceed with a deportation hearing (since Doherty was in the U.S. illegally), or to go to the Supreme Court. In the end, deportation proceedings opened which lasted until 1991, and the case was brought before the Supreme Court.

In the meantime there were several other developments in the long-running controversy over extradition. One concerned a twenty-eight-year-old Belfast man, Jim Barr, who was arrested in Philadelphia on May 29, 1984, and eventually served with an extradition warrant; the other, more momentous, development was the signing of a new extradition treaty between the U.S. and U.K. governments in June 1985.

The Barr case proved to be anomalous. The British wanted him for allegedly taking part in an attack on a British army patrol in the summer of 1981. But the only evidence they offered to sustain their warrant was the testimony of a former member of the left-wing Irish National Liberation Army (INLA), Harry Kirkpatrick. Kirkpatrick had turned informer after he was sentenced to over a

*This proved to be Friendly's final work. The eighty-two-year-old judge was found dead on March 11, 1986, shortly after the opinion was written and just before it was made public. It was believed he committed suicide in grief at the loss of his wife and his own failing health. Friendly, who the *New York Times* noted was a conservative Republican, was highly thought of for his well-grounded and lucid opinions. The fact that he had so clearly supported both the Mackin and the Doherty decisions indicates the strength of those interpretations of the treaty, and certainly underlines the absurdity of the government and popular-press contention that they are a product of some aberration of the law.

thousand years in prison for a series of murders. In return for his testimony Kirkpatrick was not given a recommended minimum sentence, so that although it was one of the longest ever handed down, he could be released after as little as five years. Barr was one of the twenty-seven alleged members of the INLA arrested on the strength of Kirkpatrick's testimony alone. After being let out on bail, Barr fled from Northern Ireland and made his way to the United States.

Kirkpatrick's testimony was voluminous, but the two-page affidavit submitted in support of the extradition request contained only the briefest passing reference to Barr. Kirkpatrick claimed that as an INLA unit was getting ready to ambush a foot patrol, Barr, "a volunteer in the Andersonstown unit" of the INLA, was told to "scout around the top end of Clonard Street for any other foot patrols." The testimony did not even go on to say whether or not Barr had actually complied with these orders and did not mention him again. While testimony as skimpy as this has been found sufficient to convict hundreds of people in Northern Ireland's juryless courts, including all of those held on Kirkpatrick's word, it was not enough for Judge Clarence Newcomer. He heard the case in August 1985 and dismissed it on the grounds that the requesting party had not shown "probable cause" for Barr to be extradited.

The defense did not need to claim the political-exception clause. The Barr case remains interesting chiefly for the comparison it affords between what is acceptable evidence in a Northern Ireland juryless court and what an American judge regards as acceptable. Informers like Kirkpatrick—so-called supergrasses—were the main prop of the British security-judicial system in the mid-1980s. The courts' reliance on such support surely casts considerable doubt on their ability to function fairly in general, and, regardless of other considerations, on the wisdom of returning any fugitive into their custody, whether or not the evidence against him is more than the mere word of an informer. The Barr case is also interesting for the sidelight it throws on Irish-American anxieties. Because of his allegedly "left-wing" connections, Barr was ostracized by Irish-American groups in general. Only a few individuals, acting on their own initiative, rallied to his support in Philadelphia.

Of more immediate relevance to the political-exception clause was the Supplementary Treaty drafted by the British and American governments and signed on June 25, 1985. The Reagan administration had decided that since the law was proving troublesome it had to be changed. The new treaty (kept secret until after it was signed) contained four key articles, which amended the 1972 treaty in crucial ways. In article 1, the new treaty listed crimes to which the political-exception defense may not apply. These crimes, according to the State Department, were those "typically committed by terrorists." They were aircraft hijacking and sabotage; crimes against internationally protected persons, including diplomats; taking hostages; murder; manslaughter; malicious assault; kidnapping; and "specified offenses," in the State Department's words, "involving firearms, explosives, and serious property damage."

The supporters of the new treaty argued that these crimes must be separated from what they regarded as genuine political offenses—which, according to their definition, included only offenses involving free speech, the right of assembly, organizing, and espionage. That is, they maintained that armed rebellion or insurrection was never to be considered legitimate or worthy of consideration as a political act. (It is interesting to note that some of the crimes included in the list of nonpolitical offenses were those which, one hundred years before, the British tried to have made extraditable when they were attempting to get their hands on the "dynamite miscreants"—the American Fenians—who they held were responsible for the bombing attacks in English cities between 1883 and 1885.)

Article 2 of the Supplementary Treaty amended the clause dealing with the statutes of limitations. In the 1972 treaty the fugitive could appeal to either the statute of limitations of the requested or the requesting party. Under the new provisions, however, the only limitations statutes to apply would be those of the requesting party. And the United Kingdom had no statute of limitations for the crimes listed in the Supplementary Treaty.

Article 3 gave the requesting party sixty days following the arrest of the fugitive to prepare its case against him. The 1972 treaty provided for forty-five days. Finally, article 4 would enable the requesting party to seek the extradition of a fugitive wanted for a crime committed before the treaty went into force. Treaty proponents argued that this article would enable them, upon passage of the treaty, to secure the extradition of Doherty, despite the fact that a decision barring his extradition had already been rendered.

President Reagan submitted the new treaty to the Senate on July 17, 1985. It seemed a perfect time for the administration to effect its quick ratification. The early summer was full of terrorist atrocities. The memory of the American airline hijacked by Shi'ites in Beirut and their brutal murder of an American, Robert Stethem, was still vivid and bitter. There had been a lethal bombing in a Japanese airport; on the same day an Air India jumbo jet disintegrated in mid-air in an explosion caused by a bomb, killing over three hundred people. (Sikh extremists were later held responsible for both bombings.) People, justifiably horrified at these crimes, would certainly welcome any measure that purported to curb the kinds of organizations or individuals responsible for such wanton disregard of life. Reagan's crusade against "international terrorism" had taken on a new and powerful urgency. State and Justice Department experts who submitted their views to the Senate on the new treaty were eager to stress its importance as a weapon in this crusade. The ugliness of the summer's violence was the perfect background against which to present the case for a quick passage of the treaty. The two men who were responsible for advancing it before the Senate were Abraham Sofaer, chief legal adviser to the State Department, and Lowell Jensen, a deputy attorney general in the Justice Department. Sofaer was a former federal judge, an ex-colleague of Judge Sprizzo, whose decision in the Doherty case he was trying so desperately to undermine. An Indian-born Jew of Iraqi and Egyptian ancestry, he had been at the department only since June 1985, but in that short time had won a reputation as a pugnacious and vigorous exponent of neoconservatism. He was an active defender of President Reagan's decision to disavow the World Court's jurisdiction during the dispute over the mining of Nicaraguan harbors. Close to Secretary of State Shultz, Sofaer was known to take a much more prominent role in State Department affairs than is usually the case with its advisers. (The *New York Times* wrote of Sofaer, "In the past, Secretaries of State and their political deputies have often complained that Foreign Service officers found reasons why the secretaries could not pursue the course of action they wanted to. By contrast, insiders say, Mr. Sofaer has told Mr. Shultz on several occasions that he could do what he wanted and that there was legal justification for it.")[10]

On August 1, 1985, Jensen and Sofaer presented their case for ratification before the Senate Foreign Relations Committee. Sofaer quickly set the context for the Senate's consideration of the new treaty. Listing the recent terrorist atrocities just mentioned, Sofaer told the committee that "the criminals who commit these types of barbarous crimes against the citizens of other nations, and manage to get to the U.S., are often able, under current U.S. law, successfully to invoke the political offense exception and thereby escape extradition . . . the treaty amendment before you would prevent such travesties of justice with respect to extradition requests between the United States and the United Kingdom." (This and following quotes from the statement by Abraham Sofaer before the Senate Foreign Relations Committee.) "Terrorism," said Sofaer, "is rampant in the world today and we are a favorite target. The United States and the other democracies are anathema to terrorists, murderers, and hoodlums. We believe in ballots and judges. They believe in bullets and bombs. We believe in majority rule. They believe in rule by terror. We are now in the midst of a worldwide struggle against terrorism and the sponsor states of terrorism. It is in the context of this struggle that you must consider the treaty before you."

Lowell Jensen, the Justice Department's representative, sang the same song: "The 1985 Supplementary Extradition Treaty," he submitted to the senators, "is designed primarily to address an issue of concern to all civilized nations: terrorism. The issue of terrorism is of particular concern to the United States and the United Kingdom since the citizens of our two countries are primary targets of international terrorism. . . . The British government has concurred in our view that it is unacceptable that a criminal may commit a heinous offense which shocks the sensibilities of all decent people; flee the country which he has terrorized; and find a safe haven in another country by labeling his crime a political offense. The United States cannot condemn terrorism committed abroad against our citizens and then provide shelter on these shores for perpetrators of such atrocities against the citizens of other countries."[11]

Their argument was summed up by Sofaer: "The rationale for this new Supplementary Treaty is simple," he argued. "With respect to violent crimes, the political offense exception has no place in extradition treaties between stable democracies, in which the political system is available to redress legitimate grievances and the judicial process provides fair treatment."

Sofaer was particularly emphatic about the "basic fairness of the British system of justice, even under the extraordinary situation that Britain has faced in Northern Ireland." His love for Great Britain was evident throughout the hearing. Talking of political dissidents, he was moved to say, "There is no more free a nation than the United Kingdom. I know you have seen people allowed to make speeches and engage in other nonviolent political actions. There is no place like the United Kingdom in those terms." Listening to Sofaer made one wonder at times why it had been necessary for the American separatists to rebel against such a nation in the first place. He defended the nonjury courts in use there to try terrorist-type offenses. (In doing so he quoted from Judge Sprizzo's decision in the Doherty case. Sprizzo had rejected the notion that Doherty would not get a fair trial if he returned to Northern Ireland. The judge held that the nonjury courts were scrupulous and fair in their treatment of both republican and loyalist prisoners. He did not mention the use of "supergrass" statements as the only evidence in some cases to convict large numbers of suspects; nor did Sofaer.)

It was clear that Northern Ireland and its political upheavals were to be treated as just another instance of the worldwide international terrorist conspiracy. The administration's case received wide support in the popular press. The *New York Times* editorialized in favor of the Supplementary Treaty.

However, the eleven senators from the Foreign Relations Committee who listened to the arguments and evidence advanced by the administration on August 1 were not all convinced. Senator Dodd of Connecticut expressed reservations about the provision allowing the U.K.'s statute of limitations to apply to the listed offenses, as well as that on retroactivity. He told Sofaer, "I suspect, Judge, that there are some people in Britain who would like to go back to the Easter Rebellion, if they could, and retroactivity would allow them to go back that far." Senator Kerry of Massachusetts was disturbed by the broad sweep of the new provisions and the language of the treaty. When Sofaer attempted to suggest that opposing the changes implied the support of violence, Senator Kerry was clearly irked. "I don't think," he said, "the issue, Judge, is so much whether or not anybody here, by approving or disapproving of this language, approves or disapproves of violence. . . . There is nobody here who does not disapprove of violence." But the strongest opposition came from Senator Biden of Delaware.

Biden wanted to keep the discussion firmly placed in the Northern Ireland context. "There is an incredible reluctance on the part of this government to criticize one of our closest allies for what I believe to be an absolutely outrageous position which they have continued to maintain with regard to Northern Ireland," he began. His statement that he was going to use the hearing "to do what we have been unable to do so far"—that is, critically examine Britain's role in Northern Ireland—signaled to the administration the unwelcome news that its hopes for a swift, controversy-free passage of the Supplementary Treaty would not be fulfilled. Biden asked Sofaer to do a comparison for the committee of the emergency legislation in Northern Ireland and that in South Africa.

"They have nothing to do with one another. They are not comparable at all," Sofaer answered.

"How is that? Tell me why," the senator pressed him. The administration's expert was clearly reluctant to do so. He said he would, however, provide the committee with an analysis of the juryless courts in Northern Ireland.

"That's not what I'm looking for," Senator Biden told him.

"And I will compare—" Sofaer continued, but Biden interrupted him with growing impatience. "My job is to ask the questions and yours is to answer them. If you are not going to do it, say no," Biden said.

"Well, to the extent that I can and am able to, consistent with my duties, I will do it."

"What do you mean by that?" Biden asked.

"Well, I mean, I don't see why we should be having to justify and engage in an analysis of judicial systems—"

"Because I asked," Biden put in: "Because a senator asked." He told Sofaer, "Either I'm new in this system, after thirteen years, or you're new to the State Department." Bidden was obviously annoyed at the aggressive and rather arrogant manner with which the administration was urging the new treaty. He warned Sofaer, "I will probably have questions for months and months on this treaty."

Sofaer also ran into troublesome questions from the ranking Democrat on the committee, Senator Pell, who made the commonsensical observation: "I think this whole question revolves around the business of one country's freedom fighters being another country's terrorists. It depends on how you look at it." Pell pressed Sofaer on a comparison between the attitudes embodied in the treaty under review with the administration's views on the Contras, who were trying violently to overthrow the Nicaraguan government with the aid and support of the U.S. The Contras used violence and tactics that could be considered terrorism, yet the administration called the Contras freedom fighters; Reagan had even compared them to George Washington.

"I don't want to comment on Nicaragua," Sofaer replied. But then he went on to say that there was "no free political system in Nicaragua," which apparently made Contra violence morally and politically acceptable. (This was part of the same rationale that the administration advanced for arguing that the political-exception clause was redundant for countries where there were free elections, since violence in those circumstances could never be a legitimate means of achieving political change. If this were to be applied to Ireland, it would mean, for instance, that the 1916 rebellion would be regarded as illegitimate, since free elections—at least for adult males—were available at the time. If the Supplementary Treaty had been in force then, political extremists like Eamon De Valera would have been liable for extradition from the U.S.)

There were so many doubts expressed in the committee that another set of hearings had to be scheduled to allow the opponents of ratification to give their contribution.

On September 18, 1985, the committee met again. This time

the hearing room was so packed, mainly with Irish Americans there to oppose the new treaty, that people had to line up against the back wall. Outside, the corridor was crowded with others hoping to get in to hear the discussion. This time, however, there were moments of tension and disruption, mainly due to Senator Thomas Eagleton's adversarial questioning. During his probing of Representative Mario Biaggi—who, though supposedly an opponent of the new treaty, seemed to end up supporting it—and of Senator DeConcini, Senator Eagleton was moved to describe the IRA as "murderous thugs." At this the audience erupted angrily. The hearing room echoed to shouts of "IRA Freedom Fighters!" "They're soldiers!" and "What about the hunger strikers—remember Bobby Sands!"

Senator Trible, who chaired the hearings, had to make it clear that another such interruption would lead to the room's being cleared of all spectators. A lawyer who had come to oppose the new treaty said to a companion at this point, "I feel like I'm on the Titanic." If the opponents of the new provisions could be identified as nothing more than a mob of IRA supporters, their opposition to them, however well founded, would certainly be doomed.

This pessimism proved premature, however. A succession of thoughtful and authoritative figures—political, legal, and academic—advanced a series of cogent objections to the proposed changes. Among the most impressive were Senator Eugene McCarthy and Dr. Christopher Pyle.

McCarthy, the former presidential candidate, presented a venerable figure with his gray hair and slightly stooping gait—the very image of a Yankee statesman. He also presented cogent arguments against the treaty. With gentle, chiding humor, he treated the committee—on which he had sat—to a history lesson that began with a quotation from Tacitus, the greatest of the Roman historians. That lesson suggested strongly that the new treaty should not be ratified. The history of Ireland was such, according to McCarthy, that he would never return an IRA fugitive to either Northern Ireland or the Irish republic, under any circumstances. If the committee endorsed the treaty, he said, "It'll be an endorsement of the hard-line policy of the British government." He received a round of applause from the audience as he left the room. It was an ironic moment, which he doubtless savored. Those applauding him would never have voted for him, in all probability, when he ran for president, since his very liberal politics would have been anathema to most Irish Americans.

For his part, Christopher Pyle, professor of politics at Mount Holyoke College in Massachusetts, delivered a brief but substantive history of extradition law and the political-offense exception. His submission (not all of which he had time to deliver) criticized the Supplementary Treaty from many different angles. From the point of view of the treaty's general purpose, he said, it was not "directed at assisting 'democratic' governments with 'fair' legal systems," as the State Department was arguing. Rather, said Pyle, we must be realistic and acknowledge that it is "directed at helping our friends and allies suppress any and all rebellions against their authority. The spirit behind this scheme is not the spirit of the liberal democratic governments that created the political-crimes defense to extradition; it is the spirit of the authoritarian regimes that opposed it in the nineteenth and twentieth centuries. It is the spirit of Tsarist Russia, Austria, Prussia, and the Soviet Union, not the spirit of Great Britain, Belgium, France and Switzerland."

He also expressed his alarm at the vagueness of the language of its provisions. "This treaty . . . would allow for extradition for acts that, on their face, could be entirely innocent but which, by the testimony of a prosecution witness desperate to earn immunity, could be transformed into criminal acts. It would also allow extradition for 'conspiracy to cause . . . an explosion': the very sort of charge that can easily be trumped up against exiled dissidents . . . with the help of coerced or bribed witnesses." Pyle compared it to the treaty negotiated between the U.S. and the Philippines in 1981 that led to warrants being issued for the arrest of many Filipino political exiles, including Benigno Aquino, who was accused, primarily on evidence from a police informer, of conspiracy to cause an explosion. (Rather than wait for an extradition request to be filed against him, Aquino decided to return to the Philippines—in the words of Professor Pyle, to confront Marcos as "a free man." He was murdered on his arrival.)

At the time the Philippines treaty was drafted, the U.S. ambassador to Manila was Michael H. Armacost. As undersecretary of state, he signed the Supplementary Treaty between the U.S. and the U.K. In his comparison between the two treaties, Pyle pointed out that the Philippines treaty contained a provision guaranteeing that extradited persons would not be tried by "extraordinary or ad hoc tribunals"—a safeguard that the Supplementary Treaty does not contain.

The Philippines treaty was destined never to reach the Senate. The Reagan administration decided that it was too controversial and that if defeated it could undermine the government's overall campaign to get rid of the political-offense exception. The State Department informed the Senate that it was not being submitted because the administration was awaiting the progress of a congressional bill designed to deprive the courts of jurisdiction in applying the political-offense exception clause. But that bill, the Extradition Bill of 1981, also became bogged down. And five years later, events in the Philippines swept away any further thought of reviving the treaty.

As the second round of hearings concluded, it seemed like a similar fate was awaiting the U.K.-U.S. treaty. Even Senator Eagleton, who had shown himself to be the most hostile in his questioning of the opponents of the new provisions, admitted that the Supplementary Treaty was "flawed." Senator Dodd's remarks that it "would have to go back to the drawing board" summed up most observers' feelings at the time.

A third session of hearings was held in November 1985 to allow opponents of the new treaty who had not been heard in September to state their case. Among the witnesses who appeared then were Frank Durkan, a prominent New York lawyer who had been a senior member of the legal team that had defended Dessie Mackin; and Raymond Flynn, the mayor of Boston, who is active on the Northern Ireland issue. At its conclusion, no further hearings were planned. This confirmed the feeling that the Supplementary Treaty would go the way of the proposed treaty of 1886—first talked and nibbled to death, then shunted away into a legislative limbo where it would be quietly forgotten. However, following the signing of the Anglo-Irish Agreement in November 1985, Britain's ambassador to Washington, Sir Oliver Wright, expressed his confidence that it would only be a "matter of months" before the new treaty was endorsed. In March 1986

Senator Lugar, the chairman of the Senate Foreign Relations Committee, stated that he would make the aid to Northern Ireland—promised as a result of the Anglo-Irish Agreement—contingent on the endorsement of the treaty.

By the spring of 1986 the administration was still lobbying for its new treaty.* Some of the activity on Capitol Hill concerning extradition involved yet another congressional bill attempting to standardize extradition proceedings on a general basis—rather than, as the administration proposed, treaty by treaty.

In its campaign to eviscerate the political-offense exception, the Reagan administration was driven to misrepresent not only the legal facts but the historical facts about Northern Ireland. In its haste to persuade the courts and the Senate of its case, the administration constantly asserted that as the U.S.-U.K. treaty stood, it allowed terrorists a haven to run to and escape justice. Before the Foreign Relations Committee, Judge Sofaer indulged in this kind of misrepresentation when he told Senator Pell that the men who had murdered Lord Mountbatten and his three companions (two of whom were teenagers and the third a grandmother) in Ireland in 1979, could, if arrested in America, successfully invoke the political-offense exception, claiming that their acts were political. What the government's expert chose to ignore was that in 1981, in the Abu Eam case, a U.S. judge had found that for the purposes of the political-offense exception "indiscriminate bombing of civilian populace is not recognized as a political act. . . ." He also chose to ignore the progress of the courts in their rulings on the political-offense exception, which have shown a clear and decided narrowing of its application—as was demonstrated

---

*Pressure to ratify the treaty increased considerably after the administration's retaliatory strikes against Libya in April 1986, during which Britain had provided vital facilities. Prime Minister Margaret Thatcher claimed outspokenly that because of the help Britain had given the U.S. at that time, the latter had an obligation to assist Britain in its light against "Irish terrorism" by enacting the treaty. The *New York Times* quoted Thatcher as saying: "What is the point of the United States' taking a foremost part against terrorism and then not being as strict as they can against Irish terrorism, which afflicts one of their allies?" Editorials in the *Washington Post*, the *Wall Street Journal*, and the *Times* of London vociferously supported her in this demand.

in the Doherty case and in the Quinn ruling in early 1986.

When confronted with the Abu Eam ruling, Sofaer said he did not see any difference between the killing of civilians and the killing of a soldier. However, the point was that he was trying to suggest that the courts made no such distinction in their evaluation of the political-crimes clause, when in fact was clear that they did make this distinction.

Before the Senate, in the courts, and in the media, the administration experts continued to misrepresent the legal situation by pretending that such distinctions had not been made. With strident rhetoric, they advanced the proposition that the political-offense exception was an open invitation to kidnappers, airplane hijackers, and mad bombers to do as they like, and then to come to America, where a welcoming committee in the form of a sympathetic judge would be there to greet them and set them up for life. Typical was the article by Terrell E. Arnold published in the *Washington Post* in support of the Supplementary Treaty. According to Arnold, a former deputy director of the State Department Office of Counter-Terrorism and Emergency Planning, the existence of the political-crimes exception meant that the people who bombed the Harrods department store over Christmas 1983, or those who blew up the Air India jet over the seas near Ireland in June 1985, or the Islamic gunmen who hijacked the American airliner in May 1985, as well as any Red Brigades, Red Army Faction, or Direct Action gunman or bomber, if caught in the U.S., would not be extraditable. He even asserted, "With the safe haven of an extradition law such as ours, a future Oswald or Sirhan Sirhan could kill a national figure, flee the country and forever escape prosecution from the crime."[12]

As Sofaer and Jensen did before the Senate, Arnold, with a blunderbuss of assertions, attempted to create an impression of a law so lax as to be indefensible. He did not inform the reader of the 1970 Hague Convention for the Suppression of the Unlawful Seizure of Aircraft, which placed airplane hijackings outside the scope of the political-exception defense; nor was any reference made to the 1973 Montreal Convention on aircraft seizure, which explicitly made hijacking an extraditable offense in all the member countries—including the U.S. and Great Britain—that signed it. Of course, the Abu Eam decision, which excluded bombings or attacks against civilians—"wanton crimes"—from the scope of that defense, was not analyzed, nor did Arnold note that since the late nineteenth century those charged with anarchistic acts had not been able to appeal to the political-exception clause. Arnold, like Sofaer and Jensen, spoke of the U.S. as a "safe haven for terrorists" thanks to this clause, creating the impression that the courts had been blithely freeing gunmen and bombers. In fact, Joe Doherty had been in jail since June 1983, held without bail, though he had won three judicial rulings; and Bill Quinn—an American citizen—had been in jail for almost five years without bail before the 1986 ruling approving his extradition for the killing of a London policeman. Far from being a "terrorist haven," the U.S. offered the likelihood of indefinite incarceration for any fugitive wanted for violent political acts.

The Reagan administration's attack on the political-exception offense was accompanied by an attempt to wrest the power to hear such cases from the courts and place it in the hands of the executive branch of government. However, the various bills the administration sponsored with the aim of doing this became stalled in Congress. Professor Pyle described this effort as an attempt to return to "the jurisprudence of the Stuart kings," where decisions on matters involving individual liberty would be made on the basis of political expediency rather than on a detached evaluation arrived at by the courts.

Governments that are fiercely ideological—whether of the left or the right—view the law as primarily a servant of their ideology. If the law should prove to be a recalcitrant one, as in the troublesome political-offense exception, then their response is to change it, as the Reagan administration tried to do in its campaign against the political-exception clause after 1981. Mary Pike, who, along with Stephen Somerstein, defended Joe Doherty, summed it up: "There is something ominous about an administration which regarded the court's stoical application of the law that was there to apply as an excuse to change the law." In order to effect those changes, the administration had to misrepresent the truth about extradition and political offenses. But this involved misrepresenting the political and social problems of Northern Ireland. It had to be shown, after all, that the situation there was just another example of "international terrorism."

All ideological world views tend toward reductionism and reliance on conspiracy theories that conveniently link together all those regarded as their enemies. Such reductionism dangerously ignores the historical and political roots of individual conflicts. Against this process, the U.S. courts were a bulwark. By insisting on weighing the particular circumstances, they helped reveal the complex circumstances of the Northern Ireland problem—in defiance of the simplifying ideologues who would sacrifice such realities on the altar of political expediency.

Postscript

By May 1986, it seemed that in spite of the help Britain had given the U.S. during the Libyan bombing raids, the Supplementary Treaty would remained stalled in the Foreign Relations Committee. However, on May 31, President Reagan himself made a direct appeal to the senators to pass the treaty on to the floor of the Senate for ratification. In a radio broadcast he said that the treaty was designed to "prevent terrorists who have kidnapped, killed or maimed people in Britain from finding refuge in our country. Today, these people are able to do that by labeling their vile acts as political." He repeated the kind of misrepresentations which had been characteristic of the administration's efforts before the committee during the hearings. And he made it clear that what was involved was more than just concern for the prevention of "international terrorism"—there was a debt to be paid.

"Any rejection of this treaty," the President declared, "would be an affront to British Prime Minister Thatcher, one European leader who, at great political risk, stood shoulder to shoulder with us during our operations against Qaddafi's terrorism.

Reagan tied his prestige to the acceptance of the Supplementary Treaty. Several weeks after his broadcast, the Foreign Relations Committee voted on what was called a modified version of the treaty, and it passed 7 to 2. At once, everyone claimed a victory. Senator John Kerry, who had opposed it in the committee, said he was "exultant" at the compromise that had been reached. Meanwhile, the British Government was reported to be "delighted."

It would appear that the British had more cause for glee than the treaty's opponents. The principal modification had merely removed conspiracy and possession of firearms from the list of offenses now regarded as always outside the scope of the political-offense exception. The British had won their campaign to have violent acts, including murder, voluntary manslaughter, assault, and any involving the use of bombs, grenades, rockets, etc., excluded from consideration as political offenses.

Kerry and other treaty opponents, including the Reverend Sean McManus of the Irish National Caucus, were consoling themselves with modifications which would allow the courts to consider evidence that the fugitive was being sought because of his or her race, religion, or political opinions, and which would safeguard him or her from being subject to an unfair trial. But both these additions were beside the point. The first, to be effective, required that the fugitive prove that he or she in particular would be treated unfairly—it did not suffice to prove that the person sought was a member of a group (such as Northern Ireland's Catholics) that had been subjected to unfair or biased treatment in the past. Such a requirement would be extremely difficult to meet. As for the fairness of the Northern Ireland courts, that would not be an issue that would protect fugitives from extradition. Statistics could be mustered to show that both Catholics and Protestants were given a "fair" trial before the juryless courts in Northern Ireland. (In his decision in the Doherty case, Judge Sprizzo praised the "impartial justice" of the courts.)

In any case, it must be remembered that the struggle was about the preservation of the political-offense exception as it has been applied and interpreted since the nineteenth century. And with the Foreign Relations Committee's vote in June 1986, that struggle was over; the Supplementary Treaty was certain to be ratified when it went before the full Senate.* The political-offense exception was dead.

*It was subsequently ratified on July 17th.

6
COVERING THE NORTHERN CRISIS: THE U.S. PRESS AND NORTHERN IRELAND

If the U.S. courts provided an opportunity to challenge certain assumptions about Northern Ireland, the U.S. press usually did not. Three things emerge from a review of the often extensive coverage Northern Ireland received in the American press. The first is that there existed a general consensus on Northern Ireland among the major newspapers and magazines. Second, the consensus was basically the same as that of the British government. Third, this consensus was remarkably consistent until about 1979. Then, and increasing after the hunger strikes of 1981, a shift toward an attitude more critical of Britain's role can be detected.

Though Northern Ireland received great attention, only two U.S. newspapers have had fulltime correspondents based in Ireland—the *Christian Science Monitor* and much later, in the 1990s, the *Boston Globe*. A semi-retired New York Times reporter began filing from Dublin also in the early 1990s, but the paper's coverage was still run from its London office. Northern Ireland was usually the responsibility of the London office, while reporting the day-to-day violence generally became the responsibility of the wire services—Associated Press (AP), United Press International (UPI), and Reuters. Press attention, of course, experienced peaks and troughs, yet it has been fairly constant since 1969. As a gauge of this level of interest, in 1985 four papers—the *Chicago Tribune,* the *New York Times,* the New York *Daily News,* and the *Boston Globe*—accounted for at least a thousand pieces of commentary and analysis alone, not including reports.

Local U.S. newspapers, of which there are estimated to be almost 1,500, generally relied on wire services (either those just mentioned or those of the major newspapers) for the bulk of their coverage. More often than not they took their editorial line from big-city colleagues.

Like the British government's official "line" on Northern Ireland, that of the major newspapers and magazines in the U.S. held the problem to be a sectarian conflict between recalcitrant religious groups kept apart only by the intervention of Britain acting as a kind of "bobby." The view of Britain was that of a detached, patient, and objective arbiter doing its best to convince two irrational, hate-filled communities to live together in harmony. Constantly undermining these noble efforts was the IRA, portrayed as a gang of mindless criminals and psychopaths bent on destruction. In later years, this portrait was touched up somewhat by the rising concern over "international terrorism"; into the picture was dutifully painted various "links" with other equally anathematized groups and individuals, such as the Palestine Liberation Organization and Colonel Qaddafi of Libya.

This consensus excluded from serious debate on Northern Ireland the other view, what might loosely be termed the "republican" analysis. In one form or another, this view is accepted by all the non-Unionist political parties in Ireland. It sees the Northern crisis as the offspring of the partition of Ireland, and the war as political rather than religious. It holds that as long as Britain maintains a presence in Ireland, the problem will never be solved, and argues that in the long term the only hope for permanent peace and stability is some kind of unified state. The moderate Social Democratic and Labour party (SDLP), the Fianna Fail party, the Fine Gael party, and the Irish Labour party all agree on this. So does the IRA. They differ in that the establishment parties do not think that violence is justified in achieving the goal they share; the IRA does.

In the pages that follow, it is not proposed to conduct a polemic on behalf of this view. Rather, it is hoped it will be shown that the U.S. press, by excluding it from its terms of reference, lacked not only explanatory power but reliability when covering the Northern crisis.

The "Inexplicable Irish"

The Northern Ireland crisis first received extensive coverage in August 1969. Up until then, although Catholic civil-rights marchers demanding reforms in housing and job opportunities had met with Unionist opposition on the streets, the confrontations had not gotten out of hand. That month, however, there was widespread and serious rioting. Loyalist mobs attacked Catholic homes. Eight people were killed, six of them Catholic, five of whom had been killed by police gunfire, including a nine-year-old boy and an off-duty British soldier. On August 14, British troops came onto the streets, partly because an exhausted police force had lost control, and partly because it was clear that, being mostly Protestant, the police were more of a provocation than a help in the circumstances.

Even at this early date, the *New York Times* quickly established certain stereotypes. Its reporter, Gloria Emerson, wrote: "In London there was a sense of something dark, inexplicable and strange in the Irish soul that foreigners cannot explain—or quite ignore."[1]

The "inexplicable" Irish soon became a fixture of the coverage. Benignly, the inexplicable nature of the Irish could be expressed in terms of mystery. Or it could be seen malignantly, as an explanation for the religious hatred which the press regards as a cause of the violence. In early 1972, *Newsweek* lamented the prospect of England's being dragged into "the deadly Irish quagmire" by "two fanatical religious armies—i.e., the Catholics and the Protestants. The image of the unreasoning, fanatical Irish (the negative side of the "inexplicable" soul) suggested something primitive. *Time* wrote that the crisis was due to the "truculent tribalism" of the Northern Irish.[2] Thus the magazine could imply that the Irish needed the British. After the failure of a British initiative, *Time* said, "The trouble, as the past few weeks have tragically demonstrated, is that the Irish cannot run Ireland either."[3]

Irrational sectarian hatred as the cause of the problem readily appealed to the *New York Times* reporter who wrote: "As the demands for reform were being made, and beginning to be met, however, members of the lunatic fringe—which is quite a long, thick fringe in Northern Ireland—got going, and coerced their co-religionists into supporting them. . . . Then the bomb-throwing and gun psychopaths of the Provisional IRA wing went to work."[4] The *Boston Globe* writer concurred on the subject of the backwardness of the warring Irish tribes: "The British army is separating the combatants in Ulster's guerrilla war because the people of Northern Ireland proved incapable of governing themselves. . . ."[5] Obviously, victims of such tribal, irrational hatreds could not possibly run a modern state.

New York Times liberal columnist Anthony Lewis, espousing the more benign view of Irish irrationality, wrote: "A mystic might say that there is some special fate bedeviling the two islands, close neighbors that need but cannot understand each other."[6] He goes on to quote a British official as theorizing that there is "too much myth in the way. Or perhaps too much history to let reason work." Lewis continued: "His voice sounded near despair as he discussed the alternatives open to Britain." One year later Lewis came to the conclusion that the only hope for Northern Ireland was for Britain to pursue a policy of "enlightened colonialism."[7]

Lewis, a well-known defender of various liberal causes, had written the first piece quoted above a few days after British paratroopers gunned down thirteen unarmed civilians after a civil-rights demonstration in Derry. Like most commentators and reporters at that time, he was content to revert to atavistic, sentimental, racist-style stereotypes of the inexplicable Irish and of how the British continue to "misunderstand" them. As an explanation of a brutal mass murder it was hardly adequate. Yet that a prominent liberal could find it so is one indication of the lack of objective critical analysis by those in the press who evaluated the events in Northern Ireland. That a liberal could go on actually to hope colonialism would save the Irish might be thought extraordinary. But it was, unfortunately, in keeping with the infatuation of

American liberal intellectuals with England, which led them to ignore Northern Ireland—perhaps because it provided too many startling contradictions to their own rather sentimental notions about English civilization. (The liberal American literary intelligensia generally shied away from the Northern Ireland issue. That bastion of enlightened and progressive thinking, *The New York Review of Books,* for instance, almost completely ignored Northern Ireland and the various issues involved, while providing regular features and reviews about other international crises.)

The "inexplicable Irish" view of the crisis, though less obvious, remained until the 1980s. In an article welcoming the Anglo-Irish Agreement, *Time* magazine's report opined: "In another part of the world, it would be called tribal warfare. In Northern Ireland, the shootings and the bombings that have taken more than 2,500 lives over the 17 years are more primly referred to as 'the troubles.' The spasms of killing have followed the ebb and flow of ancient hates and fears that divide the British province's Protestant majority and its Catholic minority."[8]

By reducing the problem to this level of "ancient hates and fears," the press succeeded in removing it from the realm of serious political debate. The reader came away asking himself what such an anachronistic conflict had to do with modern politics and why he should bother thinking about it. In this way, the coverage reinforced Britain's propaganda that Northern Ireland's problem was a product of irrational fears and hatred manipulated by gangsters, deserving of little sympathy or concern among right-thinking, intelligent people.

The British "Tommy" to the Rescue

Having established the truculent tribes of inexplicable Irish full of ancient hatreds, the press has conveniently opposed to them another stereotype: that of the patient, all-suffering Britisher. An internal memo sent between *Newsweek's* London and New York offices in July 1970 shows that this stereotype was set up from the very beginning. It read: "We're particularly interested in putting together a separate sidebar on the impossible task of the British soldiers caught in the middle between the warring Catholic and Protestant communities." That the role of the British soldier was that of a referee was taken for granted. And the use of the word "Tommy" to describe the soldier conjured up a memory of the chirpy little World War II trooper in a soup-plate helmet—an anachronism that ignored the fact that the British army in Northern Ireland was an army of volunteer professionals, not of conscripts as was the case in the 1940s. "The British army," lamented one writer, "continually deals with two potential enemies. . . . The Tommy stationed in Ulster should have the two-faced head of a Janus as well as the patience of Job."[9] After a series of bombings in Belfast that in one day (called "Bloody Friday") killed eleven people, the *Boston Globe* reporter surmised: ". . . if British soldiers do not keep the Catholics and Protestants apart, 'Bloody Friday's' 11 deaths and 130 injured from bombings will be only the beginning."[10] Years later, the *Boston Sunday Globe* would call British troops "military hostages to political failure" (July 21, 1977), continuing to purvey the concept of an almost passive, helpless soldiery, whose only function was to act as referee in a religious war while being shot at and abused. Following the collapse in 1974 of the power-sharing government, the first to include Catholics, *Time* resorted to the image of the soldier it loved most, as the London government "was forced to reimpose direct rule from Westminster and the British Tommies once again were on the alert to prevent Irishman from killing Irishman."[11] According to the *New York Times* reporter, the army was there as a "neutral peacekeeping authority between the warring Protestant and Roman Catholic communities."[12]

This was a constant refrain throughout the press coverage from the beginning of the conflict. It withstood several shocks that should have been traumatic enough to make observers question it as a basis for understanding Britain and her army's role in Northern Ireland.

For instance, after internment was introduced during which 342 men were arrested and held without trial—the press followed the government's line that internment was necessary to halt the violence. Even though it provoked the worst violence the state had yet seen—within four days twenty-two people died, all but three of them civilians, and by month's end there had been over one hundred explosions in Belfast alone—the coverage in general emphasized the British line.

"How can Catholics of this community," fumed Anthony Lewis of the *Times*, "be associated with protests that lead to the death of women and children—even last night to the fatal shooting of a priest as he gave the last rites to a wounded man. . . ?"[13] Lewis did not mention, or did not know, that the gunman who had killed the priest was a loyalist paramilitary, and the wounded man the priest had been attending was a civilian shot by the army. But the whole of the *Times* story was framed so that, despite the British action, blame was pinned only on the IRA. It was invoked to explain Catholic disaffection with the army. ". . . affection has gradually given way to hatred—perhaps an inevitable result of the army's view that it alone must bear security responsibility with no private armies. . . . The IRA fanned hatred by staging incidents and shooting isolated soldiers. The army, which showed incredible patience, was bound eventually to make mistakes and kill innocents. . ."[14]

Conveniently ignored in this purported analysis of how the relationship between the Catholics and the army had deteriorated was the fact that since the summer of 1970 the army had (with Conservative government approval) adopted a much more aggressive counterinsurgency role, which was directed exclusively against Catholics. This role could not be maintained along with that of the objective referee keeping two sides apart, because it was predicated on the belief (either of mere convenience or of true conviction) that the Northern Ireland problem was not caused by discrimination and injustice against Catholics, but by left-wing IRA subversion. Such was the thesis of the Unionists, and when the Conservatives were elected in June 1970, they saw to it that it was acted upon. Though there is little hint of this in the *Times* coverage, a feeling of disquiet did manage to creep into the editorial page.

"It may be argued," reflected the newspaper a few days after internment, 'that the Prime Minister acted unwisely in resorting to the arbitrary arrest of IRA leaders. . . ."[15] Even here, the *Times* modifies its reservations in asserting the London line that in spite of the violent backlash from the Catholics the procedure had succeeded—at least to the extent of netting the "IRA leaders."

Yet, within days of internment, the IRA held a press conference in a school in the heart of the Falls Road area—the area worst hit by the swoop at which the IRA's Belfast leadership was able to appeal for help. Joe Cahill, one of the movement's leaders in Belfast, chaired the conference. (He subsequently went off to the U.S. for a fund-raising tour in the hope of cashing in on the surge of sympathy and support that internment had created; but he was stopped at Immigration and sent back to Dublin.) It proved to all—as later testimony has substantiated—that internment not only led to an increase in violence, but blatantly failed in its original object of damaging the IRA through rounding up its "leaders." Yet no word of this was mentioned in the *Times* editorial.

Perhaps an even stronger jolt to the image of the imperturbable Tommy caught up in a religious war came with Bloody Sunday, and the shooting dead of thirteen civilians at the end of a civil-rights demonstration in late January 1972.

The following day—January 31—the major newspapers led with stories (mostly from the wire services) reporting a shootout between Catholic gunmen and British paratroopers. The British army claimed that eight of the dead were wanted, and several had been found with weapons. Within hours, this story was withdrawn. Only four, it appeared, were wanted IRA men, and only one was said to have been carrying a weapon—a "nail bomb." However, over the next day or two, even this claim was abandoned, as it was gradually acknowledged that none of the thirteen dead was in the IRA, and none was wanted for any offense. The local people's assertion that the shooting had come solely from the army gained credence. However, the U.S. press, particularly the *New York Times,* continued to assert the army's original story. In early February, the week after the shooting, *Newsweek* described it like this: "A Catholic demonstration in Londonderry degenerated into a melee of fighting with British troops, and in the confusion, thirteen marchers were shot to death." The *Times* preferred the idea of "misunderstanding" as the explanation for the butchery: "Bloody Sunday, as it is being called, is likely to go down as another landmark in the long record of misunderstanding and hatred in British-Irish relations."[16]

On the West Coast, the Irish case fared no better. The day after the shootings, an editorial in the *San Francisco Chronicle* blamed "history" (repeating a familiar theme), but did not suggest that the British troops were responsible.[17] An editorial in the *Los Angeles Times* called for an "international inquiry" and suggested a U.S. presence. It went so far as to blame the British government for allowing discrimination to continue. But the weight of its condemnation fell on the IRA, whose activities, it argued, had led to Bloody Sunday. The Irish government was also held to bear some of the responsibility. In general, while the horror of the killings was described effectively, neither in the reportage nor in the editorial comment was the culpability of the British "Tommy" emphasized.

The *Chicago Tribune* took a somewhat different tack. Though never actually coming out and condemning Britain, its editorial held that "defying prohibitions of street demonstrations, stoning British troops, and shooting civilians *with or without provocation* lead to no reduction of hostility" [my emphasis]. Thus it at least raised the possibility that the shootings were unprovoked. The editorial called for the abolition of the Unionist government at Stormont and the imposition of direct rule from London. It concluded: "The Irish conflict involves contrasting reports of fact as well as incompatible policies. The fair and cool reporting of who did what when is of the utmost importance, and makes a necessary foundation for constructive action by people in authority."

The *Chicago Tribune* was one of the only papers that in its actual reporting of the shootings featured strongly Catholic counter-allegations. In the second paragraph of its front-page report it quoted Catholic leaders as calling the killings "awful slaughter" and mass murder."[18] But the Catholic version—much of which was based on the eyewitness accounts of people who were at the march—had to wait six months before it received substantial American support beyond expressions of outrage from Irish Americans. In June 1972 some American lawyers issued an independent study of the circumstances surrounding the killings. The study, "Justice Denied," was written by Professor Samuel Dash, director of the Institute of Criminal Law Procedure of Georgetown University Law Center in Washington and a former chairman of the American Bar Association. A former dean of Yale Law School, Louis Polak, worked with Dash, as did John Carey, the chairman of the International League for Human Rights, which published the report. It substantiated the eyewitness reports that maintained that the first shot was fired by British troops as they left their armored personnel carriers. There had been some stoning sometime before the arrival of the troops at the scene of the march, which was dispersing when the shooting started. However, Dash insisted that the responsibility for the deaths rested with the army command, and that there was no level of violence sufficient to warrant the army's attack.*

In the days following the Bloody Sunday massacre, some papers amused themselves with discussing other sidelights rather than pursuing questions such as what had actually happened and whether or not the British account was the whole truth. Bernadette Devlin, the civil-rights activist, was at that time a member of the House of Commons for the Northern Ireland constituency of Mid-Ulster. A fiery but intelligent and articulate young woman, she was a cogent orator on behalf of nationalist concerns (one Unionist MP called her a "miniskirted Castro"). She was popular among Irish Americans when she arrived here, in 1969, on a fund-raising tour that netted some £50,000. (Her subsequent association with the Black Panthers, however, somewhat soured Irish-American feeling toward her.) On January 31, the day after the shootings, during a debate in the House of Commons, she strode across to the government benches and struck the British home secretary, Reginald Maudling, accusing him of lying about the events in Derry. The *Chicago Daily News* reported: "Bernadette Devlin, being female and Irish, is a mystery in her behavior to the British public. They are still mulling deeply over her indecorum in slugging Home Secretary Maudling, a genial, slow-spoken family type. Even more puzzling, Miss Devlin, after she cooled off, failed to do the gamesmanlike thing demanded of all Britons . . . apologize and shake hands. She said she wouldn't mind another try. This simply isn't done, even in Parliament. To the puzzled British this failure makes more acute the question of what makes Bernadette run. . . ."[19]

The report, by George Weller, went on to quote the *Daily Tele-*

---

*Dash found that shots were directed against the army, but only some time after the troops had commenced shooting, when the marchers lay wounded and dying.

graph of London, which jokingly suggested that the cause of Devlin's impassioned attack on Maudling was frustrated love. The *Telegraph's* story, in the form of a letter to a woman's advice columnist, and her reply, were given at length in the *News*.

This was no more than a day after Ms. Devlin had been a witness at one of the most brutal shootings in recent Irish history—shootings carried out by troops answerable to the government of which Mr. Maudling was a prominent member. Obviously, Mr. Weller and his newspapers did not see the irony of the remarks about British fair play and "gamesmanlike" behavior: the British had just gunned down thirteen unarmed civilians in front of thousands of people in circumstances that, regardless of whether the authority's story was acceptable or not, should have been the grounds for serious questioning of Britain's role in Northern Ireland. Instead, the incident was ignored in the report, and Ms. Devlin's behavior in the House of Commons became the excuse for condescension and vulgar sexist stereotyping. The *Chicago Daily News* also used it as an opportunity to dust off the jaded old cliches about the "mystery" of the Irish, with all its implied sympathy for the patient and understanding British. Anyone reading such stuff would not have imagined that it was the Irish who had been at the receiving end of a recent and brutal attack. Later, Ms. Devlin—now Mrs. McAliskey—said that the British reaction showed a lot about their attitudes toward Ireland; the assault on Maudling was greeted by more outrage than the paratroopers' killings in Derry. In turn, the reports of it in papers like the *Chicago Daily News* showed a lot about how the U.S. press viewed the Irish situation and Britain's role in it.

The One-Sided Sectarian War

The press always represented Northern Ireland as the victim of a bloody sectarian war. This emphasis generally led to a neglect of the complex role Britain has played in defending Northern Ireland, as well as simplifying the nature of groups like the IRA. It was also based on the assumption that there was a "tit-for-tat" sectarian conflict, with Catholics and Protestants killing each other routinely. The facts, however, pointed to a rather different picture of the situation, one that indicated that the press consensus was in grave error about the nature of the Northern Ireland conflict. Beginning with the riots of 1969, the overwhelming impression was of violence between Catholics and Protestants. Most U.S. newspapers relied for their day-to-day coverage on wire-service reports. Brief, and without much embellishment, these stories used the sectarian model for such explanation as was offered. "[Police found] the body of a middle-aged man. . . . The discovery raised the death toll in three and a half years of Catholic and Protestant strife in Ulster to 649."[20] "He was the 730th person killed in sectarian strife in Northern Ireland in three and a half years."[21] "He had been shot in the head—the usual method of killing in the silent clandestine struggle between the province's Protestant and Catholic communities."[22]

Even when the victim was killed by the British army, the sectarian angle was still emphasized. Reporting the death of a Belfast teenager shot by troops at a checkpoint, the Associated Press summed it up: "His death brought the toll since the outbreak of sectarian warfare in the British-ruled province in 1969 to at least 1,836. So far this year 35 persons have died in the fighting between predominantly Roman Catholic Irish Republican Army militants and Protestant extremists."[23] When the *Los Angeles Times* came to do a retrospective history of the crisis, it explained the origin and nature of the violence in these words: "What had been largely a civil rights movement deteriorated into guerrilla warfare, with Catholics and Protestants killing one another in ever increasing numbers."[24]

The sectarian-war thesis was, of course, intimately linked to the view that the IRA was the villain and that Britain, represented by the anachronistic "Tommy" image, was the patient and detached referee. When one reviews the coverage, it is noticeable that when sectarian warfare was mentioned, it was usually only one organization (if any) that was named as a participant in the war—the IRA. The IRA was referred to as the cause of the deterioration into violence, and was credited with perpetuating it. "Rock-throwing rioters gave way to deadly snipers," wrote *Newsweek*, explaining the development of the situation in April 1972; "Pitiless terrorists from the Irish Republican Army (IRA) from the South began to infiltrate Ulster in specially trained bomb squads." Ten years after the commencement of the crisis, the *Los Angeles Times* ran a long article on Northern Ireland by UPI correspondent Donal O'Higgins. He wrote: 'The British army, with its guns, tanks, and armored cars, remains, caught in the middle of a vicious struggle between Protestant paramilitaries and the outlawed Irish Republican Army, the oldest underground organization in the world."[25]

O'Higgins mentioned the "Protestant paramilitary." Compared to the constant and repetitive emphasis on the IRA and the Catholics, coverage of the Protestant violence was slight. When Protestant paramilitaries were dealt with, the treatment usually followed lines rather different from those typically applied to the IRA. It is extremely doubtful, for instance, if even an attentive reader would have been aware of the names of the Protestant paramilitary groups, never mind being able to discern from what he read their actual role in the Northern Ireland violence. The major Protestant paramilitary group was the Ulster Defense Association (UDA), a legal organization with headquarters in East Belfast. At one time in mid-1972 it claimed about 20,000 members, making it one of the largest paramilitary groups in the world. But its numbers fluctuated according to the circumstances, with marked increases only when a major crisis or increase in tension occurred.

In the early 1970s, when sectarian violence was at a bloody peak, the UDA gave many interviews to visiting journalists. *New York Times* reporter Tom Buckley interviewed UDA spokesmen at length for an "in-depth" article. "I decided they were rather sinister," wrote Buckley, "and, for people who never tired of waving the Union Jack, crashingly un-British." But his talks with them convinced him that, "As I saw it, the degree of prejudice to which the Catholics were subjected had been somewhat exaggerated, and it seemed to me that they had brought a good deal of it on themselves by pretty much refusing, right up to the time of the first civil rights marches, to do anything for themselves. . . ." So, he concluded, "By the time I left I can't say that I became particularly fond of any of the militant Protestants I had met, but I was somewhat more sympathetic to their point of view."[26]

A few months before, *Los Angeles Times* correspondent Tom Lambert spoke with a UDA representative and reported: "But the UDA has nothing against Northern Ireland's Roman Catholics, and will only try and persuade them to repudiate the IRA, he promised."[27] The story was headlined PROTESTANTS THREATEN WAR ON IRA, and continued: "The threat . . . raised the possibility of increased sectarian clashes in Northern Ireland. . . ." He said, "Some observers were inclined to take that threat seriously." At the same time, the *Boston Globe's* man in Belfast, Jeremiah Murphy, was also talking to the UDA. He interviewed Ernie Elliott, a leading member of the organization from the loyalist Shankill Road area, who expressed his anxiety over the effect the IRA's campaign was having on his men. "It's tough to hold the boys back now," he told Murphy, "they wanna have a go at them Catholics." Murphy commented: "If British soldiers do not keep the Protestants and Catholics apart . . . that would just about complete the Northern Ireland tragedy."[28] The UDA relied on the pretense that it was acting as a brake on sectarian violence, and the press repeated it for them. UDA leader Andy Tyrie told the *Christian Science Monitor's* Irish correspondent that "the UDA would end its own ceasefire and retaliate with an all-out anti-terrorist drive" if the British gave concessions to the IRA.[29] And yet at the same time it was observed (being the substance of the daily reports of violence throughout the 1970s) that Catholics were suffering heavy casualties at the hands of Protestant extremists.* How did this fit into the UDA's constant claim, reported in the U.S. press, that it was doing its best to "hold the boys back"?

In the beginning, if Protestant extremists were blamed, it was usually those belonging to the Ulster Volunteer Force (UVF)—a smaller, illegal group that predated the UDA. Indeed, at one time, AP pinned "97 percent of the Protestant violence" on the UVF.[30] Then, in 1973, the Ulster Freedom Fighters (UFF) emerged,

---

*According to statistics compiled by the European Commission on Human Rights in the mid-1970s, of the 121 victims of sectarian murder in 1972, eighty-one were Catholics and forty Protestants; in 1973, the breakdown was fifty-six Catholics and thirty-one Protestants; in 1974 it was sixty-one Catholics and thirty-one Protestants. It has remained fairly constant at the rate of two Catholics for every one Protestant assassinated. The commission also categorized the data according to which section of the community was responsible for the murders. This was a much more uncertain undertaking, but it generally revealed that almost 50 percent of all Protestants assassinated were assassinated by Protestant groups. The percentage of Catholics killed by the IRA in factional or "execution-style" murders was much smaller.

claiming responsibility for killing Catholics. The authorities went ahead and outlawed it. But the UDA remained, issuing statements, meeting reporters and government officers, occasionally lamenting that it was doing its best to keep control of the beast of sectarian war but if there were any more concessions to the IRA, it couldn't guarantee what might happen. "These men who are killing Catholics are just wildcats. . . . They are not acting under UDA orders. We are trying to stop it, but we do not know who they are,"[31] Reuters quoted a UDA leader as saying in the aftermath of one of the most vicious bouts of sectarian bloodshed Ireland had ever seen.*

The UDA were not the only ones who affected puzzlement as to the identity of these "wildcats." The Northern Ireland police were equally stumped. "We're getting these sectarian killings now that make no sense at all. . . . As many Protestants as Catholics have been killed," a police spokesman was quoted as saying in the *New York Times*.[32] In fact, the ratio of Catholics killed to Protestants was normally two to one, though Catholics were a minority of the population. No matter. When it came to the actual sectarian killings of Catholics in the much-referred-to sectarian war, nothing seemed certain. When an old Catholic couple was machine-gunned to death, UPI's story in the New York *Daily News* ran: "The Police said it was not yet known whether the killings were connected to the past four years of violence among Northern Ireland Catholics and Protestants."[33]

An anomaly was becoming apparent in the way the authorities were treating the sectarian war, and in the way it was being reported. Though it was said to be two-sided (since every war needs at least two sides), only the actions of one side, the IRA, were attributable, while those on the other remained not only "inexplicable," but even "motiveless" (a favorite word the police used to describe murders of Catholics). Though it is not clear how the killings of one side in any sectarian war can be called "motiveless," this police evaluation was allowed to go unchallenged by the press. The activities of the Protestant extremists were never brought into clear focus. Indeed, the leader of the largest Protestant

---

*There were twenty-three assassinations between January and June in 1972, and thirty-six in July alone, the bulk of them the work of the UDA.

paramilitary organization, the UDA, always used the press to dissociate his group from sectarian violence. In the mid 1980s, he told a *New York Times* correspondent, "I'm totally against sectarian conflict." However, he did not dissociate himself from attacks on what he and his group would regard as military targets—"if people who are involved in violence deal in purely selective military targets, you'd find that quite a few people, decent Catholics, would be quite happy to see some people within the IRA assassinated."[34] However, these "people who are involved in violence" seemed to have a very wide definition of a "military target." In November 1985, they murdered Kevin McPolin, a young worker with no affiliation to any nationalist organization. He was merely a Catholic who happened to work in a Protestant area. At the beginning of 1986, assassins murdered another Catholic as he slept in his bed. Like McPolin, he had no known connection with the IRA or Sinn Fein. He happened to be a bartender who worked in a club where, unusually for Belfast, both Catholics and Protestants drank. The UFF claimed both killings. Perhaps the UFF had recruited the "wildcats" among the Protestants. The authorities seemed to think so, for they had banned it shortly after it made its appearance in May 1973.

The press, like the authorities, was capable of great tolerance when it came to UDA disavowals. Take, for example, the period between December 1971 and December 1972. During that time, the press interviewed several UDA leaders, including Ernie Elliott, known locally as "the Duke," who told the *Globe* of his difficulties in "holding the boys back." One can estimate the extent of his difficulties by counting the number of sectarian killings for the period: 136, 96 of whom were Catholics and 40 Protestants.* Something was wrong with the UDA's control mechanism; even though it was allowed occasionally to go on joint patrols with the British army, with whom its members would sometimes be seen playing football, it seems never to have been a very effective participant in making sure the neighborhoods were "safe." Just how ineffective it was emerged in late December 1972, when Ernie

---

*On December 4, 1971, loyalists bombed a Catholic pub in Belfast, killing fifteen people. For a fuller discussion of the attack, which was attributed to the IRA, see my book *Too Long a Sacrifice*.

211

Elliott's body was found in a box in the back of a car. He was one of the forty Protestants murdered that year. Superficially, his death would have been attributed to the IRA-versus-Protestant-extremist bloodbath in which Northern Ireland was supposedly steeped. In fact, UDA men murdered Elliott in a drunken brawl in a Protestant club. In that, his death was no different from those of the other victims of the sectarian conflagration. For the truth is that the UDA was responsible for the bulk of all sectarian killings in Northern Ireland.

At the time Elliott was being interviewed, he was a member of one of the most active UDA assassination squads roaming West Belfast. Other UDA gangs operated from the Shankill Road; one had its headquarters in the building where the UDA gave interviews to many reporters, including the *New York Times* correspondent. (It was an old pub called the Bricklayer's Arms, since demolished.) Victims were taken there and tortured before being shot.

During research completed in 1977 by this author and David McKittrick of the BBC for a history of the UDA, figures gathered showed some 540 Catholics were murdered by Protestant extremists between 1971 and 1977. Of those, the UDA was responsible for approximately 400. After that, sectarian killings were less frequent. But they still occurred, and the UDA usually was responsible. As for the UFF, it was merely a name of convenience invented by the UDA in 1973.

What is remarkable is how little attention was paid to this murder campaign, at the same time that the press was writing about the "Catholic-Protestant conflict," which, the reader was told, the British were preventing from getting out of hand. Once again, the consensus the press adopted was that of the British government. The British chose to ignore the UDA as much as possible. In early 1973, after a bomb attack on a busload of Catholic workers, the authorities were forced to intern UDA men. They arrested two.

The *Wall Street Journal* observed: "Until the two Protestants were jailed, only Roman Catholics had been singled out on terrorist charges."[35] At the time, hundreds of Catholics were being held without trial, and the army constantly raided Catholic areas, arresting dozens of men. No more than a hundred Protestants were interned in the two years between that date and December 1975, when internment ended, compared with nearly two thousand Catholics.

Britain's reluctance to tackle the UDA was not based on ignorance of its activities. After all, the police came from the same community as the UDA; contact between them was frequent; information was exchanged; and by the mid-1970s the security forces had a wealth of often detailed data on the organization. The British view of the Northern crisis as a purely sectarian war initiated by the IRA allowed them to maintain that the Protestant violence was a product of IRA violence, so that it was essential to concentrate on stopping the IRA.

Time magazine summed it up: "British army officers seem to agree that the Protestants will stop if the Catholics do. Lately, the British have been applying most of their weight against Ulster's Catholics."[36] For the most part, the U.S. press accepted this as a justifiable explanation for the comparative lack of action against Protestant extremists, and did not allow it to interfere with their simultaneous description of the British as the even-handed "Tommy," doling out justice with patient detachment.

Nor was the press given much pause for thought by the fact that during the two periods when the IRA called a truce and halted its campaign the sectarian violence actually increased dramatically. The *Christian Science Monitor* reported that politicians' fears of further violence "are fed by sectarian killings of Catholics and the burning of Catholic-owned buildings, which have gone on almost daily since the IRA declared its latest ceasefire."[37] While this seeming contradiction did not go unreported, it generally went unanalyzed. Nor was it remembered that sectarian violence had begun in 1966 when two Catholics were murdered, and reached a peak in 1969—long before the IRA's current campaign against Northern Ireland had started, and before the IRA existed as an active threat at all.

The problem was that the press's adoption of the British consensus meant a narrowing of its ability to scrutinize the story, even in the face of evidence that contradicted that consensus. Scientific theories are rejected when evidence accumulates for which they cannot account. The consensus of the press on any given political situation is not as objective as this, because it is loaded with political arid social assumptions that need to be defended. In the case of Northern Ireland, the evidence contradicted the theory of a Protestant-Catholic tit-for-tat sectarian war; instead, it pointed to a different kind of sectarian war, in which the victims were mainly Catholic. This not only discredited the Catholic-versus-Protestant theory; it also threatened to undermine the whole consensus, which was based on the thesis that the British were in Northern Ireland to keep the two sides apart.

Naturally, then, the press showed great reluctance to examine the UDA's role, just as the British did. Nor did it deduce from the abundantly available evidence the sectarian nature of the Protestant commitment to Northern Ireland, though this was clear from the beginning. In August 1969 *New York Times* reporter Gloria Emerson had an encounter with a Protestant woman. "'We are not animals who need to be locked in, but they are, down there, the filthy scum, those papists,' a twenty-seven-year-old housewife, with badly dyed blond hair and a torn raincoat, screamed at the top of her lungs." In June 1972, Bernard Nossiter of the *Washington Post* observed: "Protestants, particularly those in the upper class, have a contempt for Catholics that verges on racism." He interviewed a UDA man, a small business contractor, who said of Catholics: "IRA lazy Fenian bastards don't want to work. . . . they just want to stay in their bloody pubs and drink. There is no such thing as a good Catholic. They're a dirtier class of stinking people and I'm paying to keep them up. We could stop the IRA bombing in a month. We could shoot them. We don't need the uniform to do anything." Such loathing is characteristic of the loyalist propaganda that emanated from the various paramilitary organizations. Militant nineteenth-century Unionism established similar themes of Catholic inferiority, propounding a sectarian equivalent of the racist "white man's burden," with "Protestant" being substituted for "white" in the Ulster context. It expressed itself most gruesomely in the tortures inflicted on some Catholic victims of the UDA and UVF before they were shot.

Though grisly killings of this kind were reported as common on both sides (as in the AP story that concluded: "So far this year at least 105 others—70 Catholics and 35 Protestants—have been slain in much the same way, often after being bound and tortured, burned with cigarettes, branded or had bones broken"[38]), this was not the case. Such acts were exclusively the responsibility of Protestant extremists.* Catholic anger was directed against the state, its security forces, and its various institutions, and did not involve the urge to degrade or humiliate the victim before killing him.† Did not the IRA take part in the sectarian violence also? Yes, it did, but only at certain times and then—ironically enough, in view of the press consensus that Protestant violence was a reaction to that—of Catholics—generally as a retaliation against UDA or UVF attacks on Catholic areas. Only once, in the summer of 1975, can it be said to have become a part of IRA policy. On that occasion, during an IRA ceasefire, the IRA leadership did issue a statement warning loyalists that it would take retaliatory measures if their attacks on Catholics did not cease. Unfortunately, the consensus in the American press imposed restrictions on its coverage that prevented such complex realities from being exposed. Without thorough reporting of these realities, the tangled nature of the Northern Ireland crisis could not be understood.

Looking for Scapegoats

By the mid-1970s, the U.S. press had established guidelines concerning Northern Ireland coverage: the "Tommy" keeping the sides apart, the religious fanatics, the conflict as a sectarian

---

*The nature of their violence is comparable to that directed against black Americans by the Ku Klux Klan, who came to embody the fears and often psychotic insecurities of white racism.

†IRA punishment shootings, such as kneecappings and the killing of alleged informers, were often horrific and brutal. This however, does not negate the validity of distinguishing between such violence and that motivated by the hatred of a dominant, repressive group acting out of insecurity when it believes that dominance threatened, which was the motivation behind Protestant sectarian killings.

‡Major bouts of IRA violence directed against Protestants occurred on several occasions. In November 1974, a tit-for-tat pattern was established for a short time, mainly in North Belfast. Then, during the summer of 1975 and early in 1976, IRA members (acting either on their own behalf or with the sanction of local leadership) retaliated against Protestant targets. However, this was something of an aberration and was stopped in 1977 with the rise of new, left-wing leaders in Belfast.

war.* Another aspect of the prevailing consensus concerned the IRA. Not only was it blamed for starting the "troubles"—either by infiltrating the civil-rights movement or "fanning" hatred of the British troops—but it was often described as coming from outside Northern Ireland to do so. The Republic of Ireland was either explicitly or implicitly held to be responsible for allowing the IRA to operate.

In 1972 there was a series of bombings in Dublin. *Newsweek* headlined its story IRELAND: THE BOMBS COME HOME—the clear implication being that the bombs that had been devastating Northern Ireland came from the republic. (Its report said: "Over the past three years, as the militant Provisional wing of the IRA has escalated its terrorism against the Protestant majority in Northern Ireland, officials in the Catholic Republic in the South have gradually unveiled an ambitious scheme for the eventual reunification of the divided nation."[39] The reader might be forgiven if he thought that the Dublin government and the IRA were working hand in hand.)

When bombers again attacked Dublin in 1974, the press attitude was that the South now knew what it felt like. Richard Eder at the *New York Times* reported from Dublin: "The tendency here not to think about the problems of the North and the consequent lack of any strong public pressure to take action against the gunmen operating from the Republic's territory came from something more complex than complacency. Partly it was the residual sympathy for the tradition of violent action to obtain a united Ireland. . . ."[40]

The following day Eder reported that the bombings were carried out by Protestant terrorists "who wanted to give this predominantly Roman Catholic country a taste of the kind of violence served on the North by the Provisional wing of the IRA."[41] A columnist in the paper had earlier suggested (July 9, 1972) that there was some equivalence between how the Catholics were treated in Northern Ireland and how Protestants

*The alternative view—that the problem was a political one stemming from the nature of partition and aggravated by British policy—continued to be ignored.

were treated in the South.* Already, the South had stood condemned at least for letting the "pitiless terrorists" of the IRA "infiltrate Ulster in specially trained bomb squads."

It was convenient for the British government to find a scapegoat for the crisis in Northern Ireland. Not wanting to admit that its policy and the conduct of its security forces had something to do with the violence and Catholic support for the IRA, it turned to the south of Ireland. In the newspeak of the 1980s, it implied that the Irish Republic was a "sponsor state" of terrorism. While there is no doubt that the IRA operated back and forth across the border between the two states, this was in spite of often massive Irish security operations. To suggest, as *Newsweek* and other reputable newspapers continually did, that the IRA was an outside force sent into Ulster was absurd. If the correspondents in question had merely visited Long Kesh internment camp and looked at the list of the inmates' home addresses, that particular theory would have been seen for the transparent propaganda it was.

When the Irish government brought a case against Britain before the Strasbourg Court on Human Rights, the British were outraged. Ireland alleged that British security forces had used illegal methods of interrogation on IRA suspects in August 1971, consisting of a series of sensory-deprivation techniques. The European Commission on Human Rights investigated the allegati6ns to see if the Irish had a case to bring before the Human Rights Court. It produced one of the most detailed and exhaustive documents on the Northern Ireland situation ever published. It was also the first non-British enquiry into the Northern situation. The commission's report, 563 pages long, was released in September 1976. It found that the British forces were guilty of violating article 3 of the European Human Rights Convention, which states, "No one shall be subjected to torture or to inhuman or degrading treatment or punishment." The case was then allowed to proceed to the court at Strasbourg for judgment.

---

*"In the South, Protestants are second-class citizens; in the North the Catholics are second-class citizens. . . ." (July 9, 1972). Mr. Sulzberger ignored the *fact* that much of the wealth of the Irish Republic was in the hands of a rich Anglo-Irish Protestant minority.

The British had attempted by various means to stall the commission's inquiry. They had also tried to undermine the Irish government's suit by alleging that it was detrimental to their fight against the IRA. And when the commission's result was revealed, the British attacked the Irish government. This is what the *New York Times* chose to emphasize, rather than the report's findings. Its story was headlined BRITISH ACCUSE IRISH ON TORTURE REPORT (September 6, 1976), a reversal of events that, though it must have pleased the British government, hardly constituted a fair or balanced assessment. The *Times* report ran: "British officials today accused the Irish Republic of deliberately embarrassing the British Government and thereby endangering joint efforts by the two countries to combat terrorism in the United Kingdom."[42] Only in the second paragraph was the Strasbourg report accusing Britain of using "torture" on Irish prisoners mentioned: "The accusation followed the formal release in Dublin and London of a report by the European Commission on Human Rights that found the British guilty of torturing suspected terrorists in Northern Ireland in 1971.

"The report said that in 1971 special British instructors had briefed local police in Ulster in interrogation techniques that were eventually put into practice." The report had said much more than that. The "five techniques," as they were known, had already been declared illegal by a British inquiry in 1972.* The Human Rights Commission found that their use had been approved at a very high level. That is, the five techniques constituted what is termed "an administrative practice." The implication was clear that the British government itself had authorized the use of illegal methods of interrogation in Northern Ireland. However, instead of pursuing this line of inquiry, the press for the most part preferred to lament the detrimental effect it would supposedly have on antiterrorist efforts. A combined wire-service story in the New York *Daily News* said, "The action by the Republic of Ireland in pressing the charges before the Rights Commission strains its relations with Britain at a time when both Governments are battling terrorists."[43]

The report in the *Christian Science Monitor* on September 6,

*The Minority Report of Lord Gardiner, March 1972.

1976, headlined BRITIAN DISMAYED OVER TORTURE ISSURE, also stressed the British government's upset. A scandal of potentially Watergate dimensions involving British ministers authorizing army officers to break the law was lost in the rush to describe British government "embarrassment" and annoyance at being pestered by the Republic of Ireland over such a matter.*

In January 1978, the Human Rights Court, after considering the report, passed its judgment. It found Britain guilty of violating article 3 of the convention. The judges found that the "five techniques" constituted "inhuman and degrading" methods of interrogation, but they did not consider them as "torture," in spite of the commission's finding. The reaction in the U.S. press was predictable: RIGHTS COURT ABSOLVES BRITISH IN IRA CASE proclaimed the headline in the Reuters story carried by the *New York Times* on January 18, 1972. "The European Court on Human Rights cleared Britain today of charges that its security forces in Northern Ireland had tortured suspected members of the IRA." Then the report went on to say that the court had found "evidence" that the British had used "inhuman and degrading treatment" in their interrogation methods in 1971. Only in the third and final sentence of the opening paragraph does the reader learn that the court actually found Britain guilty of breaking article 3 of the Human Rights Convention.

On the West Coast the coverage of the story gave a more balanced view. An AP report in the *San Francisco Examiner,* headlined COURT SLAPS BRITAIN FOR IRISH ACTS, said that the court had condemned the British for letting its troops use "inhuman and degrading third-degree methods of questioning suspected members of the IRA in 1971." AP said that the court had "turned down a recommendation of its European Commission on Human Rights that the interrogation techniques be called "torture."[44] It went on to describe briefly the five techniques. Likewise, the *San Francisco Chronicle,* under the headline COURT ASSAILS BRITISH TREATMENT OF IRISH CAPTIVES, managed at least to convey that it was the British and not the Irish who were on trial. The report quoted

*A full description of the commission's inquiry and the British government's coverup of responsibility will be found in my book *Too Long a Sacrifice,* chapter 3.

Irish government officials as saying that the judgment was "of major importance" because it formally condemned the interrogation methods.[45] The *Los Angeles Times* ran a report similar to that from AP in the *Examiner.*

Unfortunately, these reports did little to lift the coverage of the Strasbourg hearings above the general level of pro-British posturing, which had managed to distort the story so much in the influential *New York Times.*

On a different level, the press continually sought to blame Irish Americans for Northern Ireland's troubles. It also excoriated anyone of any political standing who seemed to be pursuing a course more favorable to the republicans. Congressman Mario Biaggi is a case in point.

In early 1978, when the Irish prime minister attacked the congressman in a letter that was made public, the press eagerly joined in ". . . the encouragement of Ulster extremists by thoughtless and ill-informed politicking in this country hurts the chance for peace over there,"[46] said the editorial in the *Washington Star.* The *Baltimore Sun* denounced Biaggi's association with the Caucus and Sinn Fein, which it claimed "he has taken as representatives of Ireland." The *Sun* called Sinn Fein "a handful of people who could never get elected," and accused Biaggi of "spurning those whose legitimacy like his own survives the test of fair and free elections."[47] One wonders if Sinn Fein's subsequent electoral successes would have caused the *Sun* to be less critical of any congressman who now chose to meet with them.

The idea that a Bronx congressman should presume to concern himself about Northern Ireland seemed to cause extreme irritation in editorial offices all over the U.S. The only serious exception to this almost universal condemnation was a significant one—the New York-based *Irish Echo,* the country's largest Irish-American newspaper. Calling Biaggi a "Friend of the Irish," the paper said that Biaggi had "time after time on a variety of issues . . . stood for what is right and just."[48]

Few papers, apart from the *Echo,* paused to reflect on the extremely unusual nature of the event on which they were editorializing. That is, a head of a friendly government had publically berated a member of the House of Representatives. (The *Manchester Union-Leader* did refer to it as an "unprecedented step" and advised that "private persuasion might have been more in keeping with diplomatic niceties."[49] Nor did the press take time to consider the possibility that in order to understand a guerrilla war it might be necessary to meet with and talk to all the participants. Whether one condones their activities or not, getting "the whole story," as the *Echo* put it, is a legitimate aim for anyone concerned with a situation like that of Northern Ireland. It is ironic that it is the newspapers themselves who have to be reminded of this.

However, the British consensus upon which much press coverage was based did necessitate finding scapegoats. It did not matter if today's scapegoats—say, the Irish government when it was bringing the British before the Human Rights Court—became an upholder of that consensus tomorrow, as when someone like Biaggi, who dared to stray outside it, was condemned. The main purpose of the consensus was to prevent the raising of certain questions potentially critical of Britain. The dissenter must be slapped down, and the basis of the consensus protected, regardless of facts.

Blaming the Judge

The press reaction to the courts' refusal to extradite IRA fugitives provided one of the most egregious examples of unbalanced coverage. But this bias was drastically increased because although the press generally reported and editorialized on each decision, none of the major newspapers ever actually covered the hearings themselves. When the finding was announced, the reader had nothing to guide him other than a report outlining it and an editorial condemning it virulently. The detailed testimony preceding the judgment was never reported, probably because so much of it was unfavorable to the British and would certainly challenge the consensus that the American press generally relied on to guide its Northern Ireland coverage. But without that context, the editorial opinions condemning the judge's decision could not possibly be fairly weighed by any reader not directly familiar with what went on in the courtroom.

Press hostility to the courts' continual rejection of extradition warrants against IRA fugitives reached a peak in late 1984 with the handing down of the Doherty decision. The editorial reaction to that decision will be looked at in detail, since it followed the lines of previous opinions on the outcome of earlier cases, except that over Doherty most of the major newspapers lost any semblance of fairness.

Manhattan Federal Court Judge John Sprizzo handed down his decision rejecting the British extradition request for IRA member Thomas (Joe) Doherty on December 13. (For a detailed examination of that hearing and others, see chapter 5.) The *New York Times* headlined its December 14 report on the judgment: U.S. JUDGE REJECTS BID FOR EXTRADITION OF IRA MURDERER.[50] The New York *Daily News* story on the decision carried the headline: CONVICTED IRA KILLER WINS A COURT VICTORY.[51] And the *New York Post* greeted the decision with: IRA GUNMAN CAN REMAIN IN THE U.S.[52] (The *Post* did not say that remaining in the U.S. meant continued incarceration without bail. Doherty's victory did not free him; he remained in jail until 1992, when he was deported to Britian. On the West Coast, the *San Francisco Chronicle,* using an AP story, headlined it U.S. JUDGE BARS EXTRADITION OF IRA KILLER.[53] These set the tone for the editorials and generally unsympathetic coverage that followed. The New York *Daily News* was one of the first to editorialize on Sprizzo's finding. Entitling its piece FIGHTING TERRORISM—EVERYWHERE, the *News* began unequivocally: "Thomas Doherty is an Irish terrorist who murdered a British soldier and ought to be extradited to face charges." It went on, referring to Sprizzo's decision, "It's a crazy ruling. Imagine the outcry if some foreign government refused to extradite an FALN bomber because it's a 'political' struggle. The IRA members are terrorists just as much as the Puerto Ricans who tried to kill Harry Truman, or the Moslem fanatics who killed the Marines in Beirut, or the hijackers of the Kuwaiti plane who murdered two Americans." The editorial then listed a series of acts committed by the IRA, including the 1984 bombing attack on the hotel where the Conservative party leaders were staying, and the bombing of department stores and restaurants. "Sprizzo would presumably call all these 'political' attacks. . . . It's a ridiculous argument," the *News* asserted. "Terrorism is a plague, afflicting Americans as well as British, Irish, Israelis and Lebanese. . . . The U.S. insists, rightly, that the nations of the world must unite to fight terrorism. It's a hollow protest if a U.S. judge can wrap an Irish murderer in the American flag."[54]

Other editorials which followed in the *Wall Street Journal*, the *New York Post*, the *New York Times*, and the *Chicago Tribune* all made similar points, comparing Doherty's acts to other sensational, headline-grabbing attacks and concluding that these, too, would be protected by Sprizzo's decision. The *Wall Street Journal*, referring to Sprizzo's description of the IRA as a disciplined group, which he found distinguished it from amorphous terrorist groups, claimed the finding could be used to protect Mehmet Ah Agca, "whose attempted assassination of the Pope has behind it the organization, discipline and command structure of the Soviet Government." *The Journal* held the decision to be "another setback in the war against international terrorism."

The author of the editorial in the *New York Post* was equally outraged: "Terrorists the world over owe a vote of thanks to Manhattan Federal Court Judge John Sprizzo who refused to allow the extradition of an IRA assassin Thomas Doherty, convicted of the ambush and murder of a British soldier." It accused the judge of "giving aid and comfort to the cause of terrorists everywhere. He has issued an open invitation to these killers to pursue their bloody work—after which they can flee to the U.S., where sympathetic judges are available to hear their pleas that their crimes were 'political.'" The political-offense exception was not allowed to stand in the way of the *Post's* anger at the findings. To give that exception any credence at all, according to the *Post*, "is precisely the sort of reasoning that has been used to excuse the PLO and the Red Brigades—organizations allied to the IRA—and has helped create the atmosphere in which terrorists thrive."[55] In another, later editorial, the *Post* compared the Doherty decision to one in which an anti-abortionist plants a bomb in an abortion clinic and kills a janitor. "Arrested later in France," and facing extradition back to the U.S., "he would presumably plead that his crime was political because he had acted from passionate opposition to the Supreme Court's ruling on abortion." In what must be a record for muddled thinking in so short a piece of prose, the *Post* alleged that Sprizzo's ruling would make the killing of a supreme court justice a political offense. The editorial stumbles along, finally resorting to this crutch for a conclusion: ". . . a crime is a crime is a crime however lofty the motives."[56] The words were (appropriately enough) British Prime Minister Margaret Thatcher's, uttered in 1981 when she was refusing to concede to the republican hunger strikers' demands for political status.*

The *Chicago Tribune* accused Judge Sprizzo of misusing the power to forbid extradition. It acknowledged that he had "acted within the law and his powers, but he certainly violated the clear rules of common sense." It said the judge had "conferred upon the IRA the political and military status that has been denied it" by both British and Irish governments, and "gave blessing to the myth" that the IRA is involved in a struggle to free Ulster from British rule. ". . . in reality," the *Tribune* explained—trotting out the well-worn consensus view that the press has followed from the beginning—"the struggle there is tragically medieval. . . . The IRA has exploited that strife to fight both the British and Irish Governments, to prey in street-gang fashion upon both Protestant and Catholics and to harass, frequently with violence, the chief Catholic political party in Ulster."[57] Here the *Tribune* was referring to the SDLP. But there were actually few known instances of the IRA's attacking the SDLP. An AP story of May 8, 1974, reported the murder of the Catholic couple by the IRA because the wife was an SDLP member and the party had condemned violence. In fact, the murders were carried out by the loyalist UVF for purely sectarian reasons.

The editorial then went on to make the familiar argument that Sprizzo's ruling would protect those who attempted to blow up Prime Minister Thatcher and would also protect Lebanese bombers. It urged congressional action to close the "loopholes" in the extradition treaty.

The *New York Times* referred to the decision as "an undesirable result." It took a line critical of the political-offense exception as

*The *Post's* editorial had referred to the case of a British soldier convicted of murdering a Catholic. The decision came just after the Doherty decision and was made much of as proof that the British courts are fair. In fact, though the security forces had killed an estimated 163 civilians, mostly Catholics, between 1969 and 1985, no soldier had ever before been convicted in court.

a whole, calling it a "hangover from the 19th century, when revolutions in Europe engendered sympathy in Great Britain and the United States for some fugitives from authoritarian governments."* It argued that the Doherty case made clear "the need for reform" of the handling of extradition proceedings, and suggested that as things stand judges "have been required to exercise too much judgment." The *Times* concluded: "And the Administration's original plan, to get the courts out of the political thicket entirely, now looks even more desirable. Some countries should not be trusted to deal fairly with some fugitives. America's diplomats are better judges of which countries these may be."[58]

There were few papers that took any other line. Among those that hailed the Sprizzo judgment was the *Philadelphia Daily News,* which attacked "the same newspapers that condemn repression in South Africa" for complaining about the judgment. It noted that the British used the same arguments against Doherty as they did when "hunting down many of the men who became the leaders of Israel."[59]

The weekly *Irish Echo* in New York defended the decision, calling it "a very correct ruling." "Sprizzo ruled that Doherty could not be extradited because his was a 'political offense.' The judge is correct on the facts and correct on the law. His detractors should be ashamed of themselves. And they should try to get their facts straight."[60] The *National Law Journal* agreed with the *Echo.* Its editorial, entitled FOLLOWING THE LAW, defended the judge against his detractors in the administration. For administration officials to attack Sprizzo, as they did after his finding was announced, the *Law Journal* said, was "to demean the judicial process and the Justice Department itself." It pointed out that Sprizzo's decision "was fully supported by the facts and the law."[61]

The exasperation and dismay expressed in the *Echo's* editorial is justified considering the quality of the major newspapers' response to the Doherty ruling. To draw analogies, as they did, with an attack on an abortion clinic, the attempted assassination of the

---

*Among the revolutions then that did not engender sympathy of the *Times* was Ireland's struggle against England. The *Times* supported sending Fenians back to Great Britain to stand trial.

Pope, and the various atrocities committed in the Middle East, was to show ignorance of the law on the matter, as well as apparent ignorance of the decision itself, that is truly inexcusable in any press organ with a reputation for serious reporting. The editorial writers of the New York *Daily News*, the *Wall Street Journal*, and the *New York Post* should have known that the wanton-crimes exception enunciated in such cases as Abu Eam's (1981) would have doomed to failure any appeal to the political-exception defense for crimes against civilians or other atrocities. And by no stretch of the imagination could the judge's ruling be made to cover isolated acts of violence.

As Sprizzo made clear in his very precise and pithy decision—all of thirteen pages long—one of the factors necessary before the political-offense exception could be successfully appealed to was the existence of a widespread uprising or rebellion in which government authority was being challenged by the rebel group. Sheer indifference to the facts, or willful ignorance, may not be sufficient to explain how editorial writers could pretend to find that factor in the acts of an abortion-clinic bomber or a fanatic assassin who tries to kill the pope. Obviously, as with the administration's policy toward the extradition law, there was a preconceived and weighty body of political opinion operating in the background to distort and warp the press's attitude toward, and reporting of, these judicial matters. Once more, and perhaps more blatantly with the extradition cases than with any other aspect of the Northern Ireland problem, the U.S. press showed itself to be almost an arm of the government rather than a mediator responsible for presenting its readers with a version of events approximating to the facts.

When the Senate Foreign Relations Committee met to consider the proposed revisions to the U.S.-U.K. treaty in the summer and fall of 1985, the press repeated its performance of December 1984. The new treaty proposed to make the political-offense exception inapplicable when the accused was alleged to have committed acts of violence, which the new clauses specified. The *Times* hailed the new treaty with the headline SEALING A TERRORIST FOXHOLE.[62] When the revision did not get the easy passage that was hoped for, the *Washington Post* called it "disgraceful," alleging that the impediments were due to a lobbying campaign by "supporters of the IRA in this country."[65] (Legal experts like Professor Pyle of Mount Holyoke College and senators like Eugene McCarthy who gave their considered views on why it should not be ratified might be surprised to hear themselves described as such!) The editorial rehashed all the fallacies concerning the current application of the political-exception defense, alleging, for example, that it would prevent the extradition of those responsible for the attempted assassination of Margaret Thatcher. The fact that attempts on the lives of heads of state, or the killing of civilians, do not come within the scope of the political defense as it now stands, was not allowed to trouble the editorial writers in their unseemly haste to make a purely political point. The political point was the same as that made by the administration throughout all of the extradition cases: that it was politically and diplomatically embarrassing to have these fugitives described as political offenders, regardless of the nature of the struggle in which they were participants. The chief yardstick used was the political and diplomatic self-interest of the United States in relation to its ally the United Kingdom. Legal standards were ignored, or addressed without detachment, and the press was once more content to recycle the usual errors and misleading comparisons. The terminology of the editorials on the new treaty, as on the extradition decisions, was that of the administration, providing another unsettling example of the merging of press and government consensus in dealing with this controversial issue.

Sentimental Tough Guys—
Hero Reporters

Among American journalists, few broke through these self-imposed limits and restrictions. There was, however, a group of Irish-American columnists who produced work which was decidedly more sympathetic to the Irish nationalist view. Indeed, Pete Hamill, who wrote for the New York *Daily News* and the *Village Voice,* Jack McKinney of the *Philadelphia Daily News,* and Jimmy Breslin, a syndicated columnist with the New York *Daily News,* often wrote fiercely from that viewpoint. Unfortunately, they generally relied on stereotypes and used stylistic characteristics that threw little light on the situation. Rather, this style tended to throw light on the writers' connection with that situation, which they viewed through the eyes of a "sentimental tough guy" persona derived, it would seem, from popular American detective fiction.

Breslin mixed the sentimental—which enabled him to describe Northern Ireland in maudlin terms as "a wet, soft, beautiful, bitter little country"—and the street-tough attitude, which viewed people from Belfast as hard-drinking, ballad-singing "characters" obsessed with murder, or with talking about murder. For example: "After the singing ended, the old woman again began talking about another killing up at the end of her street in Belfast. 'These two men got on a bus and pulled out guns and . . .'" Breslin's version of a Belfast taxi driver was a ghoul who rambled on: "'On the Antrim Road we have marder male' ["murder mile"], the one called Liam said. His words came out of a long, sad face."[64] Such ghouls were as much a caricature as were the inexplicable natives and truculent tribes who typified the coverage of the *New York Times, Time,* and *Newsweek.*

The sentimental tough guy reached something of an apotheosis in the work of Hamill. At one time, the most vigorously engaged in the Northern Ireland question of any American journalist, Hamill could be credited with hard-hitting work. When the *New York Times* was apologizing for internment, Hamill, writing in the *New York Post,* actually described an army raid on a Catholic home. He wrote about the horrors of the prison protests in the early 1980s. And he was probably one of the few American reporters to sit down and interview Gerry Adams before the peace process, when it became fashionable to do so.

On the debit side, however, Hamill's work was marred by sentimentalism. There was a vicariousness in his writing on the IRA, for instance, which tended to intrude constantly between the reader and the subject matter. Responding to Governor Hugh Carey's attack on the IRA in April 1977, Hamill wrote: "In that province [Northern Ireland] I have met cowards and fools and liars. But I have also met some of the bravest men and women on this earth, and all of them have been in the Provisional IRA." He cannot resist injecting himself into the story. "Twice," he continues, "on my visits to Northern Ireland, they saved my life. On more times than that, I listened to them as they discussed strategy and decided against actions that would have killed innocent people."[65]

He does not say how his life was saved by the IRA. But the article extols the IRA as model freedom fighters and ends in a blaze of sentimentality: "I wish I could provide [Carey] with the names of some people to whom he could send his apologies. Unfortunately, most of them are dead. They died without ever seeing Regine's or 21 or P. J. Clarke's. They died without ever knowing whether their children would live in freedom. They died without ever seeing the tricolor billowing in the breeze over the rooftops of Derry. They died for Ireland. Maybe they were fools. But they were better men than Hughie Carey and it will take someone better than me to forgive him for this one."[66]

The object is blurred by melodrama. The Northern Ireland issue becomes a backdrop to the drama of the journalist's feelings about it. In the process, negative stereotypes about the sentimental, maudlin Irish are reinforced. This of course does little to raise the level of debate on to the rational, critical plane where it has to be dealt with if any understanding is ever going to filter into the public awareness. Unfortunately, the arcadian disposition accepts this kind of sentimentality readily; sentimental reveries come more easily to it than analytical thinking. This partly explains the appeal of Hamill's writing on Northern Ireland to Irish Americans, and indicates something about the Irish-American community's arcadian view of Ireland as a Garden of Eden spoiled only by the serpent England. Clearly, it is too narrow a basis on which to give a complex and stimulating analysis of the crisis.*

---

*It is interesting to contrast the Irish-American view with the intellectual history of American Jews, which draws on rich traditions with strong roots in European radical and Marxist thought. The Irish-American community had a vibrant and varied intellectual life in the nineteenth and early twentieth century which developed from similar traditions, but in more recent years these traditions have become all but extinct as an important part of that community's culture. Some have attributed this to the ascendency of conservative elements within the Catholic church. There is some sign, however, that younger Irish Americans are once more reviving some of the intellectual vigor that characterized the last century.

The Post-Hunger Strike Coverage

In the late 1970s and early 1980s, two major factors influenced the U.S. press and made it somewhat more critical of the British government's role in Northern Ireland. The first was the growing access that the Irish diplomatic service had to the editorial rooms of major newspapers like the *New York Times* and the *Los Angeles Times*. This was itself due to the growth in Irish influence in Washington already noted. The Irish government was eager to detach the press from its reliance on London's view of Northern Ireland as an out-and-out sectarian war for which Britain had little responsibility, while at the same time anxious that it not let up on its critical view of the IRA and the Irish Americans who supported it. In this it was more or less successful, though not entirely through its own efforts, because the other major factor was a powerful one: the hunger strikes of 1981 and the subsequent rise to political power of Sinn Fein, the political wing of the IRA. The hunger strike was undoubtedly one of the major news stories of the last twenty-five years in Ireland. An estimated four hundred journalists gathered in Belfast from all over the world, with a heavy representation from all the major U.S. newspapers and network television stations, to watch as Bobby Sands, the first of the hunger strikers, died.

The death of Sands, which was followed by the deaths of nine other prisoners (all of them either members of the IRA or INLA), provoked the most critical editorials the British had yet seen in papers like the *New York Times*. "By willing his own death," the *Times* wrote, "Bobby Sands has earned a place on Ireland's long roll of martyrs and bested an implacable British Prime Minister. . . . Mrs. Thatcher deplores the IRA terror, but seems unable to address the grievances that make terrorists like Bobby Sands heroes to the Catholic minority. Power remains in the hands of an unyielding Protestant majority, whose leaders, in 1914, preferred mutiny against the Crown to Home Rule."[67] The paper went on to advise Mrs. Thatcher to negotiate, as she had in Rhodesia.

In an editorial dated May 1981, the New York *Daily News* called for a British withdrawal and demanded "a break-up of the covert alliances between Protestant paramilitary groups and military and police organizations in Northern Ireland." This was remarkable, considering that the *Daily News* had almost completely ignored such stories in its regular reporting. Mike Daly, a *News* columnist, wrote about the UDA in the winter of 1980. This was one of the rare acknowledgments of the loyalists' contribution to the violence, and was probably the inspiration for the editorial's assertion. Even the *New York Post,* usually so pro-British and pro-Thatcher, exclaimed editorially: "That Northern Ireland is now a colony is beyond argument. That is exactly how Britain treats and rules it, albeit prolonging the agony."[68] And as another hunger striker neared death, the *Times* upbraided Thatcher for her intransigence, predicting: "The cry of 'Brits Out' may yet come true."[69] The old consensus was broken; the idea that Britain was partly responsible for the Northern Ireland mess had taken hold.

The hunger strike set off a chain of events whose reverberations are still being felt. It created a power base for the politics of Sinn Fein. No longer could it be said—as the press had throughout the 1970s—that the IRA's cause had no support among nationalists. This in turn started a frantic effort in the moderate nationalist political camp to build a new platform on which to appeal to nationalist voters. From this came the 1984 New Ireland Forum, an attempt by the SDLP and the Dublin government under Garret Fitzgerald to present a reasonable nationalist alternative—or set of alternatives—to the "Brits out" demands of Sinn Fein. When the Forum report was published in the early summer of 1984, the American press welcomed it wholeheartedly; in an editorial entitled "Ireland makes its move," the *Chicago Tribune* sympathetically reviewed the report's proposals. Margaret Thatcher was criticized for her "great fondness for the status quo" in Northern Ireland, and for maintaining her position that "nothing will be done without the approval of the province's Protestant majority." The *Tribune* reminded Thatcher that "the lack of a political solution has cost an insupportable price in violence, bloodshed, economic decay and loss of public treasure. Attempts to maintain the status quo have always led to a change for the worse. Ireland has made its move. Now, urgently, it is Britain's turn."[70]

Equally positive about the report was the *New York Times,* which in a May editorial called UNDER TWO FLAGS suggested that the idea of joint authority, which was one of the alternatives discussed in the report, was a worthy one that deserved serious study in London.

Seven months later, Thatcher and Fitzgerald met in London. After the meeting Thatcher gave a press conference at which she dismissed in staccato fashion (the famous "Out, out, out" speech) the three major alternatives described in the report. The U.S. press reaction was swift and hostile. Forty-seven editorials appeared, generally critical of Thatcher's position. THE IRA WINS AGAIN proclaimed the *Chicago Tribune*.[71] THATCHER SAID TOO MUCH was the response of the *San Francisco Examiner*.[72] In an editorial entitled THE INS AND OUTS OF IRELAND, the *New York Times* said of the British prime minister: "No one doubts her courage in opposing the demonic fanaticism of the IRA. But she has yet to show the same resolve in dealing with Northern Ireland's Protestants, who refuse to share power or even symbols with the oppressed minority."[73] The *Washington Post* said that the bridge-building efforts of Fitzgerald and the New Ireland Forum had been "undermined by Mrs. Thatcher's brusque and dismissive comments," and warned that "terrorists can only find comfort from the failure" of the cooperative efforts of Dublin and London.[74]

"Prime Minister Margaret Thatcher," declared the *Boston Globe,* following the summit debacle, "rightly prides herself on her toughness and determination. Her grave mismanagement of affairs in Northern Ireland, however, calls into question her imagination and sensitivity. It does no good to have a will of iron if that will is in the service of an obtuse sensibility and a mind choked with prejudices. . . ."[75] It was probably one of the most outspoken attacks on a British prime minister ever to appear in a major American newspaper.

The barrage of criticism had some effect. When Thatcher came to Washington early the following year to address both houses of Congress, she was a different figure from the Iron Lady usually presented to the press. Instead, she made conciliatory remarks on Northern Ireland, which emphasized the cooperative effort with Dublin. Later that year, she signed the Anglo-Irish Agreement with Prime Minister Fitzgerald, giving his government some role in the affairs of the North for the first time. Undoubtedly, hostile response of the press to her earlier position played a part in that development.

The press universally welcomed the agreement. In doing so, however, they were occasionally involved in contradictions such as that demonstrated in the *Los Angeles Times*. The paper reported on the need for the agreement's provision to give Ireland a role in the North; this way, it was thought, the alienation of Catholics from institutions like the courts might be reduced. Yet in the same issue an editorial said, "The system of British justice applied in Northern Ireland has shown every sign of working fairly."[76] Presumably, if the courts were working fairly, there would be no need for said provision.

Overall, the agreement was greeted as a viable solution that would undermine support for Sinn Fein and the IRA. It led to a modification of the old consensus, which had already been revised after the 1981 hunger strikes. In the new, post-agreement consensus, the London–Dublin nexus, which the agreement held up, was regarded as the only hope for peace. Therefore it had to be defended against the onslaught of the IRA and the intransigence of the loyalists, both of whom were viewed as twin enemies of the agreement; their every action was treated as if it were designed to thwart it. In the new alignment, the Protestant majority, which opposed the agreement, and whose rights as the majority had been for so long defended against nationalist claims to a united Ireland, were now being told that they had to accept the new plan—being a majority obviously no longer carried the democratic mandate it once did, an interesting shift which was generally not commented upon in the eulogies of the agreement in the press.

Conclusion

In the winter of 1978, the magazine *Index on Censorship* published an article by British reporter and author Peter Taylor.* Taylor,

---

*His book *Beating the Terrorists* is a detailed investigation of allegations of brutality made against the Northern Ireland police in the mid- to late 1970s.

who worked for both the BBC and independent television networks in Britain, and who wrote about the Northern Ireland question in depth, was considering the difficulties British journalists faced in covering "the troubles." He was particularly concerned about the increasing reluctance of the networks to handle controversial stories on the crisis which departed from the accepted consensus derived from the British government's view. He said: "Northern Ireland is different. . . because the nature of the consensus that exists makes any informed discussion of the problem difficult, if not increasingly impossible." His description of that consensus is much the same as that outlined at the beginning of this chapter. The remarkable thing about the American press was that in general it stayed closer to the British government consensus than did its British counterpart. British reporters, in both print and broadcast media, showed more willingness to question the British government's attitude to the Irish conflict than did American journalists, and managed over the years to produce a respectable body of work delving into the genesis and development of the situation.* The same daring cannot be said for their American counterparts. What was noticeable, even among the handful of reporters in America willing to break the mold, was the almost complete absence of any detailed or extended treatment of the complexities of the crisis. The consensus view—of religious fanatics held back by a kindly British referee—suffocated any intelligent discussion of Northern Ireland in the U.S. throughout the 1970s.

Such limitations took their toll. A *Time* magazine story began: "By now the Ulster problem probably bores the world."[77] Another commented almost petulantly, "This time for what it was worth, the blame for the outburst of violence could be leveled at the Protestant side. . . ."[78] Around the same time the *New York Times* reporter was also suffering from ennui: "It is all old and stale: the army patrols, the stone-throwing—some of the 7-year-olds

---

*As a result, the British government has frequently sought to suppress coverage it regarded as too unfavorable to its views. This happened in 1985, when the BBC was forced to drop a documentary, *At the Edge of the Union*, because it contained an interview with an alleged IRA leader. The decision caused a strike of BBC journalists. (The documentary was shown later.)

started when they were 4—the resentment and weariness of the soldiers. . . ."[79]

What is never stale is good, vigorous reporting that is not afraid to challenge accepted stereotypes. But instead the American press for the most part preferred to reiterate the tired and weary cliches handed on from the British government. To then blame Ulster for "boring the world" was to exhibit extraordinary arrogance papering over ineptitude. What bored the world was precisely the way Ulster was covered in the press!

Things began to change with the hunger strikes of 1981. The coverage of the peace process in the 1990s helped confirm that the old British-dominated consensus that characterized U.S. coverage was broken. The *New York Times* editorialized in favor of granting Gerry Adams a visa in January 1994. When Adams first arrived in New York in early 1994, he was a media celebrity. The man routinely denounced as an apologist for terrorism received fairly positive coverage, including a profile in the *New York Times* penned by Edna O'Brien. Adams has since been profiled and interviewed extensively in a manner unthinkable a decade before. Most Americans wanted to celebrate the IRA and Sinn Fein's involvement in the peace process as a positive step, and the British government's reluctance to engage with them after the IRA cease-fire in 1994 was criticized. It was a far cry from the coverage that typified the 1970s, when the acceptance of the British government's consensus on Northern Ireland provided a worrying example of how in democratic societies a free press could be used to stifle controversial matters and to make sure that challenging questions about a tragic crisis are not admitted into serious debate.

7
CONCLUSION: THE DECLINE OF THE REBEL

America has been the destination for many generations of Irish men and women. But in some ways it has also been Ireland's destiny. The Irish have flourished in America in a way impossible in Ireland. In America, the population of Irish descent is eight times the present population of Ireland itself. In America, the Irish have achieved political and economic power far in excess of anything they could have hoped for in Ireland. In America, they have achieved the prosperity, security, and acceptance that was denied their ancestors and that is still beyond the reach of significant sections of the population in Ireland's northeastern counties. It might well be argued that Ireland's destiny and its true significance can be discerned not only in its own history, but also in the history of the Irish experience in America. But of course the two cannot be separated. The American connection, at all its different levels, from the gunrunners to the political elite in Washington, is a testimony to their continued interdependence. Ireland's relationship to America remains as unusual as its history as a Western European nation. Its history of conquest, colonialization, famine, and oppression is not that of the postimperial western nations that are its closest geographical neighbors, but that of the third world.

For Irish Americans, that history provided their point of departure, and helped shape their subsequent connection to the land of their ancestors.

The unresolved issue of Irish nationalism—the creation of one unified Irish nation—has meant that in some way or other, for many Irish Americans their sense of what it was to be Irish was never completely satisfied. It remained a nagging counterpoint to their own progress and success in becoming assimilated into the mainstream of American society. As the years passed, however, it was alleviated by political success in Ireland—the achievement of some degree of autonomy in 1921, and by the increasing economic and social success in America.

In many different ways, the American connection has shaped the course of events in Northern Ireland since then; it can even be credited with helping to bring about some of the most crucial developments, including the Anglo-Irish Agreement, which some see as the first step along the path that led to the peace process and the Good Friday Agreement over a decade later, with its provisions for power-sharing between Catholics and Protestants and cross-border institutions. In the 1990s, President Clinton put Northern Ireland on his agenda and, for the first time, the issue went beyond the politics of Irish America and entered the U.S. political mainstream. But had it not been for the Irish-American involvement in the first place, this development might never have occurred, and the current settlement, in which Clinton has been credited with playing a central role, might never have been reached. (See Chapter 8)

The historian Thomas Brown has said that there have always been two dominant and contrasting figures in Irish-American political life—the rebel and the politician.[1] The contrast is between idealism and pragmatism; romanticism and reality; the politics of the cause and the politics of power. (Though it is not a contrast between sentimentality and real feeling: Tip O'Neill the politician probably drank more green beer than, say, George Harrison the rebel.) Recent history would seem to indicate that the rebel's dominance is finished, while that of the politician has increased. The decline of the rebel has actually been in process for at least a generation; only the renewal of the nationalist problem through the Northern Ireland crisis has given him a sudden and unexpected new lease on life. But it will probably prove temporary.

George Harrison, the quintessential Irish rebel, is now in his eighties. There is no one in the same mold to replace him. Even the up-and-coming younger leadership of organizations like NO-RAID, for example, springs from a different world. Martin Galvin, NORAID's most prominent spokesman, was a young former assistant district attorney—a politician, really, who would be very much an establishment figure were it not for the aberration of his commitment to extreme Irish nationalism.

Since the 1950s, there has been no major influx of IRA men fleeing defeat to perpetuate their struggle from the shores of America. Certainly the Troubles produced many IRA fugitives, hiding out in Irish-American communities from San Francisco to New York. In the 1970s and 1980s, however, America was not so welcoming as the federal authorities tightened the extradition law. Even if IRA fugitives succeeded in court they faced the prospect of deportation, as witnessed by the fate of Joe Doherty. With the development of the peace process, things changed somewhat. Deportation proceedings against a score or so of Irish republicans were suspended. Much depends, of course, on whether or not the current peace process succeeds and the Troubles end for the foreseeable future. There remain unpredictable factors and organizations still prepared to resort to violence. Already, republican splinter groups that do not recognize the peace process have received aid from supporters in the U.S., but on a far smaller scale than did the IRA over the decades.

Yet even if the violence in Northern Ireland were to increase again, the powerful social and economic forces that have been at work since the fifties in the Irish-American community have made changes that are irreversible, and which have transformed the American connection. If Irish America's point of departure was the desolate landscape and tortured history of famine and post-famine Ireland, its destination and its destiny was a landscape of a wildly contrasting character.

During the last forty years, Irish Americans have merged rapidly into the vast American middle class, where old ethnic traditions become blurred, or remain as mere decorative emblems. Theirs is the landscape of leafy suburbia, ordered, subdued, where the pursuit of happiness has become the pursuit of comfort. Inevitably, political changes have followed. At least at a national level, more and more Irish Americans are voting Republican. In 1984 they helped give a conservative Republican, Ronald Reagan, 55 percent of the Catholic vote nationwide. The Democratic party pointed to its detailed Irish policy—which affirmed the party's "strong commitment to Irish unity achieved by consent and based on reconciliation of all the people of Ireland "—in vain. Democratic vice-presidential candidate Geraldine Ferraro's strong record of interest in Northern Ireland proved to be of secondary importance even to those Irish Americans active on the issue; many of them showed that they were more concerned with attacking her for her pro-choice position on abortion than they were with supporting her because of her commitment to human rights in Northern Ireland. (This was the experience of politicians at local levels as well. Several who had been active on Northern Ireland found themselves banned from addressing Irish-American meetings, or threatened with pickets from the so-called Right to Life movement because of their pro-choice voting records.)

Of course, Ronald Reagan had made his much publicized "roots" pilgrimage to Ireland in June 1984. But until then his administration's most widely known Irish concern was its determination to extradite IRA fugitives and draft legislation to prevent Americans from supporting Irish republican groups in Ireland. (The government's involvement in the Anglo-Irish dialogue was largely unknown then.) His Irish trip, however, proved something of a shock to many Irish Americans, and indicated the gulf that has opened between them and the Irish. Everywhere he went were thousands of pickets to greet him and protest his foreign policy, particularly as it affected Central America, with which the Irish, through Catholic church missions, had considerable ties. The land of a thousand welcomes became, for Ronald Reagan at least, the land of a hundred thousand pickets. Irish Americans were furious, and for the most part uncomprehending. At that point, the experience of the Irish in America and those in Ireland clashed. Regardless of what he did or did not do about Northern Ireland, Irish Americans were proud of Reagan because he represented the success as well as the charm of the Irish in America. He also happened to reflect the views of many of them on matters like abortion and family values—though Irish-American conservatism on other issues (such as American foreign policy) should not be exaggerated.

The Irish, on the other hand, for the most part indifferent to the American obsession with success, saw his charm as vulgar and his Irishness as shallow as a career in Hollywood could make it. Those who supported the IRA also disliked him because of his ideological identification with Margaret Thatcher. This was a particularly touchy matter for Reagan's Irish-American supporters, especially those who regarded themselves as pro-nationalist. To even suggest to such people that Reagan and Thatcher were ideological partners was tantamount to treason. When this author wrote a column in the New York *Irish Echo* about the Reagan-Thatcher relationship, an irate reader denounced it as "degrading and insulting"; another wrote that it was an insult to a good and decent man. A subsequent column that pursued the same topic was dropped by the publisher because he feared an angry backlash from his readers. Irish-American supporters of Reagan simply ignored or rejected such contradictions between their professed Irish nationalism and their identification with a politician so sympathetic to Thatcher, a woman they habitually denounced as an ogress. They seemed content to enjoy the president's continuing Irish antics, which he obligingly kept up: on St. Patrick's Day in 1986, Reagan was given a surprise in the form of a green-clad dwarf representing an Irish leprechaun, a "fair colleen," also clad in green, and an Irish tenor, all beaming "top of the mornin'" smiles and prancing and singing before him.

Meanwhile, Garret Fitzgerald, the Irish prime minister, presented the president with a crystal bowl full of shamrocks. Reagan was clearly genuinely delighted. The leprechaun charade indicates the vulgarity and crassness to which St. Patrick's Day celebrations in America can sink. But the Irish themselves—or at least their government—were quite prepared to pander to Irish-American sentimentality when it suited them.

Lauding Reagan while condemning Margaret Thatcher was one of the many contradictions of Irish-American political life. As has been argued earlier, Irish America's view of Ireland tends to be arcadian—a reverie of the past in which the world was innocent, free from contradictions, rural and simple. It has been vulgarized by the tourist industry, with its trite sentimental image of the Emerald Isle, an image that has eclipsed the Ireland of the rebel with its desolate landscape of suffering and its endless litany of sacrifice. In any case, one cannot imagine exiled Irish rebels being at home in the middle-class suburban world of modern Irish America where the vulgarized image of Ireland as arcadia prevails. Warring ideologies and the rhetoric of deeply felt wrongs find no resonance there.

Of course, Irish-American working-class neighborhoods still exist in Boston, New York, and elsewhere. In Boston, it once was not an unusual sight to see walls daubed with IRA slogans. But even in such areas where nationalist feelings are still strong (if residual), Irish Americans face contradictions, as do any Irish republican activists who hope to appeal to them. These contradictions might be summed up by the observation that spokespeople like Bernadette McAliskey are not welcome in the working-class areas of Irish-American Boston. Nor would the IRA's left-wing sympathies have found any resonance among the people there who supported its war against the British. The sort of redneck racism which is frequently found in such communities would be uncomprehending of the IRA's political development in Northern Ireland, or even of the experience of that province's Catholic population. Indeed, it is a frequent observation made by Northern Ireland Catholics who have some experience of the Irish-American community and America in general that they feel closer in many ways to American blacks than to their American cousins. This is not surprising, given their historical experience, which has given American blacks and Northern Ireland Catholics at least this much in common: historically, they are both outsiders in their own societies. Irish Americans, for the most part, are insiders.

Those Irish Americans who have been left behind in the general upward movement into the middle class, as in the poorer areas of Boston, are most given to racism simply because they feel they are "insiders" who have been cheated of the privileges that go with that status. Ironically, their experience is closer to that of Northern Ireland's poor Protestants than it is to that of the Northern Ireland Catholics. It is among the poorest sections of the Protestant community that one finds the worst anti-Catholic bigotry. Having been brought up to believe that they are part of the dominant group, they find their poverty inexplicable and in rage turn on the "inferior" minority, whose every social, economic, or political gain is perceived as a dire threat.

Underprivileged Protestants have also attacked the more well-off, middle-class Protestants, whom they blame for "selling out" to Catholic demands.* The crisis in Boston over busing between the poorer Irish Americans and blacks has many similarities to this situation. Like the underprivileged Protestants, the working-class Irish Americans turned on their wealthier brethren, accusing them of being "limousine liberals" who make generous concessions to blacks at the expense of poor Irish-American neighborhoods.

However, the situation of underprivileged Irish Americans remains something of an anomaly, unrepresentative of that community as a whole. Equally unrepresentative, but deserving of note, is the fact that though suburbanization may be the dominant influence in current Irish-American social and political development, radicalism, at least among the younger generation, has not entirely vanished. Indeed, since the 1960s there has been something of a revival of more challenging views among Irish Americans, a revival that has even affected the Catholic church in America.† Following the upsurge in the black civil-rights movement—in which some Irish Americans like Paul O'Dwyer played a role— young Irish Americans developed not only a new political interest in their history, but also became concerned about the survival of Irish culture in America. This has spawned many Irish-American Irish-language groups, as well as societies devoted to Irish arts and music. (The Irish Art Center in New York is among the best known of such organizations. It holds readings by Irish and Irish-American writers, Irish dancing events, folk-music concerts, and political lectures.) Younger Irish Americans in quest of their roots have found them in the older, more radical left-wing traditions once vigorous in America and Ireland, and so have brought a deeper and welcome alternative to the shallow sentimentalism about Ireland more typical of middle-class Irish-American visions of the Irish arcadia.

---

*For a fuller analysis of the social tensions behind Protestant working-class attitudes see my book *Too Long a Sacrifice: Life and Death in Northern Ireland Since 1969.*
†Irish-American activists in the church have often been at the forefront of more radical approaches. The 1950s Catholic Worker Movement and its various offshoots involved many Irish Americans. During the Vietnam War, Irish Americans like the Berrigan brothers were prominent in many areas of the antiwar movement in which the church became involved.

If Ireland remains for most Irish Americans an image of arcadia (however trite), then America remains their utopia—the land of the future that they have helped forge over generations of exile in a struggle that has brought them the many comforts and privileges of suburbia. Pride and a sense of security derived from that achievement have largely replaced the old bitterness and sense of wrong. The Irish-American politician, triumphant figure in the landscape of Irish-American political life, is there to proclaim that achievement—and dares anyone to challenge it. Meanwhile, the ranks of the rebels grow thin, perhaps reaching their last generation, as Ireland's American destiny merges into the calm innocuous suburb. And Irish revolutionaries turn elsewhere—to the postcolonial chaos of Africa and the Middle East, for example—hoping to forge other connections, ideological as well as material, that may sustain them in their long struggle. The triumph of the politician has made that inevitable. He is the American connection now, and the rebel has no place there, being either a threat to the utopia of his America, or a blot upon the arcadia of his Ireland.

8
AFTERWORD:
NORTHERN IRELAND
IN THE CLINTON ERA

The crowd was waiting expectantly under the tent on the south lawn of the White House, sheltered from the evening sun which in the second week of September was bathing Washington in a last burst of summer. There were about 1,000 mostly Irish and Irish Americans gathered, facing the empty stage and podium, talking somewhat uneasily. The reason: They were there to see president William Jefferson Clinton receive an award named in honor of the Irish American civil rights activist Paul O'Dwyer who had died that July. It was September 11, 1998. The report of the Special Prosecutor Kenneth Starr was at that very moment—a first in history—being disseminated via the internet. A veritable stella nova of scandal was irradiating the Clinton presidency with allegations of sexual misconduct with Monica Lewinsky explored in the 454-page report in minutest, crudest detail. The nation was in a state of bewilderment and anxiety, and on the White House lawn, the mood was uneasy.

The Paul O'Dwyer Peace and Justice Award was being given to Clinton for helping bring about a peaceful settlement in Northern Ireland. This was a real political achievement, one that ten years before would have been unimaginable for two reasons. First, because most observers long ago came to the conclusion that the Northern Ireland crisis was perpetual—a problem without a solution. And second, even if there was a solution, the idea of a U.S. president being closely involved in its formulation and implementation would have been out of the question. Yes— Jimmy Carter did make his Ulster speech in August 1977, breaking the long tradition of official U.S. support for Britain's position that Northern Ireland was an internal matter for the U.K. Yes—eight years later, President Reagan did throw his weight behind the Anglo-Irish Agreement. But this was the extent to which U.S. presidents until Clinton were prepared to go. They would nudge here, apply a little private pressure there on their oldest and closest ally, Great Britain, but that was all. And even these developments were a matter for comment and controversy. Northern Ireland, it seemed, would never become more than a side issue for the U.S.

The Clinton presidency changed all that.

He was supposed to appear at 5 P.M. It was put back thirty minutes and then another thirty minutes. The trepidation in the air was increasingly palpable. The Starr Report was at the center of a whirlwind of media attention which swept away consideration of every other issue. And Irish Americans were not known for their liberal views on sexual behavior. At the moment which should have been a straightforward celebration of his Irish triumph, he was being subjected to the most tawdry and vulgar public exposure, which would have been as unthinkable a decade ago as the proposition that a U.S. president would one day help solve the Ulster crisis.

It was almost 6 P.M. before President Clinton finally appeared with his wife Hillary, along with former Senator George Mitchell, Senator Ted Kennedy, Vice-President Al Gore, and Brian O'Dwyer, Paul's son, who was to give the award.

The crowd rose to its feet as one and began to applaud. Whatever signs of unease there were earlier vanished as the applause grew more vigorous. One minute passed yet there was no sign of anyone wanting to resume their seats. On the contrary, they continued to applaud with increasing enthusiasm. Some began to cheer and holler and stamp their feet. There was an overwhelming, spontaneous feeling of solidarity in the audience as they cheered and clapped the president. His smile had at first been uncertain. But as the applause continued, it spread across his face. His looked towards his wife, who was standing across from where he sat. They both realized this was real, undiluted enthusiasm of the kind they had experienced on their two trips to Ireland. After three minutes Al Gore attempted to get people to be seated, but to no avail. His appeals simply provoked louder applause. It was not just coming from the Democrats in the audience. The Republicans there were applauding as well. At around four minutes into the proceedings, Clinton stood up in an effort to persuade the audience to be seated and only succeeded in inspiring an even wilder wave of enthusiasm, marked with hoots, waves and cheers. Finally, after almost five minutes of a standing ovation, the guests began to sit down, reluctantly, in order to give the ceremony a chance to proceed.

The Starr Report was clapped and stomped into the background, at least for the time being. "You make us feel like we're back in Ireland," said Mrs. Clinton, genuinely moved.

The day before, on September 10, back in Ireland, another extraordinary event had taken place that helped explain the enthusiasm of many on the south lawn that evening. The leader of the Ulster Unionist Party, David Trimble, met with the president of Sinn Fein, Gerry Adams, for one-on-one talks that lasted an hour in the old parliament buildings in Stormont near Belfast. This was the first time that such a high-ranking Irish republican had held talks with a senior Ulster Unionist since IRA leader Michael Collins met with Unionist Party chief James Craig in 1922 to try and end the sectarian violence then gripping Belfast. Trimble was First Minister in a new Northern Ireland assembly, in which Adams' party held seventeen seats. Discussions were under way about the setting up of a shadow executive that would reestablish ten different departments, allocated to the assembly parties according to their strength. Sinn Fein, the IRA's political wing, which spent twenty-five years justifying IRA attempts to physically destroy Northern Ireland, was now on the verge of entering its government.

The dubious obsessions of Ken Starr's report consumed the attention of the U.S. media at a moment of profound historic change in Ireland, a change which would not have come about without Bill Clinton—the American connection in the most powerful and decisive form it has ever taken.

By the late 1980s, the Northern Ireland stalemate seemed un-breakable. The republican movement's dual strategy of fighting elections and conducting an armed campaign was effectively con-tained, after some initial victories, including the election of Gerry Adams to Westminster. Even though Sinn Fein ended its tradi-tional policy of refusing to recognize the Dail (Irish Parliament) in 1986, it was obvious that Sinn Fein's base of support was not ex-panding outside the working-class districts of Belfast, and in some rural areas near the border. Talks opened in 1988 between Adams and the SDLP leader John Hume, to see if a way could be found to accommodate the physical-force republicans and the constitutional nationalists. Sinn Fein also looked to the U.S. to see if its support there could be expanded.

But there, the party also faced problems. A handful of Irish Americans were opposed to the new strategy. George Harrison, formerly the IRA's main arms supplier, and Thomas Falvey, who had been part of the old arms network, saw the change, of course, as a worrying sign.

They issued a statement condemning it:

> We categorically reject any move for elected representation of Sinn Fein to enter the Leinster House government, an institution im-posed on Ireland by British guns and bayonets, to serve the inter-ests of British imperialism. . . . We reaffirm our support to those who stand solidly behind the traditional Republican policy of ab-stention or boycott of all British-imposed institutions of servility and replace not reform them with Republican institutions of liber-ty and freedom.

Harrison threw his support behind Daithi O'Conaill and Ruairi O'Bradaigh who had established their own political party, Republican Sinn Fein, which held fast to the movement's original abstentionist position. Secretly, O'Conaill also set up an armed wing, the Continuity IRA, though the IRA leadership warned him not to do so. CIRA, however, would not become active until 1994.

Michael Flannery was also a supporter of O'Conaill and O'Bradaigh but remained in NORAID which he had helped found. Others broke away to set up the Friends of Irish Freedom. In 1989 Flannery joined them, and remained a member until his death in September 1994. NORAID's role continued as before, though its fund-raising abilities were reduced. Throughout the late 1980s it was remitting less than $200,000 a year to the IRA prisoners' dependents fund in Ireland, according to figures submitted to the Justice Department.

In the late 1980s Sinn Fein was eager to break out of its political isolation, both in Ireland and in the U.S. The party sent a fact-finding delegation to America in 1988 to look at the situation. Later that year, NORAID leaders were asked to attend a meeting in Dublin at which they were told that the group's efforts were too limited, and that it would have to build contacts with "progressive" organizations in the U.S. Sinn Fein's leaders felt that the group was becoming moribund. Flannery and others were unhappy with the new role. He saw NORAID as a fund-raising organization, not an extension of Sinn Fein. In 1989, he resigned and joined the Friends of Irish Freedom, which soon began to provide a forum for people identified with Republican Sinn Fein. However, it quickly became apparent that this was a rearguard action and that the momentum lay elsewhere.

A new alignment was taking place in the republican movement. As it explored ways of broadening its support, the IRA leadership was coming to the conclusion that the conflict would have to end sooner rather than later. Secret contacts opened up between the British government and the IRA in 1990. The following year, the secretary of state for Northern Ireland, Peter Brooke, made a statement declaring that Britain had "no selfish, economic or strategic interest in Northern Ireland." It would accept a united Ireland if it came about with the consent of the majority in Northern Ireland. This was an overture to the IRA, who Brooke had earlier conceded could not be defeated militarily. When Sir Patrick Mayhew replaced him in 1992, the new secretary of state reiterated Brooke's statement. He said that if the IRA's campaign of violence was called off, Sinn Fein could be included in the talks process. Behind the scenes, the contacts between the republicans and the British continued, with the IRA trying to establish the exact dimensions of any British concessions that would come if it called an end to its campaign of violence. Also in 1992, Hume began another series of exploratory talks with Sinn Fein leaders, in an effort to convince them to get the IRA to call a cease-fire.

In the meantime, Irish America was in need of some sort of morale booster. In February 1992 Joe Doherty's long struggle to stay in the U.S. ended in defeat after almost nine years of incarceration without bail, during which he fought first the British government's extradition demands and then a series of deportation attempts. The case went right up to the Supreme Court when the attorney general argued that he had it within his power to order Doherty deported without benefit of an asylum hearing. The Supreme Court ruled in the attorney general's favor. Shortly afterwards, Doherty was handed over in chains to the British authorities, much to the fury of Irish Americans who had been active in his campaign. There were riots in the New Lodge area of Belfast, where Doherty grew up, when news spread that he was being returned to prison.

The British press gloated at the decision, representing it as the British government's triumph over Irish American influence in Washington. They conveniently ignored the fact that what had prevented Doherty from being handed back to the British was not some mythical Irish American lobby, but the decisions taken by the U.S. judicial system, which at almost every step in the process ruled in his favor. Nor did they explore the legal implications for other political refugees in the U.S. The British government was delighted, of course, to get Doherty out of the U.S. where he had become something of a media figure, representing the Irish republican side of the story with an intelligence and charm that the IRA's "mad gunmen" were not supposed to possess. By March, Doherty was in the Maze Prison with his IRA colleagues to serve out his life sentence. In deference to his long American sojourn, his fellow prisoners devised a new slogan at mealtime: "French fries for Doherty, chips for everybody else."

In a move that to Doherty's supporters seemed particularly vindictive, the British government later decided that his time spent in U.S. jails would not be taken into account when deciding on how long he had left to serve of his recommended thirty-year sentence before being considered for bail hearings.

Meanwhile, another four IRA men, Pol Brennan, Jimmy Smith, Kevin Barry Artt, and Terence Kirby, all escapees from the Maze Prison during the mass breakout of September 1983, were arrested on the West Coast in 1992 and served with extradition warrants.

It was against this acrimonious background that in April 1992, Governor Bill Clinton of Arkansas, who was running for the Democratic nomination for president, agreed to attend a forum on Irish issues being held in the Sheraton Hotel in Manhattan organized by Bronx assemblyman John Dearie. California Governor Jerry Brown also attended the event. Dearie wanted to put Ulster on the presidential agenda. George Bush's administration's interest in Northern Ireland was limited to hounding Joe Doherty to make sure he was returned to Britain. Unlike Reagan, Bush did not possess even a vestige of political concern with the problem.

Dearie wanted to ensure that whoever the Democratic nominee was, he would make Northern Ireland an American issue. He was to succeed beyond his wildest imaginings.

When questioned by a panel of Irish American journalists, both Clinton and Brown (who appeared separately) committed themselves, if elected president, to putting Northern Ireland on their agendas. The issues that concerned the panel were the appointment of a special envoy to act as an intermediary in Northern Ireland; extradition; getting a visa for Gerry Adams to visit the U.S.; the MacBride Principles on fair employment; and human rights abuses on the part of the British security forces. On all of the issues, both men gave satisfactory answers and showed that they had at least taken the time to read up on the subject of the Ulster conflict. But it was Clinton's commitment to the special peace envoy that caught people's attention. When asked if elected president would he appoint one, he replied: "The short answer to your question is 'Yes.'"

Clinton's comments about appointing an envoy made headlines in the Irish newspapers the following day. Sir Patrick Mayhew, the Northern Ireland secretary of state, was not amused. "We do not need a peace envoy," he was quoted as saying. "What we need is a settlement as a result of the talks process."

The fact that Martin Galvin of Irish Northern Aid was among those who questioned the candidates greatly irritated British newspapers. He was "one of the IRA's most visible supporters in North America" as one put it.[1]

Candidate Clinton's responses convinced a cadre of Irish-American activists to form "Irish-Americans for Clinton-Gore," which played a role in winning back some Irish American support from the Republican party, where it had drifted during the Reagan years, and was to help the former governor of Arkansas become the forty-second president of the United States. However, most commentators reassured themselves that Clinton's campaign promises would be about as reliable as those of a drunk man.

Few expected a Clinton administration to act in a way that would deeply anger Britain, given the importance of the strategic relationship between them.

One observer of the Irish-American political scene said, "If he's elected, all his promises to interest groups will get snowed under. When he is reminded of his promises, the likelihood is that the State Department will ensure that they never become policy."[2]

However, with the ending of the Cold War and the collapse of the Soviet block, the balance of forces that determined the special relationship between the U.S. and Great Britain was changing. It would affect the British–U.S.–Irish alignment profoundly, though this was far from obvious in the early 1990s.

On April 9, 1992, a few days after candidate Clinton attended the Irish forum in New York, Adams lost his West Belfast seat in the British general election that returned John Major, leader of the Conservative party, to power. It was a bad blow to the Sinn Fein leader and his party in more ways than one. As Clinton settled into his presidency, his Irish-American supporters waited for him to act on his Irish commitments, especially regarding the envoy and the Adams visa. Boston Mayor Ray Flynn and former congressman Bruce Morrison who had been active on "Irish Americans For Clinton-Gore" were pressing him to fulfill promises on both issues. During the 1993 St. Patrick's Day festivities, when the Irish Taoiseach Albert Reynolds arrived in Washington, the subject of the envoy was discussed at length. John Hume met with the president over a lunch hosted by Tom Foley, the Democratic Speaker of the House. Hume came away deeply impressed with Clinton's understanding of the Northern Irish question.

"I was astounded by the depth and detail of his knowledge," Hume told reporters. "This is a major and very positive development."[3] Unfortunately, neither Reynolds nor Hume had much else to show in the way of actual U.S. policy change on Northern

Ireland. Following the mounting speculation that he would nominate Foley, who was known to be strongly against further U.S. involvement in the Northern Ireland quagmire, Clinton hesitated on the envoy issue. He said he would postpone his decision until May, much to the disappointment of his Irish-American supporters. They saw the envoy issue as the catalyst for a peace process and grew impatient at Clinton's hesitation.

Clinton was reluctant to intervene not on principle but because the Irish situation was far from clarified. The Provisional IRA campaign continued, making it difficult for any peace initiative to succeed. The president was being advised that a peace envoy would be more useful after there was an Irish initiative that looked as if it might produce results. Before such a development, any U.S. envoy dispatched to broker a deal would have difficulty in winning Unionist support, which was crucial to any settlement. Irish Americans were further disappointed when, at the beginning of May, Adams' application for a visa to come to New York was turned down.

The reason given for Adams' visa rejection was his continued support for terrorism. That is, "that he advocates or teaches . . . the duty, necessity or propriety of the unlawful assaulting or killing of any officer or officers (either of specific individuals or officers generally) of the Government of the United States or of any other organized government . . . that he has abetted and organized and/or participated in such activities." However, the administration did say that the denial was not based on a general ban of Sinn Fein members who wanted to visit the U.S. Morrison for one took some slight consolation in this as "progress." But NORAID was outraged. A spokesman declared: "How could Irish-Americans take seriously government pledges to monitor British human rights violations or religious discrimination while Sinn Fein, the party whose members are victimized, cannot be heard in the United States?"[4]

Though Adams was involved with Hume in a series of exploratory talks, he was still too closely identified with a violent campaign which in mid-1993 showed no signs of abating. Just before Clinton arrived at his decision to deny him a visa, the IRA detonated a huge bomb in the center of London, killing a press photographer. Until there was an IRA cease-fire or an assurance that serious moves were being made to bring one about, the president could not revise his policy without the risk of handing the IRA and their Irish-American supporters an enormous propaganda victory.

For Clinton it was a matter of timing. In principle he remained committed to doing something about the interminable question of Ulster. The dynamic changed as the Hume-Adams initiative continued throughout the summer of 1993. They issued a statement in September committing themselves to a peaceful and just solution. Hume claimed that the outcome of their meetings could form the basis for a permanent end to the conflict. The same month Bruce Morrison headed a delegation to Belfast on a fact-finding mission. To coincide with the visit, the IRA halted its campaign. These hopeful signs were dashed on October 23, when an IRA bomb exploded prematurely on the Protestant Shankill Road, killing ten people, including the bomber, Thomas Begley. Adams lost his temper with the head of the Belfast IRA and its chief bomb-maker, whom he blamed for jeopardizing his peace efforts.

Though the White House squashed another application for an Adams visa, events took a dramatic turn in November. It was revealed that for the past three years the British government was secretly in contact with the IRA, passing on information about the course of various political initiatives, and even allowing Sinn Fein a preview of speeches by Northern Ireland Secretary of State Sir Patrick Mayhew and Prime Minister John Major. At one point the British government's representative who met with the republican movement told it that a united Ireland was going to come about and that British efforts at marginalizing Sinn Fein had failed. This revelation clearly made it more difficult for the British to oppose others who advocated talks with Adams.

In early December 1993 another delegation from the U.S. arrived in Belfast. At its head was New Jersey lawyer Edmund Lynch and he was coming specifically to look at how the visa ban on Adams might be lifted. The RUC Special Branch closely monitored his meetings with Sinn Fein and other officials. On his return he went to Washington D.C. for a supposedly confidential meeting with Jane Holl, the Director of European Affairs on the National Security Council. Within days the Special Branch in Belfast knew what transpired. Holl told Lynch that the president had expressed interest in the Hume-Adams initiative and that the administration would reconsider its visa ban on Adams if he received another invitation to come to the U.S.

The Holl-Lynch meeting took place on December 14, the day before the Irish and British prime ministers, Albert Reynolds and John Major, made public the Downing Street Declaration. It was partly based on the Hume-Adams proposals (which were never published), modified in a way that it was hoped would not alarm Unionists. It proclaimed that Britain had no "selfish strategic or economic interest" in Northern Ireland but wanted to see peace, stability, and reconciliation established through agreement between all parties to the conflict. "The British government agree that it is for the people of the island of Ireland alone, by agreement between the two parts respectively, to exercise their right of self-determination on the basis of consent, freely and concurrently given, North and South, to bring about a united Ireland if that is their wish." It also committed the British government to allowing Sinn Fein into a talks process if the IRA ended its campaign.

It was a far cry from the republican movement's demands for a declaration of intent to withdraw, or even from its later position, apparently reiterated as part of the Hume-Adams proposals, that Britain should persuade Unionists to join a united Ireland. Both Hume and Reynolds, in chorus with Major, heralded it as the basis for a peace process. But Adams and the republicans held back from endorsing it. Instead, they requested "clarification."

The Irish government saw it as an opportunity to use U.S. influence to advance the process and pressed ahead. In the meantime, Adams was invited to speak before the National Committee on American Foreign Policy in New York City on February 1, 1994. Reynolds told the president that granting Adams a visa would help swing the IRA behind the new initiative. The new U.S. ambassador to Ireland, Jean Kennedy Smith, also proved a powerful advocate for lifting the visa ban. Kennedy Smith persuaded her brother Senator Edward Kennedy to press the administration to change its policy. The combination of forces on the Hill, added to the Irish government influence and the more hopeful developments in Northern Ireland, overcame the fierce British opposition to removing the ban. On January 29 Clinton approved a "limited duration" visa for the Sinn Fein president. Two days later, Adams arrived in New York proclaiming: "This generation of young republicans will see peace in Ireland."

For a couple of days, Adams was a celebrity. He appeared on Larry King Live, and Irish novelist Edna O'Brien wrote a gushing profile of him for the Op Ed page of the *New York Times,* comparing him to Michael Collins. (O'Brien was having something of a fling with former republican activists. Earlier, in 1993, she had struck up a relationship with Dominic "Mad Dog" McGlinchey, former leader of the Irish National Liberation Army.) But Adams' message was not what everyone in the Irish-American community wanted to hear. It was more about peace than a United Ireland. Traditionalist NORAID activists such as Martin Galvin were left out in the cold. Adams' new American friends were now people such as Bill Flynn, former CEO of Mutual of America (who had arranged his speaking engagement before the National Committee), billionaire businessman Chuck Feeney, and Niall O'Dowd, publisher of the New York weekly, the *Irish Voice.* None of them were known for their republican credentials. However, they had something more important: connections. The truth was that Sinn Fein and the republican movement were moving into a new phase in which those connections—to the corporate world and the political establishment—would be needed; the time for shaking cans for dollar bills in Bronx bars was passing. The English novelist and journalist George Orwell once defined a revolutionary as "a social climber with a bomb in his pocket." The subsequent evolution of Sinn Fein and the IRA would prove the accuracy of his definition. But first there was the little matter of the armed campaign to deal with.

Back in Northern Ireland and Britain, the IRA was still, technically speaking, at war. Not long after Adams got home it launched a mortar attack on London's Heathrow Airport. The mortars were intentionally not primed. It was a mere demonstration of what the IRA could do if it wanted. Its aim was to emphasize to the British government that if the IRA was moving towards peace it was not out of military weakness. The violence continued but at a much lower level, with loyalist paramilitary groups killing more people than the IRA. By June it was obvious to those with good sources in the republican movement that a cease-fire was coming—it was only a matter of when.

At first, the speculation was that the IRA would call a limited cease-fire, as it had in 1974–75, reserving the right to take retaliatory action for attacks on nationalists. To the Irish government, however, this was anathema. Reynolds wanted a complete cessation and nothing less. There could be no forward movement, no inclusion of Sinn Fein in the peace process unless this condition was met. "It's either all or nothing," Reynolds said.[5] On August 31 he got his wish. The IRA's leading body, the Army Council, issued a statement, 146 words long. It declared that "recognizing the potential of the current situation and in order to enhance the democratic peace process and underline our definitive commitment to its success the leadership of Oglaigh na hEireann [Irish Republican Army] have decided that as of midnight, Wednesday, 31 August, there will be a complete cessation of military operations. All our units have been instructed accordingly." The statement claimed that the republican struggle had seen "many gains and advances made by nationalists and for the democratic position. We believe that an opportunity to create a just and lasting settlement has been created. We are therefore entering into a new situation in a spirit of determination and confidence . . ."

There was jubilation in nationalist areas of Belfast and Derry. Among Protestants there was suspicion—they feared a deal with the British had been done behind their backs. "The rank and file unionists are still wondering what the hell the IRA have been given," James Molyneaux, the Unionist Party leader, commented to the Dublin *Sunday Tribune* not long after the cease-fire announcement. In Irish America, prominent figures such as Senator Kennedy welcomed it. But others asked themselves the same question as Molyneaux's: what had the IRA received in return for a cessation of violence? There was unease in the ranks of the old can-rattlers, British consulate pickets, and raffle-ticket sellers of NORAID. They recalled the promises the IRA leadership made throughout the decades that there would be no end to the armed campaign until the British declared their intention to withdraw. Yet the armed campaign had ended and the British were blatantly still there. Unease increased when Sinn Fein announced that it was opening a "Friends of Sinn Fein" office in

Washington D.C. to lobby Capitol Hill to promote the new party line and raise money. Chuck Feeney would pay the rent on the premises. Its first director was a prominent Sinn Fein party member, Mairead Keane.

On a visit to New York in September, Adams was welcomed by Mayor Giuliani, who in the mid-1980s had earned the opprobrium of Irish Americans because of his zealous prosecution of Joe Doherty. But a new politics was taking shape that would see sometimes strange alignments. Would there be a place in them for NORAID?

Support for the IRA's political violence had always kept NORAID on the margins of political life, and restricted its appeal to a handful of traditional Irish republicans and Irish American activists such as Galvin. Being marginal figures themselves, they could not broaden the republican movement's support base in the U.S. In the new circumstances, there would have to be changes.

From the very moment of the IRA's cease-fire, Galvin's shortcomings were obvious. He said that NORAID would support a resumption of the "fight for Irish freedom" if necessary. It was the wrong response, framed in terms of conflict at a time when the republican movement was moving into conflict resolution. Rumors of a split within NORAID increased when in September, *The Irish People*, NORAID'S weekly, ran a long letter from George Harrison denouncing the cease-fire as a "surrender" and a sellout. Many saw this as a deliberate slap in the face to Sinn Fein. Galvin was far from popular with some prominent figures in the republican movement such as veteran IRA man Joe Cahill, who was a member of the IRA's Army Council. Cahill was extremely sensitive to any criticism from Harrison, who had been close to him in the 1970s when he used the Harrison home as a base when making illegal visits to the U.S.

Jack Kilroy, a Cleveland lawyer, had already replaced Galvin as National Director of Publicity. There were rumors that Galvin had quarreled with Adams and would be removed as editor of *The Irish People*. Controversy deepened when a personal letter from Kilroy was made public. It accused Galvin of mismanaging *The Irish People* and insulting women in the office. Sinn Fein continued to deny there was trouble with Galvin or within NORAID. It denounced as "scurrilous" and "untrue" any reports to the contrary.

Richard McAuley, a Sinn Fein spokesman, and Adams both defended Galvin and claimed he still enjoyed the confidence of the party. Adams affirmed that Galvin had his "full backing." However, within two months, Galvin was ousted from *The Irish People*. Several of the organization's units, mainly in New York, resigned in protest or joined the Friends of Irish Freedom. At the NORAID annual conference held in New York in 1995, only seventy-five people showed up, almost none of them from the city. Galvin was further demoted and before long was off NORAID's board of directors of which he had been a member since 1979.

NORAID still survived but it was becoming increasingly redundant in the new climate. Said one Irish-American activist at the time: "NORAID do not matter if you're doing your political business through the Kennedys."[6]

The Irish People, always a big money loser, struggled along. But by the mid-1990s, Niall O'Dowd's *Irish Voice* had in effect become the Sinn Fein leadership's American mouthpiece. Its editorials promoted the party line on the peace process and other issues, and it carried a regular column by Adams. The older Irish American activists resented O'Dowd's influence bitterly. To them he was an upstart and an opportunist, with no track record as a republican; they pointed out that he had not even bothered to attend the Irish forum in April 1992 where Clinton appeared to answer questions. (The *Irish Voice* in fact endorsed Jerry Brown as the Democratic candidate.) But O'Dowd was now useful to Sinn Fein and the traditionalists were not. In the real politics of the peace process, that was what mattered.

Things were moving fast elsewhere. In October 1994 Anthony Lake, the chairman of the National Security Council, informed Adams that the prohibition on meetings between administration officials and Sinn Fein was lifted. During a trip to Washington, Adams took a telephone call from Vice President Al Gore to discuss the peace process. It was only a matter of time before he met Clinton himself. In Northern Ireland there was further good news when on October 13 the main loyalist paramilitary groups, the Ulster Volunteer Force and the Ulster Defense Association, declared a cease-fire.

In their statement the loyalists said that they were satisfied that the union with Great Britain was safe and they had been assured that no secret deal was being done with the IRA. At the end of October spokesmen for the parties representing the paramilitary organizations, the Ulster Democratic Party (UDP) for the UDA and the Progressive Unionist Party (PUP) for the UVF, came to New York and Washington at the invitation of the National Committee on American Foreign Policy, the same group whose invitation to Adams in January led to the lifting of the visa ban.

UDP leader Gary McMichael was accompanied by PUP spokesman David Ervine. In the six-man delegation was Gusty Spence, Billy Hutchinson, Joe English, and Davy Adams. Spence was a legendary figure among Ulster loyalists as the founder of the UVF, whose campaign of assassination in 1966 started the modern "Troubles." Spence served eighteen years for the murder of a Catholic barman in 1966. Before his death at the hands of the IRA in December 1987, McMichael's father John was in charge of the UDA's assassination squads. English and Adams were prominent members of the UDA. English was its chairman during one of its most violent periods. Hutchinson was a former UVF man who was convicted of murdering two Catholic half-brothers in 1974. Ervine and Adams also served time for terrorist offenses.

The six representatives of the most violent loyalist organizations in the history of Northern Ireland handled themselves before the world's media with poise and confidence, overturning the image of loyalists as inarticulate bigots. Irish Americans were for the first time exposed to the genuine voice of working-class Protestant militancy, unfiltered by polite Unionist apologetics and unwarped by the rabid religious mouthings of the Reverend Ian Paisley. They presented a view of the situation diametrically opposed to that of Adams and Irish nationalists. It was a view that Irish Americans had ignored, but they could do so no longer. They expressed that view with considerable emotion, unlike the more politically savvy Sinn Fein representatives. There was a genuine feeling from the loyalists of regret at the loss and the suffering inflicted over the years—a feeling rarely expressed by Sinn Fein with its more analytical and ideological approach.

At the same time the loyalists were adamant that they would not concede on their basic position—that Northern Ireland must remain a part of the U.K. as long as the majority wanted it. And while they were prepared to concede nationalist demands for power-sharing and some form of cross-border institutions, they insisted such institutions must not be seen as a "Trojan horse" leading to a United Ireland. "I am British. I will always be British. And I have always been British," Ervine told the hushed audience in New York. This was not the story as represented by Sinn Fein and IRA propaganda, which pushed the line that loyalists were the unwitting dupes of the British government who would embrace Irish nationalism if given the opportunity.

Throughout 1994 and 1995 the Clinton administration helped maintain the euphoria the cease-fires created. It proved much more responsive to the new situation than the British government. And it showed a willingness to defy the British government when it thought necessary. When Britain announced that Sinn Fein was not invited to take part in an investment conference it was holding in Belfast in December 1994, President Clinton's representative to the conference, Ron Brown, threatened to boycott it. The British were forced to admit the IRA's political wing. In March 1995, again against protests from Britain, Clinton said "yes" to a visa for Adams, allowing him to raise money in the U.S. On a first outing, in the Tower Ballroom in Queens, the Sinn Fein president took in $20,000. Between February and June 1995, Friends of Sinn Fein raised $900,000, a figure which would double over the next year. When the question of President Clinton's shaking hands with Adams arose, Sir Patrick Mayhew declared that "50,000,000" British people would not be pleased if Clinton did so. Yet the president shook hands with Adams on March 16, during a congressional lunch hosted by House Speaker Newt Gingrich. The gesture was, however, in private, and no photographs of the handshake were taken.

The White House 1995 St. Patrick's Day gathering was an extraordinary occasion. For the first time, Irish political leaders representing nearly every shade of opinion gathered in the nation's capital as it basked in the sunshine of an early spring. That evening, as the sunset bathed the city in vermilion, the guests assembled for a reception in the East Room. UDA chief Joe English sat with Gary McMichael a few feet away from Clinton, the First Lady, Paul Newman and his wife Joanne Woodward, and Irish Prime Minister John Bruton and his wife. A few feet behind the loyalists stood Gerry Adams, the spokesman for the organization that killed McMichael's father. Meanwhile Frank Patterson, the Irish tenor, sang "The Rose of Tralee." At the evening's end, John Hume and Adams sang a duet of "The Town I Love So Well," Phil Coulter's popular song about Derry. By that stage the loyalists had slipped away. There were no songs from their tradition at the gathering. People, while they were happy to embrace the diversity of Irish political culture, were clearly not yet ready to sing about it.

Two months later the administration played host to a Northern Ireland investment conference in an effort to shore up the political changes with economic development. In July, keeping up the momentum, Clinton announced that he would be going to Belfast at the end of the year.

In glaring contrast to Clinton, British Prime Minister John Major appeared to dither. He had greeted the cease-fire with skepticism because the declaration did not contain the word "permanent." It took his government six weeks to accept the IRA move as genuine. Then he raised the issue of the decommissioning of IRA weapons. Northern Ireland Secretary of State Sir Patrick Mayhew said some weapons would have to be destroyed or handed over before Sinn Fein and the other political representatives of the paramilitary groups could enter the talks process. The IRA rejected this out of hand. In September 1995 it stated: "There is no possibility of disarmament except as part of a negotiated settlement . . . The demand for an IRA handover of weapons is ludicrous." Republican leaders accused the British of trying to achieve a victory over the IRA, something which they had been unable to do during the twenty-five-year-long conflict. IRA leader Martin McGuinness on a trip to New York warned that if the British continued to insist on disarmament, it would jeopardize the whole peace initiative. Adams later accused the British of "subverting" peace. Then in October, the IRA's leadership body, the seven-strong Army Council, of which McGuinness and Adams were both members, met in Donegal. Over a year had passed since the cease-fire and still Sinn Fein was kept waiting at the door, unable to gain entry to the talks. They suspected Britain was deliberately prevaricating in order to undermine the IRA, knowing that the longer the organization remained inactive, the more difficult it would be for it to resume its campaign. At that meeting, the Army Council decided that, barring a sudden change in British policy, the cease-fire should end. The question was when.

At the same time, officials were making plans for Clinton's visit to Ireland, unaware of the drastic change threatening to end the peace process that the president was coming to celebrate, being more concerned about the efforts of the British and Irish governments. They were desperately trying to hammer out an agreement that would allow them to get around the decommissioning roadblock. Without such an agreement, the whole trip would be in doubt. Just eleven hours before Clinton landed in London on the first leg of his visit, both governments agreed to adapt a twin-track approach. Former U.S. Senator George Mitchell, already acting as the president's special envoy on economic matters for Northern Ireland, would be appointed chairman of an international body to look at the controversial matter of disarmament. At the same time, the talks process should be allowed to proceed, with the aim of achieving all-party negotiations by the end of February 1996. Once more, it was the pressure coming from the U.S., with the imminent arrival of Clinton, that concentrated British minds on "moving the situation forward."

Clinton arrived in Belfast on November 30, 1995. It was a clear cold morning with only a few clouds in the sky as his cavalcade drove him, the first serving U.S. president to visit Northern Ireland, into Belfast. For years, the city was the cockpit of the Ulster conflict, but now it was at the heart of the huge welcome that was awaiting the president and the First Lady. His first stop was on the loyalist Shankill Road, a judicious decision that helped win over the Protestants, who tended to be at best skeptical and at worst hostile to U.S. involvement. (To protest Clinton's allowing Adams into the U.S., a loyalist politician had slit his thumb, smeared a U.S. flag with his blood, and waved it at the U.S. Consul General's office in Belfast.) But a visit to a flower shop and a brief walkabout was all it took to turn the Shankill residents into Clinton enthusiasts.

The spontaneity and evident goodwill of the greetings energized the president throughout the day. Thousands cheered him wherever he went. On the Falls, the heart of nationalist Belfast, there was an extraordinary turnout. There he met Adams for another, this time public, handshake. He received standing ovations at a factory in West Belfast and at the Guildhall Square in Derry where he shared a platform with John Hume. The president spoke not far from where the first Provisional IRA car bomb had gone off in March 1972. That evening in Belfast, the Clintons were in front of the Christmas tree under the ornate columns and dome of the City Hall, before a huge crowd of eighty thousand people. They looked out over a sea of American flags and smiling, upturned faces. The city's lord mayor, Eric Smyth, a Protestant fundamentalist preacher, made a speech in which he began to quote from the Scriptures. The crowd booed and someone shouted good-humoredly: "Save it for Sunday, Eric." Hillary spoke and was followed by her husband, who with a child on either side of him pulled a dummy lever to light up the tree while a city council electrician sitting in a nearby hut threw the real switch. There was an enormous roar of appreciation.

"Hillary and I thank you from the bottom of our hearts for making us so welcome," Clinton told the crowd, before being whisked off to another venue. Later he said: "I will remember this day for as long as I live with great gratitude." In many ways, it was the highlight of his first term as president. He had received a welcome of the sort that was rarely accorded to him in America. For years, Clinton would fondly recall that visit as giving him one of the most memorable days in his life.

The visit was a tremendous publicity success. But it did nothing to stop the deepening crisis that behind the scenes was about to bring the IRA cease-fire to an end. Even as the president was being cheered through Belfast, in a terraced house near the Falls Road leading members of the IRA were informing a group of Irish Americans including Bruce Morrison that it was now only a matter of time before the cease-fire crumbled.

On January 24, 1996, George Mitchell's international body overseeing disarmament published its recommendations. It concluded that the disposal of weapons should not be a precondition for entry into all-party talks. Instead, the twin-track strategy should be adopted, allowing the talks to proceed while some decommissioning took place simultaneously. Major effectively rejected the report, and also added what the IRA saw as a new precondition—that elections must take place in Northern Ireland "to secure a democratic mandate" for those who wanted to join the all-party talks.

The IRA's response came sixteen days later. On February 9, a huge bomb exploded in Canary Wharf, London, killing two people. In a statement announcing that the cease-fire had ended, the IRA alleged that

> instead of embracing the peace process, the British government acted in bad faith, with Mr. Major and the Unionist leaders squandering this unprecedented opportunity to resolve the conflict. Time and again, over the last eighteen months, selfish party political and sectional interests in the London parliament have been placed before the rights of the people of Ireland . . . The resolution of the conflict in our country demands justice. It demands an inclusive negotiated settlement. That is not possible unless and until the British government faces up to its responsibilities. The blame for the failure thus far of the Irish peace process lies with John Major and his government.

In spite of the resumption of violence, Clinton refused to cut off contact with Adams. When David Trimble, the new Unionist leader who had replaced James Molyneaux in 1995, pressed him to do so, Mike McCurry, the president's spokesman, spelled out the administration's position. "Mr. Adams is an important leader in this process because he speaks for Sinn Fein. It is hard to imagine a process making progress without him." Likewise, Hume rejected calls—some from within his own party—to break off talks with Adams. However, the Sinn Fein leader did not receive an invitation to the 1996 St. Patrick's Day gathering in the White House and was privately advised not to apply for any more visas.

The renewal of the IRA's campaign was at first confined to Britain, but then spread to Northern Ireland and the continent. A bomb attack in Manchester in June 1996 injured hundreds of shoppers, and two blasts inside the British army headquarters in Lisburn, County Antrim, the following October killed a soldier. Another soldier was shot dead in South Armagh in early 1997. Two policemen were murdered in Lurgan in July. But these were all the "successes" the IRA could claim. Their attempt to renew the armed campaign proved a disastrous failure.

Three days after the Canary Wharf bombing, the police arrested an eight-man IRA unit in Belfast during an attempted robbery;

it included one of the city's top gunmen. It was an indication of things to come. During the eighteen months or so of renewed violence, the IRA's Belfast operations were rendered ineffective by the police. Belfast was the key to any IRA campaign, and the fact that it was crippled there meant that the campaign as a whole was doomed.

By the summer of 1996 the security forces had broken the IRA's bombing operations in Britain and they had scooped up most of those involved in planning the Lisburn attack. In April of 1997 undercover soldiers seized the IRA's "A" team of snipers in South Armagh, responsible for over a dozen murders. High-grade intelligence managed to contain the efforts to renew the war, especially in Belfast where the IRA was thoroughly compromised. It was only a matter of time before another cease-fire was declared. The IRA, in effect defeated, waited for an opportunity. The May 1997 British general election saw Tony Blair and the Labour party sweep into power with a massive 171-seat majority, driving out the Conservative party after eighteen years in government. Adams also retook his West Belfast seat and Martin McGuinness won Mid-Ulster for Sinn Fein. The party saw its vote rise to over 17 percent—the highest ever.

The new government brought fresh energy to the problem. It assured Sinn Fein that if there was another IRA cease-fire it would not block its entry into the talks process. On July 20 the IRA announced an end to the campaign. Seven weeks later, on September 15, Sinn Fein formally joined the talks. For the moment, the problem of decommissioning was set aside. Blair and his newly appointed secretary of state for Northern Ireland, Mo Mowlam, set Easter 1998 as the deadline for achieving a settlement—an ambitious timetable that most thought could not be met.

In Blair, Clinton found a political leader with whom he could do business. The men liked each other. Both were pragmatists, willing to abandon or revise long-cherished ideological positions if necessary, eager to reestablish their respective parties as parties of government through recapturing the political center. There had been a real antagonism between Major and the president since the time when the Conservative party leader dispatched advisers in a failed effort to help President Bush win reelection. Relations between Clinton and Major were fraught. After Clinton granted Adams a visa to raise funds, for instance, the British prime minister went into a huff and refused to return the president's calls for five days.

That antagonism was replaced now with a common purpose. Blair recognized and did not resent Clinton's role in settling the Ulster conflict. An indication of the new situation was the appointment of Mo Mowlam as Northern Ireland secretary of state. She was at the opposite pole from Sir Patrick Mayhew, her predecessor. Bluff, good-humored, down-to-earth, and approachable, she was perhaps the first secretary of state that the British could send to talk to Irish Americans without the risk of antagonizing them.

The centrality of the administration's role was emphasized with the appointment of George Mitchell as the chairman of the all-party talks, which began in 1998 with the aim of reaching a final settlement by April 10. As former majority leader of the Senate, all his negotiating skills, and even more, his patience, would be put to the test over the difficult weeks that lay ahead. There were immediate problems. Trimble, the brash, intelligent, but somewhat irascible new Unionist Party chief, swore he would not meet face to face with Adams until the IRA began to disarm. During the entire period of negotiations, the two party leaders never actually met. Mitchell acted as a go-between. Disarmament remained the main stumbling block, with the Ulster Unionists insisting that the paramilitaries hand over or destroy at least a token number of weapons before their political representatives be allowed to take their seats in any future government.

The Irish and British governments knew that this would threaten the very existence of the republican and loyalist cease-fires. Instead, they tried to persuade Trimble to accept a commitment written into the agreement that the paramilitary spokesmen would do all in their power to influence their organizations to begin the process of disarmament which would have to be completed by the year 2000. Trimble wavered. At one point Blair was forced to physically block his path to stop him walking out on the negotiations.

At 11 P.M. (U.S. time) on April 9—just hours before the deadline—Blair telephoned Clinton and asked for his help in persuading the recalcitrant Unionists and republicans to reach a compromise. The president took his call and manned the telephone into the early hours of the morning. After a brief rest he rose again at 5 a.m. Clinton spoke with each of the party leaders on the telephone, concentrating on Adams and Trimble. The Sinn Fein leader was reassured that Washington would give attention to the matter of prisoners and policing; Trimble was told that the contentious problem of disarmament would not be ignored. Agreement was reached. On Good Friday, April 15, it was signed, giving Northern Ireland a power-sharing executive assembly, with provisions for the creation of cross-border institutions and a commitment to take the gun out of Ulster politics for the first time this century. Before the signing, Trimble's closest colleague, Jeffrey Donaldson, walked out in protest at his leader's change of course on disarmament. The Unionist Party was effectively split down the middle on the issue, a fact which would constrain Trimble in the coming months.

Elections to the new assembly were held, and then joint referenda North and South at which the population of Ireland overwhelmingly endorsed the new arrangement

Many problems remained. Nationalists and Unionists had sharply divergent views on what to do with the Northern Ireland police force, the Royal Ulster Constabulary. Nationalists demanded drastic overhauls, even disbandment, while Unionists saw the force as an institution that had to be protected. A shadow executive was supposed to have been established by the fall of 1998. But once more the controversy over disarmament prevented Unionists and republicans from agreeing, with Trimble demanding that the IRA offer some token gesture before Sinn Fein be assigned seats in the governing body, which was due to take office in February 1999. There was some unease at first over the release of paramilitary prisoners. But by December 1998 over two hundred of the four hundred or so being held were free, among them Joe Doherty. He had spent over fifteen years in jail.

For some, however, violence remained an option. The Orange marches were still a flash point for trouble, especially in Armagh where a local Orange parade from Drumcree near Portadown goes past a Catholic neighborhood each July 6, sparking dangerous confrontations. They have spilled over into widespread sectarian violence during Ulster's marching season. As well, the IRA lost some of its leaders, who defected to set up their own "Real" IRA in late 1997. They relaunched a campaign of terror the following year. In early 1998 their political representatives, calling themselves the 32-County Sovereignty Committee, came to New York appealing for support and accusing the Sinn Fein leadership of selling out republican ideals. What little response they received was drastically reduced when on August 15, 1998, the RIRA exploded a huge bomb in the market town of Omagh, killing twenty-nine people. The massacre—the worst incident in the whole history of the Troubles—was a devastating blow to the hard-line republicans, and a horrifying reminder of the kind of alternative they were offering to compromise and negotiation. The "Real" IRA subsequently called a cease-fire. By late 1998 only the armed wing of Republican Sinn Fein, the Continuity IRA, remained obdurate. (It had even received a small supply of weapons from the U.S. in 1997—a few MAC-10 machine pistols.) But it was clear that neither the CIRA or other dissident republicans possessed the power or the support to wage a sustained terrorist campaign. Ireland, North and South, was setting out along a new road.

Five months later, on September 11, 1998, the day after Trimble and Adams met for their first face-to-face discussions, the guests gathered on the White House lawn heard Mitchell declare: "I was there from the first day [of the talks] to the last. There would not have been a peace agreement in Northern Ireland without the efforts of Bill Clinton."

The age of the rebel was over. And the American connection, which for so long had sustained it, helped bring it to an end. And even these developments were a matter for comment and controversy.

Chronology of Events

IRELAND	UNITED STATES
1967	
Civil Rights Association formed in Northern Ireland. (February)	
1968	
Civil-rights marchers attacked by police. (October 5)	Civil-rights support groups formed. American Congress for Irish Freedom formed.
1969	
Riots escalate. British troops intervene. (August 14–15)	Harrison network moves carbines collected in early 1960s to Northern Ireland. Mick Flannery forms Irish Action Committee.
1970	
IRA and Sinn Fein split into Provisional and Official factions. Serious confrontations between Catholics and British troops. (July)	Leading IRA men Daithi O'Conaill and Joe Cahill arrive in U.S. Meet with Flannery and help set up Irish Northern Aid Committee. Meet with Harrison and Cotter, reactivate arms network. (January–April)

(Continued)
IRELAND   **UNITED STATES**

1970

NORAID holds big demonstration near U.N. (July 10)
FBI begins surveillance of NORAID.

1971

IRA shoot dead a British soldier in Belfast. (February)
Internment without trial is introduced. (August 9)

NORAID registers under FARA as an agent of Northern Aid Committee in Belfast. (January)
Harrison network acquires weapons including first Armalites and first M-16 rifle for IRA.
Senator Kennedy and Congressman Hugh Carey condemn British actions. (October)

1972

Bloody Sunday. Thirteen protesters shot dead. (January 30)
IRA grows in strength. Forms "no-go" areas throughout Catholic districts. Kills over 100 soldiers in one year.
Stormont Parliament suspended; direct rule imposed by British. Protestant extremists set up assassination campaign against Catholics. (March)
IRA holds talks with British government. Ceasefire established. (June)
Ceasefire collapses. IRA launches massive bombing campaign. Many civilians die. (July)

Biaggi dispatches observer to Northern Ireland.
Massive NORAID demonstration in New York. (February)
U.S. Congress holds hearings on Northern Ireland.
Five NORAID members from New York subpoenaed by Texas grand jury investigating illegal arms trafficking.
NORAID reports collecting $313,000 in six-month period after Bloody Sunday—largest amount so far.

(Continued)
IRELAND

1973

First Protestants interned. (February)
Sunningdale Agreement signed providing for a power-sharing government involving Catholics for the first time. (December)

UNITED STATES

NORAID holds first of yearly fundraising testimonial dinners in New York City. Claims over 70 units throughout U.S. (January)
FBI steps up its investigation of NORAID. Says Irish problem "has become . . . a source of embarrassment to the United States."
Interagency meeting held to discuss ways of alleviating Irish problem in U.S. (September 26). Harrison network firmly established. 200-300 weapons a year being sent to IRA; many smuggled from Camp Le Jeune, North Carolina, by George De Meo.
Irish National Caucus formed to lobby for IRA-Sinn Fein in Washington.

1974

Power-sharing government takes office. (January)
In general election in Britain, Protestant Unionists reject powersharing initiative. (February)
Protestant paramilitaries organize work stoppage to protest Sunningdale Agreement. Set off car bombs in south of Ireland, killing over 30 people. Power-sharing government falls. (May)
IRA starts bombing campaign in U.K. Birmingham pubs bombed; many die. (October-November)

Irish National Caucus active in support of IRA, including some NORAID activists. Five arrested and charged with conspiring to smuggle arms to IRA. Assistant attorney general asks FBI to "make all efforts" to halt arms and funding going to IRA.
NORAID's returns show a sharp decline from mid-1970s onward.

(Continued)
IRELAND   **UNITED STATES**

1974

IRA-British make contact on truce
  proposals. (December)

1975

Tentative truce between IRA and   IRA–Sinn Fein leaders refused
  British. (January)   visas to enter U.S.
Many sectarian killings. IRA retal-   Congressman Biaggi arrives in
  iates against Protestants. (April)   Dublin on a INC-sponsored tour.
IRA truce breaks down. (August)   Holds a press conference with
                                             prominent IRA–Sinn Fein lead-
                                             ers. Commits himself to lifting
                                             visa restrictions on IRA–Sinn
                                             Fein speakers. (April)
                                           Harrison network gets massive
                                             arms deal: 200 rifles plus 150,000
                                             rounds of ammunition.
                                           Yearly NORAID returns fall below
                                             $200,000 for first time.

1976

Sectarian killings reach peak. Ten   Harrison's colleague, Liam Cotter,
  Protestants murdered by IRA.   killed in New York. (April)
  (January)   Big raid on an armory in Danvers,
British abolish political status for   Massachusetts. M-60 machine
  paramilitaries in Northern   guns in haul.
  Ireland's prisons. (March 1)   Presidential candidate Jimmy
First IRA prisoner begins protest   Carter meets Caucus leaders.
  to restore political status.   (November)
  (September 13)   Justice Department files suit
Irish government launches diplo-   against NORAID under FARA.
  matic campaign in Washington.
  Contacts made with O'Neill,
  Kennedy, Moynihan, and Carey.

(Continued)
IRELAND

UNITED STATES

1977

Younger Northern leadership gains influence in IRA.

Undercover British antiterrorist units become active. IRA reorganized into "cell" structure.

IRA prison protests to return political status continue: prisoners refuse to wear prison clothes.

IRA continues campaign against prison officers.

M-60s arrive in Ireland. (September)

Tip O'Neill becomes House Speaker. Big Four issue first St. Patrick's Day statement condemning IRA violence and its Irish-American supporters. (March)

O'Neill meets with Carter aides to discuss possible initiative in Northern Ireland. (April)

Harrison network acquires seven M-60s from Boston contacts. Six M-60s shipped to Ireland. (July)

Carter initiative offering aid if a solution is reached. (August 30)

Mario Biaggi forms Ad Hoc Committee on Ireland. (September)

1978

IRA unveils M-60. (January)

Prison protests against removal of political status intensify. (June)

Amnesty International condemns police abuse of IRA suspects. (June)

Letter of rebuke from Irish prime minister Jack Lynch to Biaggi made public. (February) Biaggi attacked by press.

Prime Minister Lynch comes to U.S.

Big Four issue second St. Patrick's Day statement calling on Irish Americans to condemn men of violence. (March 17)

Sean Donlon appointed Irish Ambassador to Washington.

Irish rebel fugitive Peter McMullen served with extradition warrant; first in 75 years.

(Continued)
IRELAND   **UNITED STATES**

1979

Airey Neave, Margaret Thatcher's Northern Ireland spokesman, killed by saboteurs of the Irish National Liberation Army. (March) Thatcher later elected prime minister.

IRA intensifies campaign, kills 18 British soldiers in an attack and assassinates Lord Mountbatten same day. (August)

Prison protests draw more support.

Irish police capture arms haul in Dublin. Find identification marks on some guns not removed. (November)

Big Four issue statement critical of continued British intransigence. (March 17)

Magistrate rejects McMullen extradition invoking political-exception defense. (May)

Mario Biaggi succeeds in getting House to impose ban on arms sales to Northern Ireland police force (RUC). (July)

Biaggi's Peace Forum fails. (Autumn)

Harrison arranges major arms deal: over 150 weapons and 60,000 rounds of ammunition leave New York. (Autumn) Arrive Dublin. (October–November)

Major inquiry begins. Leads to George De Meo.

1980

Prison protest intensifies.

IRA prisoners go on hunger strike. (October) Called off. (December)

George De Meo convicted. Sentenced to 10 years on arms charges.

Donlon active in Washington lobbying against Biaggi. Attempts by new Irish prime minister Charles Haughey to remove him fail when Big Four say he is essential to their efforts. Their St. Patrick's Day statement once again condemns British lack of progress in Northern Ireland. (March)

De Meo approaches justice Department with deal. (August)

(Continued)
IRELAND

UNITED STATES

1980

IRA man Dessie Mackin arrested in New York and served with extradition warrant. (October)

1981

Bobby Sands begins hunger strike. (March 1)
Protests grow in support of Sands.
Sands elected member of Parliament for Fermanagh, South Tyrone, in by-election. (April 10) But Thatcher refuses to concede.
Sands dies after 66 days without food. (May 5) Northern Ireland very tense.
Francis Hughes dies on hunger strike. (May 12) Widespread violence throughout Northern Ireland.
Ray McCreesh and Patsy O'Hara (INLA) die. (May 21)
Irish Prime Minister Charles Haughey appeals to Reagan to intervene with Thatcher. General election in Ireland. Haughey's party loses two seats to prisoner-candidates. Garret Fitzgerald's coalition government elected. (June)
Joe McDonnell dies. (July 8)
Martin Huson dies. (July 13)
Kevin Lynch (INLA) dies. (August 1)
Kieran Doherty dies. (August 2)
Thomas McElwee dies. (August 8)

Donlon establishes important links with incoming Reagan administration.
Reagan visits Irish embassy on St. Patrick's Day.
Mackin extradition case heard in New York. (March)
Huge crowds gather outside British consulate in New York in support of Sands.
De Meo sets up phoney arms deal with Harrison.
U.S. court demands NORAID file as agent of IRA. NORAID appeals.
De Meo introduces Harrison and Falvey to "White." (May 17) Told major arms deal possible.
Prince Charles in New York, at Lincoln Center, met by thousands of protesters.
George Harrison and Tom Falvey arrested after making arms deal with "White." (June 19)
NORAID organizes hunger-strike relatives tour of U.S.
New York magistrate rejects extradition warrant for Mackin. (August 13)
William Quinn arrested and served with extradition warrant. First

(Continued)

IRELAND	UNITED STATES

1981

Owen Carron of Sinn Fein elected to Sands's old constituency.
Hunger strike called off. (September)
Sean Donlon appointed head of Foreign Affairs Department.

U.S. citizen to face extradition for involvement in Irish political violence. (September)
Bills go before House aimed at "modernizing extradition law." Government's appeal against Mackin decision rejected. Mackin leaves for Ireland. (December 30)

1982

General election in South— Haughey reelected. (February)
British announce plans for new assembly in Northern Ireland. (April)
IRA resumes bombing campaign in England. (July)
Sinn Fein wins five seats in Assembly elections. (October)
General election in South brings Fitzgerald back to power. (November)
First of major "supergrass" trials begins with former IRA man Christopher Black as only witness. (December)

Haughey guest at White House. (March 17)
Quinn case heard before magistrate in San Francisco. (March)
Magistrate orders Quinn to be extradited. Writ of habeas corpus issued. (September)
Trial of Harrison, Falvey, Flannery, Mullins, and Gormley begins in Brooklyn. (October)
All five found not guilty. (November 5)

1983

Irish nationalist leaders meet to consider setting up New Ireland Forum to discuss future of Northern Ireland. (April)
Forum meets. (May 30)

In their St. Patrick's Day statement, the Big Four call for face-to-face negotiations between Dublin and London. (March 17)
IRA man Joe Doherty arrested in

(Continued)
IRELAND

UNITED STATES

1983

Thatcher holds Westminster elections. Sinn Fein win one seat and over 100,000 votes. (June)
In Supergrass Black trial, 35 convicted. (August)
Irish Forum meets throughout autumn. Protestant politicians refuse to attend.
IRA bombs go off in London. (December)

New York and served with extradition warrant. (June 18)
Federal judge Aguilar overturns Quinn decision. (October)
Justice Department threatens to sue NORAID for noncompliance under FARA. (November)

1984

New Ireland Forum report issued. Offers three options: United Ireland, with federal, state, or joint authority over Northern Ireland.
Irish authorities intercept IRA arms shipment from U.S. off coast of Ireland. (September)
IRA bomb Conservative party hotel. (November)
Thatcher rejects Forum report findings. (November)

Doherty extradition hearings begin. State Department expresses alarm if political offense exception is granted. (March)
Belfast man Jim Barr arrested in Philadelphia. Served with extradition warrant on evidence of supergrass Harry Kirkpatrick.
President Reagan visits Ireland. (June)
Democratic party calls for a United Ireland in election platform. State Department denies visa to Gerry Adams, Sinn Fein president and member of Parliament for West Belfast. (July)
NORAID forced to register under FARA as agent of IRA. (August)
In presidential election, Reagan wins 55% of Catholic vote. (November)
Reagan tells Thatcher of U.S. unhappiness over lack of progress in Northern Ireland. (December)

(Continued)
IRELAND   **UNITED STATES**

1984

Federal judge rejects extradition warrant for Joe Doherty. (December 12)

1985

IRA mortar attack kills nine Northern Ireland policemen. (February)

Rumors spread that Dublin-London talks are nearing important initiative.

In local elections, Sinn Fein win 11% of Catholic vote. (May)

Irish Foreign Secretary Peter Barry says "disastrous" if London-Dublin talks fail (July)

Protestant Unionists threaten to oppose any Dublin-London settlement.

Irish Prime Minister Garret Fitzgerald and British Prime Minister Margaret Thatcher sign Anglo-Irish agreement, giving Dublin a say in running of Northern Ireland for first time and recognizing Unionists' right to remain within U.K. (November 15)

Huge Unionist rally to protest agreement. Protestants swear defiance.

Figures for 1985 show IRA violence lowest in 15 years.

Thatcher addresses joint session of Congress. Makes conciliatory remarks on Northern Ireland. (February)

Behind-the-scenes contacts between Irish officials and Reagan administration officials to gather U.S. support for a London-Dublin initiative.

Reagan administration signs new extradition bill with U.K., removing violent acts from scope of political-exception defense. (June)

First Senate hearings on new U.S.U.K. extradition treaty. (August)

Second hearings on treaty hear objections. (September)

Third hearings on treaty leave matter unresolved. (November)

Reagan and Speaker O'Neill jointly issue statements in support of Anglo-Irish Agreement. Reagan, quoting Carter's 1977 statement, promises aid. (November 15)

(Continued)
IRELAND

UNITED STATES

1986

Protestant protests continue.
Anglo-Irish Secretariat set up outside Belfast. (January)
Election shows decline in Sinn Fein vote. (January)
Widespread disruptions throughout Northern Ireland. British refuse to back down. (March)
Sinn Fein recognizes Dail (Irish Parliament). (November)
Ruairi O'Bradaigh forms Republican Sinn Fein. (November)

Ninth Circuit Court of Appeals overrules judge Aguilar's 1983 decision on Quinn and holds former IRA man extraditable. (February 18)
Congress approves aid bill for Northern Ireland. (March)
U.S. Senate ratifies new extradition treaty with Great Britain making extradition of IRA fugitives easier. (July 17)

1990

Margaret Thatcher replaced as leader of Conservative party by John Major. (November)
New Northern Ireland Secretary Peter Brooke says Britain has no "selfish" economic or strategic interest in Northern Ireland. (December)

1991

Brooke Talks begin in Belfast. (April)
Talks unfold. Wave of violence sweeps Northern Ireland. (July 4)

Joe Doherty case reaches Supreme Court. (October)

(Continued)

IRELAND	UNITED STATES

1992

Massive car bomb in London kills three. (April 10)

Supreme Court rules against Doherty. (January)

Doherty deported to Belfast. (February 26)

Democratic presidential hopeful Bill Clinton tells Irish political forum in New York City that there will be "no more Joe Dohertys" if he's elected, and commits to appointing a Special Envoy to Northern Ireland as well as reviewing visa ban on Sinn Fein president Gerry Adams. (April 5)

1993

It is revealed that SDLP leader John Hume and Gerry Adams have been involved in talks aimed at ending violence. (April)

Truck bomb in London kills one. (April 24)

IRA bomb kills ten on Protestants' Shankill Road. Loyalist retaliations leave many dead. (October 23)

It is revealed that the British government has been holding secret talks with the IRA and Sinn Fein. (November)

Downing Street Declaration by British and Irish Governments. (December 15)

Clinton inaugurated as president. (January)

Adams again refused a visa to come to U.S. Clinton also says Special Envoy on hold. (May)

U.S. delegation in Belfast to look at visa ban. Clinton administration reconsidering ban. (December)

(Continued)
IRELAND

1994

Speculation about IRA cease-fire mounts but violence continues. (June)

Loyalist paramilitaries call cease-fire. Loyalist delegations travel to New York. (October 13)

Major accepts that IRA cease-fire is genuine but insists on disarmament before all-party talks. (December)

IRA announces cessation of violence. (August 31)

1995

Irish and British governments publish Framework Document outlining plans for settlement involving a new power-sharing assembly and cross-border bodies. (February 22)

Secretary of State for Northern Ireland Sir Patrick Mayhew demands the decommissioning of weapons before paramilitaries be allowed into talks. (March 7)

Adams rejects British demands for disarmament. (June)

Serious sectarian confrontations erupt around Orange march in Drumcree, Co. Armagh. (July)

IRA leader Martin McGuinness warns that peace process is in danger. (September)

UNITED STATES

Adams visa ban lifted. He travels to New York. (January 29)

Clinton administration announces it is removing bar on meeting with Sinn Fein officials. (October 3)

President Clinton allows Sinn Fein representatives to fundraise in U.S.; shakes hands with Adams at St. Patrick's Day event in Washington. (March 16)

Administration hosts Northern Ireland investment conference in Washington. (May)

Clinton becomes first U.S. president to visit Northern Ireland. (November 30)

(Continued)

IRELAND	**UNITED STATES**

1995

At secret meeting IRA leaders decide to end cease-fire unless Britain drops demand for disarmament. (October)

British agree to set up panel chaired by former Senator George Mitchell to look at decommissioning problem, adopting twin-track strategy. (November 28)

1996

Huge bomb explodes in London as IRA announces end of cease-fire, blaming Britain for undermining peace process. (February 9)

Sectarian confrontations at Drumcree lead to province-wide violence. New group called Loyalist Volunteer Force kills Catholic and threatens more sectarian attacks. (July 6)

IRA units in Britain arrested. (July–September)

Bombs kill one soldier at British Army HQ in Lisburn, Northern Ireland. (October 7)

IRA intelligence-gathering unit broken up in Belfast. (November)

Attacks resume in Belfast, but IRA campaign falters. (December)

Mitchell committee recommends that disposal of weapons should not be a precondition for all-party talks but the two should go on parallel tracks. Major effectively rejects recommendations. Calls for elections to peace forum. (January 24)

(Continued)

1997

British soldier shot dead by IRA sniper in South Armagh. (February 13)

British arrest IRA sniping unit in South Armagh. (April 13)

British Labour Party wins crushing victory over Conservatives. Tony Blair becomes new prime minister and appoints Mo Mowlam as Secretary of State for Northern Ireland. Says no bar to Sinn Fein taking part in talks once cease-fire is called. (May)

IRA resumes cease-fire. (July 20)

Sinn Fein enters talks. April 9, 1998, set as deadline for settlement. (September 15)

Dissident IRA and Sinn Fein members break away. (November)

32-County Sovereignty Committee emerges, attacking Sinn Fein's role in peace process. Bobby Sands' sister Bernadette Sands-McKevitt is vice-president. (December)

LVF leader Billy "King Rat" Wright assassinated in Maze Prison by INLA gunmen. Sectarian violence grips Northern Ireland. (December 27)

1998

Dissident republicans attempt to smuggle bomb to England. Violence continues in Northern Ireland. (January)

Sinn Fein suspended from talks because of IRA attacks. Peace process threatened. (February)

Mortar attacks by dissident IRA men on police station; another attempt to bomb England fails. Talks continue but Ulster Unionist leader David Trimble refuses face-to-face negotiations with Sinn Fein. (March)

Talks on verge of collapse after Mitchell's outline of possible settlement rejected by Unionists. (April)

Clinton intervenes. (April 9)

Agreement reached by all parties to the talks on Good Friday, April 10. (April 10)

Referenda on agreement held North and South shows it has overwhelming support. Sinn Fein announces it will take its seats in new Northern Ireland assembly. A group calling itself the Real IRA emerges, threatening violence. (May)

Elections for new assembly give pro-agreement parties a majority. (June)

Three young brothers burned to death by loyalist petrol bombers during Drumcree confrontation. LVF calls cease-fire. (July 12)

Continued)

Real IRA bomb kills 29 people in Omagh, Co. Tyrone. Soon afterwards, it calls a cease-fire, as does INLA. (August 15)

1998

Adams categorically condemns Omagh massacre. (September 1)
Adams meets Trimble. This is the first meeting between Sinn Fein
and the Unionist Party since 1922. (September 11)
It is announced that John Hume and David Trimble will share 1998
Nobel Peace Prize. (October 16)
Joe Doherty is one of the paramilitary prisoners being freed as part
of Good Friday Agreement. (November 6)
Negotiations finally produce agreement on form of executive for
new government. LVF decommissions some weapons. (December
18)

1999

Mowlam announces that Britain will hand over powers to new
Northern Ireland government on March 10. (January 13)

Notes

1. Ireland's Arcadians

[1] W. H. Auden, "Dingley Dell and the Fleet," in *The Dyer's Hand* (London: Faber and Faber, 1963; New York: Random House, 1968).

[2] Thomas Brown, *Irish American Nationalism* (Philadelphia: Lippincott, 1966).

[3] *ibid.*

[4] *ibid.*

[5] Lawrence McCaffrey, *The Irish Diaspora in America* (Washington, D.C.: The Catholic University of America Press, 1984).

[6] Denis Donoghue, "The American Imagination," in *America and Ireland: 1776–1976,* David Noel Doyle and Owen Dudley Edwards, eds. (Westport, Conn.: Greenwood Press, 1980).

[7] John Devoy, *Recollections of an Irish Rebel* (Shannon: Irish University Press, 1969).

[8] *ibid.*

[9] Auden, *op. cit.*

[10] From "Pearse's Graveside Oration," in *Irish Historical Pamphlet 2* (1982), Kevin McEneaney, ed.

[11] *ibid*

[12] McCaffrey, *op. cit*

[13] Brown, *op. cit.*

[14] *ibid.*

[15] *ibid.*

[16] *ibid.*

[17] Devoy, *op. cit.*

[18] *ibid.*

[19] Sean Cronin, *The McGarrity Papers,* (Tralee, County Kerry: Anvil Books, 1972).

[20] *ibid.*

[21] Tim Pat Coogan, *The IRA* (Boulder: Roberts Rinehart, 1994).

[22] Cronin, *op. cit.*

[23] Cronin, *op. cit.*

[24] Paul O'Dwyer, *Counsel for the Defense* (New York: Simon and Schuster, 1979).

[25] Dennis Clark, *Irish Blood* (Port Washington, N.Y.: Kennikat Press, 1977).

[26] Clark, *op. cit.*

[27] McCaffrey, *op. cit.*

[28] *ibid.*

2. NORAID and the Northern Crisis

[1] The source for all quotes from FBI memos is file 97-5299, defendant's evidence, presented by the American Civil Liberties Union (ACLU) in the case of *The Attorney of the United States* vs. *The Irish People, Inc.*

[2] Dennis Clark, *Irish Blood.*

[3] ACLU, op. *cit.*
[4] *ibid.*
[5] *ibid.*
[6] Paul O'Dwyer, *Counsel for the Defense.*
[7] *ibid.*
[8] *ibid.*
[9] Clark, *op. cit.*
[10] *New York Times,* December 16, 1986.

[11] ACLU, *op. cit.*
[12] *ibid.*
[13] *ibid.*
[14] *An Phoblacht,* November 7, 1985.
[15] Los Angeles Times, February 2, 1981.
[16] *ibid.*

3. Of Arms and the Man

[1] Sean Cronin, *The McGarrity Papers.*
[2] *ibid.*
[3] Tim Pat Cooper, *The IRA.*
[4] *ibid.*
[5] From *The Report of the European* Commission on Human Rights, Appendix C (X). Published 1976.
[6] *New York Times,* September 26, 1985.
[7] *ibid.*

4. Congressional Conscience

[1] *Irish People,* October 4, 1975.
[2] *ibid.,* August 9, 1974.
[3] *ibid.,* November 24, 1979.

5. Northern Ireland on Trial

[1] *Magistrates Memorandum Decision,* May 11, 1979.
[2] *The Friendly Opinion,* United States Court of Appeals, Second Circuit.
[3] *New York Times,* October 26, 1983.
[4] *Matter of Doherty by Government of the United Kingdom,* 559F, Supp. 270, footnote 6.
[5] This and following quotes from *Matter of Doherty by Government of the United Kingdom,* 599F, Supp. 270.
[6] *Memorandum of Law in Support of Government's Motion for Summary Judgment.*
[7] *Defendant's Memorandum to Dismus,*
[8] *The Government's Motion to Dismus.*
[9] United States Court of Appeals for the Second Circuit, Docket no. 83-6248.
[10] *New York Times,* December 30, 1985.
[11] Statement of Lowell Jensen before the Senate Foreign Relations Committee.
[12] *Washington Post,* October 23, 1985.

6. Covering the Northern Crisis

[1] *New York Times,* August 16, 1969.

[2] *Time,* February 19, 1973.

[3] *ibid.,* June 10, 1974.

[4] *New York Times,* December 10, 1972.

[5] *Boston Globe,* July 21, 1977.

[6] *New York Times,* February 3, 1972.

[7] *ibid.,* March 24, 1973.

[8] *Time,* November 25, 1985.

[9] *New York Times,* July 12, 1972.

[10] *Boston Globe,* July 23, 1972.

[11] *Time,* June 10, 1974.

[12] *New York Times,* January 21, 1973.

[13] *ibid.,* August 11, 1971.

[14] *ibid.*

[15] *ibid.,* August 12, 1971.

[16] *ibid.,* February 1, 1972.

[17] San Francisco Chronicle, February 1, 1972.

[18] *Chicago Tribune,* January 31, 1972.

[19] *Chicago Daily News,* February 1, 1972.

[20] New York *Daily News,* December 4, 1972.

[21] *ibid,* February 23,1973.

[22] AP, *New York Times,* May 14, 1973.

[23] *New York Times,* May 8, 1978.

[24] *Los Angeles Times,* Jan. 7, 1976.

[25] *ibid.,* May 6, 1979.

[26] *New York Times,* December 10, 1972.

[27] *Los Angeles Times,* July 24, 1972.

[28] *Boston Globe,* July 23, 1972.

[29] *Christian Science Monitor,* June 6, 1975.

[30] AP, November 19, 1973.

[31] Reuters, July 8, 1972.

[32] *New York Times,* July 14, 1972.

[33] New York *Daily News,* July 8, 1973.

[34] *New York Times,* March 10, 1985.

[35] *Wall Street Journal,* February 8, 1973.

[36] *Time,* November 4, 1974.

[37] *Christian Science Monitor,* February 27, 1975.

[38] AP, December 6, 1972.

[39] *Newsweek,* December 18, 1972.

[40] *New York Times,* May 19, 1974.

[41] *ibid.,* May 20, 1974.

[42] *ibid.,* September 6, 1976.

[43] New York *Daily News,* September 6, 1976.

[44] *San Francisco Examiner,* January 18, 1978.

[45] *San Francisco Chronicle,* January 19, 1978.

[46] *Washington Star,* February 22, 1978.

[47] *Baltimore Sun,* February 24, 1978.

[48] *Irish Echo,* March 4, 1978.

[49] *Manchester Union-Leader,* May 9, 1978.

[50] *New York Times,* December 14, 1984.

[51] New York *Daily News,* December 14, 1984.

[52] *New York Post,* December 14, 1984,

[53] *San Francisco Chronicle,* December 14, 1984.

[54] New York *Daily News,* December 16, 1984.

[55] *New York Post,* December 18, 1984.

[56] *ibid.,* December 27, 1984.

[57] *Chicago* Tribune,Januarv 11, 1985.

[58] *New York Times,* December 19, 1984.

[59] *Philadelphia Daily News,* December 19, 1984.

[60] *Irish Echo,* December 29, 1984.

[61] *National Law Journal,* December 31, 1984.
[62] *New York Times,* July 11, 1985.
[63] *Washington Post,* November 3, 1985.
[64] *Daily Item,* April 1, 1977.
[65] New York *Daily News,* April 27, 1977.
[66] *ibid.,* April 27, 1977.
[67] *New York Times,* May 6, 1981
[68] *New York Post,* May 6, 1981.
[69] *New York Times,* May 10, 1981
[70] *Chicago Tribune,* May 19, 1984.
[71] *Chicago Tribune,* November 27, 1984.

[72] *San Francisco Examiner,* November 26, 1984.
[73] *New York Times,* November 24, 1984.
[74] *Washington Post,* November 24, 1984.
[75] *Boston Globe,* November 27, 1984.
[76] *Los Angeles Times,* October 21, 1985.
[77] *Time,* January 29, 1973.
[78] *ibid.,* February 19, 1973.
[79] *New York Times,* May 28, 1973.

7. Conclusion

[1] Thomas Brown, "The Political Irish: Politics and Rebels," in *America and Ireland: 1776–1976,* David Noel Doyle and Owen Dudley Edwards, eds.

8. Afterword

[1] *Independent,* October 22, 1992.
[2] *ibid.,* October 22, 1992.
[3] *Irish Times,* March 18, 1993.
[4] *Irish Times,* May 13, 1993.
[5] Conor O'Clery, *Daring Diplomacy: Clinton's Secret Search for Peace in Ireland* (Boulder: Roberts Rinehart, 1997).
[6] *Irish Echo,* September 27, 1994.

Bibliography

Auden, W. H., *The Dyer's Hand and Other Essays,* Faber and Faber, 1963; Random House, 1968.

Brown, Thomas, *Irish American Nationalism 1870-1890,* Lippincott, 1966.

Clark, Dennis, *Irish Blood: Northern Ireland and the American Conscience,* Kennikat Press, 1977.

Coogan, Tim Pat, *The IRA.,* Roberts Rinehart, 1997.

Cronin, Sean, *The McGarrity Papers,* Anvil Books, 1972.

Devoy, John, *Recollections of an Irish Rebel,* Irish University Press, 1969.

Doyle, D., and Edwards, O., eds., *America and Ireland, 1776–1976,* Greenwood Press, 1980.

Farrell, Michael, *Sheltering the Fugitive? The Extradition of Irish Political Offenders,* Mercier Press, 1985.

Gallagher, Thomas, *Paddy's Lament: Ireland 1846–1847,* Harcourt Brace Jovanovich, 1982.

Holland, Jack, *Too Long a Sacrifice: Life and Death in Northern Ireland Since 1969,* Dodd, Mead, 1981.

O'Clery, Conor, *Daring Diplomacy: Clinton's Secret Search for Peace in Northern Ireland,* Roberts Rinehart, 1997.

O'Dwyer, Paul, *Counsel for the Defense,* Simon and Schuster, 1979.

O'Hanlon, Ray, *The New Irish Americans,* Roberts Rinehart, 1998.

MacStiofain, Sean, *Memoirs of a Revolutionary,* Gordon Cremonesi, 1975.

McCaffrey, Lawrence J., *The Irish Diaspora in America,* The Catholic University of America Press, 1984.

Moody, T. W., ed., *The Fenian Movement,* The Mercier Press, 1968.

Wilson, Andrew J., *Irish America and the Ulster Conflict 1968–1995,* Catholic University of America Press, 1995.

Reports:

The European Commission on Human Rights: Report of the Commission (Ireland Against the United Kingdom of Great Britain and Northern Ireland), 1976.

Northern Ireland: A Role for the United States: Report of the Committee on the Judiciary, 95th Congress, 2d Session, 1978.

Index

32-County Sovereignty Committee, xiii, 268

Abu Eam, Ziad, 164–65, 166, 191–193

Adams, Gerry, 56, 138, 140–41, 228, 246, 247, 250, 252, 251, 253, 254, 255, 257, 258, 260, 261, 262, 264, 265, 266, 267, 268
  Hume, John, talks with, 247, 252, 253

Ad Hoc Committee on Irish Affairs, xv, 131, 139, 145, 149

Aer Lingus, 34

African National Congress, 56, 57

Agca, Mehmet Ah, 223

Aguilar, Roger P., 167–68

Ahearn, Brian, 40

Air India jet explosion (1985), 183

airplane hijackings, 192

Aitken, Sir Max, 165

AK–47 rifles, 92, 96, 99

Alcohol, Tobacco and Firearms, U.S. Bureau of, 39, 45, 84, 103, 110n

American Civil Liberties Union (ACLU), 40, 41, 46, 47–48, 60

American Committee for Ulster Justice, 38

American Congress for Irish Freedom, xv, 28

American Friends of Irish Neutrality, 23, 24, 25

American Irish Unity Committee, 235n

Amnesty International, 130, 131, 132, 139, 174

Ancient Order of Hibernians (AOH), xv, 25, 34, 117

An Cumann Carbhrach, 31

Anglo-Irish Agreement (November 1985), xiv, xvi, 115, 121, 129, 136, 142–43, 144, 148, 149–50, 151, 190–91, 200, 232–33, 237, 245

An Phoblacht, 33, 35, 51–56, 67

anti-Catholic discrimination, 27–28

Anti-Internment Coalition, 38

Aquino, Benigno, 189

Armacost, Michael H., 189–90

Armalite rifles, 82, 85, 92

arms smuggling, 71–113
  CIA connection in, 103–108
  from Europe, 108–109
  FBI investigation of, 93–101, 109–10
  1982 trial for, 102–108
  NORAID charged with, 41–45, 59–62
  police interceptions in, 108–11
  security in, 83–84
  transport methods in, 73–75, 83–84, 92–93
  weapons supplied through, 72–73

Arnold, Terrell E., 192–93

Ashe, Thomas, 65–66

Associated Press (AP), 196–97, 207

Auden, W. H., 7–8, 12, 17

Baker, James, 143

Baltimore Sun, 220

Barr, Jim, 180–81

Barrington, Carl, Jr., 103, 104, 105

bazookas, 73–74, 89

BBC (British Broadcasting Corporation), 234

Beaverbrook Newspapers, 165

Behan, Brendan, 69, 74

Berrigan brothers, 242n

Biaggi, Jackie, 119

Biaggi, Mario, xiv, xv, xvi, 36, 115, 118–21, 130–34, 145,188
  Anglo-Irish Agreement and, 149–50
  in arms sale issue, 139–40
  background of, 118–19
  peace conference proposed by, 140–41
  press treatment of; 220–21

Biden, Joseph, 134, 186–87

black Americans, 27, 241–42

Black and Tans, 66, 105

Black Liberation Army, 176

Black Panthers, 205

Blair, Tony, 265, 266

Blame, James, 156n

Bloody Sunday (January 30, 1972), 35, 119, 203–206

Boston Globe, 197, 199, 201, 209, 211, 232
Boston Pilot, 15
Boston Sunday Globe, 201
Bradshaw, Bob, 68–69
Breslin, Jimmy, 227–28
Brewster, Leo, 42
British army:
  in Bloody Sunday, 203–205
  counterinsurgency role of, 202
  in human rights violations case, 217–20
  undercover teams used by, 88–89
  U.S. press portrayal of, 200–206
British government, 248, 249, 253, 254, 255, 260, 262, 266
British policy:
  of criminalization, 158
  on extradition, 157–60, 194–95
  Irish-American politicians and, 116–17, 139–40
    Irish Republic as scapegoat for, 217
  in 1985 negotiations, 146–48
  in Sunningdale Agreement, 117
Brooke, Peter, 248
Brown, Jerry, 250, 258
Brown, Thomas, 8, 237
Bruton, John, 260
Buchard, Samuel, 156*n*
Buchwald, Naomi, 161–63, 174
Buckley, Tom, 208
Bush, George, 250, 265

Cahalane, Daniel, 42–43
Cahill, Joe, 29–30, 31, 32, 36, 59, 60, 91, 97, 98, 101, 109, 120, 203, 257
Callaghan, James, 129, 134
Campbell, Robert, 172
Camp David initiative, 140, 141
Carey, Hugh, xvi, 45–46, 116, 123, 124–25,126, 134, 139–140, 143, 228
Carey, John, 204–205
Carlin, Liam, 48
Carter, Jimmy, 114, 115, 121, 126–30, 132, 140, 143, 148, 245
Casey, Martin, 66, 67
Castioni, Angelo, 156–57
Catholics, 117, 147, 149, 151, 198, 202, 204, 213, 242
  in sectarian violence, 206–15

Catholic Worker Movement, 242*n*
Catron, John, 164
Charles, Prince of Wales, 49–50
Chicago Daily News, 205, 206
Chicago Tribune, 197, 204, 223, 224, 231, 232
Chile, 55–56, 111
Christian Science Monitor, 196, 209, 213, 218–19
Churchill, Winston, 23, 24
CIA (Central Intelligence Agency), 39, 102–108
Citizen, 16, 153
civil rights movement, 27–29
Clann na Gael, xvi, 20, 68
Clark, Dennis, 35, 43
Clark, Johnny, 87
Clark, Ramsay, 105
Clark, William, 143, 144, 147
Claudia, 109
Clinton, Hillary, 245, 246, 260, 262, 263
Clinton, Bill, 237, 244, 245, 246, 250, 251–252, 253, 254, 260, 261, 264, 265, 266, 268
  visit to Ireland, 262–63
Collins, Michael, 68, 246, 255
Collins, Patrick, 156
Conlon, James, 43
Connolly, James, 55, 170
Conservative party, 202, 251, 265
Continuity IRA, xiii, 247, 268
Cotter, Liam, 71–88, 107, 113
criminalization policy, 158
Cronin, Sean, 23

Dail, 76–77, 78, 79, 247
Daily Express (London), 165
Daily Telegraph (London), 205–206
Daly, Mike, 231
Dash, Samuel, 204–205
Davitt, Michael, 14–15, 17, 18, 26
Dearie, John, 250
DeConcini, Dennis, 136–37, 188
De Meo, George, 71–75, 81–82,88, 92, 93–95, 98, 102–108
Democracy in America (Tocqueville), 2
Democratic party, 2–3, 114, 121, 143, 155–56, 246, 250
Denman, Judge, 157
De Valera, Eamon, 18, 20–21, 22, 23, 24, 71, 76

Devine, Michael, 53
Devlin, Bernadette, 18, 28, 54,
    80–81, 105n, 173, 205–206, 241
Devoy, John, 16–17, 19, 156
dirty protest (1980), 48–49
Dodd, Christopher, 185–86, 190
Doherty, Brendan, 109
Doherty, Joseph, 170–80, 183, 193,
    222–26, 249, 250, 257, 267
Donlon, Sean, xvi, 121, 122, 132, 134,
    136, 143, 144, 145, 147
Donoghue, Denis, 10
Douglas, William O., 42
Douglass, Frederick O., 27
Dowd, Michael, 102
Downing Street Declaration, 254
Drumm, Maire, 120
Drury, Thomas, 35
Duffy, Michael, 67
Duggan, Andy, 109, 110
Duniway, Ben C., 169
Durkan, Frank, 102, 161, 190

Eagleton, Thomas, 134, 188, 190
Easter Rising (1916), xiii, 4, 11, 13, 18,
    55, 158
Eder, Richard, 216
Eilberg, Joshua, 137, 138
Elliott, Ernie, 209, 211–12
El Salvador, 55–56, 112
Emerson, Gloria, 198, 214
Erin's Hope, 3, 13
Ervine, David, 259, 260
European Commission on Human
    Rights, 209n, 217, 218
European Court of Human Rights, 28,
    161, 219, 221
European Human Rights
    Convention, 217
Extradition Bill (1981), 189–90
extradition law, 152–95
  Abu Eam case in, 164–65, 166,
    191–93
  Barr case in, 180–81
  British policy on, 157–60,
    194–95
  declaratory judgments in, 178–79
  Doherty case in, 170–80, 183, 193,
    222–26
  in 1880s and 1890s, 152–57
  executive vs. judicial power in,

    193–94
  informers and, 181
  Lynchehaun case in, 157–58
  Mackin case in, 160–65, 174, 177
  McMullen case in, 158–60, 174
  misrepresentations in cases on,
    191–92, 194
  Philippines treaty and, 189–90
  political–offense exceptions under,
    153–60, 168–70, 173–77, 179–80,
    182, 191–95
  Quinn case in, 165–70
  Senate Committee debates on,
    181–90
  statute of limitations on, 182
  as sui generis, 154–55, 157
  Supplementary Treaty on,
    182–191, 226–27
  terrorism crusade and, 160, 162,
    168, 169, 173, 176–77, 182, 283,
    185, 192–93, 194
  Thurmond bill on, 163, 178–79
  treaties on, 148, 149, 152–56, 177,
    182
  U.S. press reports on, 192–93,
    221–27

Falvey, Tom, 72, 81, 83, 88, 95,
    98–101, 247
Farrell, Michael, 157n, 165n
Faul, Denis, 136
FBI (Federal Bureau of
    Investigation), 24
  arms smuggling investigated by,
    93–101, 109–10
  NORAID monitored by, 32–33,
    38–41, 44, 45
Feeney, Chuck, 255, 257
Fenian Brotherhood, xiii, xv–xvi, 3,
    11–13
Ferraro, Geraldine, 239
Fianna Fail party, 20–21, 144, 197
Fine Gael party, 144, 197
Finerty, John, 15–16, 152–53
Finn, Pat, 66
Fish, Hamilton, 136, 137, 138
Fitzgerald, Garret, 115, 121, 144–45,
    146, 147, 149, 231, 232, 235n, 240
Fitzpatrick, Mike, 37
Flannery, Michael, xvii, 26, 28, 31, 32,
    36, 57–58, 59, 60, 85, 97, 98,

101–102, 101–106, 117, 141–42, 247, 248
Fletcher, Betty, 169
Flynn, Bill, 255
Flynn, Raymond, 190, 251
Flynn, Sean, 53–54, 59
Foley, Tom, 251
Ford, Patrick, 25, 156
Foreign Agents Registration Act (FARA), xvii, 33–34, 38–41, 45–48
Foreign Assistance Act, 139
Friendly, Judge, 164, 177, 179–80
Friends of Ireland, xvii, 143–44, 148
Friends of Irish Freedom, xvi, 30–31, 247, 248, 258
Friends of Sinn Fein, xvi, 256, 260
Fusco, Angelo, 171–72

Gaelic Athletic Association (GAA), 25
Galvin, Martin, 47, 57, 60, 238, 250, 255, 257, 258
Gamble, Bobby, 160
Gandhi, Mohandas K., 27
Garand rifles, 72–73, 88
Garret, Brian, 161
Geneva Convention, 176
Gibney, Seamus, 60
Gleason, Teddy, 52–53, 117
Good Friday Agreement, 237, 267
Goodman, William, 159, 167
Gore, Al, 245, 246, 258
Gormley, Danny, 97–98,101–102
Gormley, Patrick, 97–98
grease guns, 80
Green Cross, 31–32, 36, 60–61
Guevara, Ernesto (Che), 112
Guiliani, Mayor, 257

Hague Convention on aircraft seizure (1970), 192
Haight, Charles, Jr., 178
Hamill, Pete, 125, 227, 228–29
Harrison, George, 26, 63–113, 247, 257
   background of, 64–70
   in Dail participation dispute, 76–77
   in De Meo-Cotter network, 72–75, 81–88
   FBI investigation of, 93–101
   financing of arms from, 84–85
   in Irish-American groups, 70–71
   liberation struggles and, 111–12
   McLogan and, 76–79
   as principal IRA arms supplier, 64
   on trial, 102–108
Hart, Gary, 134
Haughey, Charles, 3, 53, 144
H-Block Armagh Committee, xvi, 54
Heaney, James, xv, 28
Heath, Edward, 38
Hillery, Patrick, 38
Hillick, Harry, 43
Holl, Jane, 253
Home Rule party, 14–15
House of Representatives, U.S., 2–3
   Immigration, Citizenship and International Law Subcommittee, 137
Hughes, Francis, 50
human rights violations, 217–20
Hume, John, xiv, 122, 124, 125, 144, 151, 247, 248, 251, 252, 253, 254, 261, 262, 263
hunger strike at Maze Prison (1981), xiii, 1–3, 6, 49–54, 57, 144, 160, 163, 172–73, 230–31
Hurson, Martin, 53
Hutchinson, Billy, 259
Hyde, Henry, 130

immigrants, Irish:
   during famine of 1845–1854, 2
   in industrial expansion, 9–10
immigration, 137
Immigration and Nationality Act, 137
Index on Censorship, 233–34
Intergovernmental Council, 147
International League for Human Rights, 204–205
international terrorism:
   in 1880s, 152–53
   extradition cases and, 160, 162, 168, 169, 173, 176–77, 182, 183, 185, 192–93, 194
   Reagan administration crusade against, 160, 173, 176–77, 183
   Rome airport attack in, 169
   in Senate debates, 187
   U.S. press on, 197, 22–24
internment policy, 201–203
Irish Action Committee, xvi, 29
Irish American Nationalism (Brown), 8

Irish-American politicians:
  British perceptions of, 158
  IRA influences in, 115
  pragmatism of, 114
Irish Americans:
  conservatism of, 21–26, 54–55
  Easter Rising supported by, 4
  in extradition controversies, 151–56,
    158, 181
  financial contributions from, 26
  funerals as historical events for, 12–13
  Irish-Irish vs., 14
  in middle class, 25, 237, 239
  nationalism of, 14, 237–43
  as nostalgic, 8–9
  partitioning and, 19–20
  political power of, 2–3
  racism among, 241–42
  radicalism among, 242–43
  Reagan and, 239–41
  as rebels, 237–38
  St. Patrick's Day and, 8-9
  working-class, 241–42
  during World War II, 23–24
Irish Art Center, 243
Irish Blood (Clark), 35
Irish Citizens Army (ICA), 170
Irish Echo, 40–41, 133, 150, 220–21, 225,
  240
Irish forum, 250, 251
Irish government (Dublin), 261, 262,
  266
  in Anglo-Irish Agreement, 115,
    148–51
  "Big Four" and, 123–25
  Human Rights Court case
    brought by, 217–20
  INC and, 117–18
  Irish-American politicians and,
    115–16
  New Ireland Forum and, 144–46
  1985 British negotiations with,
    146–48
  U.S. aid bill for, 148–49
  U.S. diplomatic involvement and,
    150–51
  U.S. government relations with,
    116–17
  U.S. press coverage of, 216–17
  U.S. pro-IRA influence and, 121–22
  U.S. visa restrictions and, 138–39

Irish Labour party, 69, 144, 197
Irish National Caucus (INC), xvi–xvii,
  117–22, 129, 130, 140–43,
  149–50
Irish National Liberation Army
  (INLA), xiii–xiv, 50–54, 96,
  180–81, 255
Irish Northern Aid Committee
  (INAC), *see* NORAID
Irish People, 34, 40–41, 45–48, 51,
  55–57, 118, 142, 150, 257, 258
Irish Republican Army (IRA), xiii,
  5–6, 246, 247, 248, 249, 250, 253,
  254, 255, 256, 259, 260, 261, 266,
  267
  Anglo-Irish Agreement and, 151
  Biaggi and, 120–21
  at Biaggi peace conference, 140–41
  bombings, 252, 253, 263, 264, 265
  border campaign of, 75–76, 79, 80
  British army tactics used against,
    88–89
  Carey's attack on, 124–25
  cease-fires, 253, 256, 263, 264, 265
  Dail participation issue in,
    76–77, 79
  De Valera's outlawing of, 22
  in Easter Rising, 4
  in extradition cases, 158–59,
    161, 162, 161–70, 171–74,
    176, 221–27
  founding of, 18–19
  guerrilla tactics of, 19
  Harrison and, 64
  human rights violations against,
    217–20
  income of, 61–62
  liberation struggles and, 51–57
  mid-1950s regrouping of, 71
  mortar attack, 255
  1977 reorganization of, 91–92
  NORAID and, 31–32, 35, 41,
    43–44, 45–47, 60–62
  partitioning and, 19, 21
  press portrayal of, 197, 198,
    202–204, 207, 213, 216
  provisional, 252, 263
  Provisional vs. Official, 29
  republican goals of, 5
  sectarian violence and, 215
  setbacks in arms supplies for, 10–11

Irish Republican Army (cont.)
  in Shammer, 61–70
  socialist tendency in, 55
  targets of, 85–6
  Thompson guns used by, 68–69
  visa issue and, 40–41, 117, 120,
    137–39
  war declaration issued by, 21–22
  weapons lost by, 86–87
  weapons used by, 68–69, 72–73,
    86–7, 90–91, 92
  during World War II, 24
Irish Republican Brotherhood (IRB),
  xiii, xv–xvi, 11, 15–16
Irish Republican Socialist Party (IRSP),
  xiii–xiv, 52–54, 137
Irish Times, 69, 75
Irish Voice, 255, 258
Irish War of Independence, xiii, 158
Irish World, 25, 156
Israel, 47, 56, 164–65

James Connolly Club, 70, 71
Jensen, Lowell, 183, 184
Joint Terrorist Task Force, 100
Justice Department, U.S., xvii, 35, 36,
  37, 40, 4142, 44, 45, 47, 52, 59, 60,
  93, 183, 184, 248

Keane, Jack, xv, 117, 130, 133
Keenan, Sean, 31, 32, 60
Kennedy, Edward M., xvi, 45–46, 116,
  122, 125, 139,143, 144, 146, 149,
  245, 254, 256
Kennedy, John F., 10, 78
Kennedy, Michael, 102, 106
Kerry, John, 186,194
Kilroy, Jack, 257
Kirby, David, 103, 105, 106
Kirkpatrick, Harry, 180–81

Labour Party, 265
Lambert, Tom, 208–209
Land League, 17
land reform, 14–15, 17–18
Langford, Steele, 166, 167
Larkin, Michael, 43
Leahy, Patrick, 134
Lenin, Vladimir, 55
Lewis, Anthony, 199, 202
Lewis, David, 102

liberation struggles, 55–57,
  111–12
Libya, 97,109, 191n
Lillis, Michael, 121,122, 123, 132,
  133–34, 147
Long Green Line, 6n
Los Angeles Times, 37, 59, 60, 204,
  207–209, 220, 230, 233
Loughran, Seamus, 118, 120
Lugar, Richard, 148, 149, 191
Lynagh, Vincent, 161
Lynch, Edmund, 253
Lynch, Jack, 131, 132
Lynch, Kevin, 53
Lynchehaun, James, 157–58
Lynchehaun Defense Committee,
  157–58

M-l rifles, 72, 73
M-16 rifles, 82, 90, 92, 101
M-60 submachine guns, 90–91, 92
MAC-10 submachine gun, 95, 96, 99
McAliskey, Bernadette, see Devlin,
  Bernadette
MacBride, Sean, 174
McCaffrey, Lawrence, 10
McCann, Fra, 48
McCarthy, Eugene, 188–89, 227
McCarthy, Jack, 31
McCartney, Robert, 174
McCloskey, Paul, Jr., 133
McCreesh, Malachy, 50, 51
McCreesh, Ray, 50
McDonald, Joe, 51, 53
McFarlane, Robert, 147
McGarrity, Joe, 20–23, 24, 57–58, 68,
  71, 112
McGehee, Ralph, 105
McGlinchey, Dominic, 255
McGlynn, Father, 156
McGovern, George, 134
McGowan, Jack, 31
McGuinness, Martin, 261, 265
McIllwee, Tom, 53
McKeon, Barney, 93, 101
Mackin, Dessie, 160–65, 174, 177, 180,
  190
McKinney, Jack, 37
McKittrick, David, 212
McLaughlin, Joseph, 102
McLogan, Paddy, 66, 71, 76–80, 83, 113

MacMahon, Kieran, 43
McManus, Sean, xvi, 117, 119–20,
    140–43, 149–50, 195
MacManus, Terence Bellew, 12
McMichael, Gary, 259, 260
McMullen, Peter Gabriel, 158–60
McParland, Paddy, 109
McPolin, Kevin, 211
Magee, Paul "Dingus," 171
Major, John, 251, 253, 254, 263, 265
Marcos, Ferdinand E., 189
Marita Ann, 110
Marshals Service, U.S., 107
Martin, John Joe, 72, 81, 87
Marxism, 54, 55, 57
Masterson, Kenneth, 161
Maudling, Reginald, 201–206
Mayhew, Patrick, 248, 250, 253, 260,
    261
Maze Prison, 249
Meehan, Eamon, 109–10
Meehan, Paul, 109–10
Meese, Edwin, 143
Megahey, Gabriel, 109,110
Meunier, Theodore, 166
Middle East, 55–56, 57
Mitchell, George, 245, 262, 266, 268
Mogulescu, William, 102
Molyneaux, James, 256, 264
Montreal Convention on aircraft
    seizure, 192
Morrison, Bruce, 251, 252, 253, 263
Mountbatten, Louis, Lord, 191
Mowlam, Mo, 265, 266
Moynihan, Daniel Patrick, xvi, 45–46,
    123, 139, 143
Mullins, Paddy, 98, 101–102
Murphy, Jeremiah, 209
Murray, Margaret, 37
Murray, Raymond, 136

Naples, Kingdom of, 156
Nation, 11
National Association for Irish
    Freedom, 38
nationalism:
    dormant period in, 23–26
    of Irish Americans, 14, 237–43
    land reform and, 14–15, 17–18
    during World War II, 23–25
National Law Journal, 225

National News Council, 235*n*
National Security Council, U.S., 147,
    253, 258
Ndaba, David, 105*n*
Newcomer, Clarence, 181
New Ireland Forum, 144–45, 231
Newsweek, 198, 200–201, 203, 207,
    216, 217, 228
New York *Daily News,* 124–25, 197,
    210, 218, 222–23, 226, 227–28,
    230–31
New York Post, 222, 223–24, 226,
    228, 231
New York Review of Books, 200
New York Times, 43–44, 107–108,
    140, 152, 155, 167, 170,177, 180*n*,
    183–4, 185, 191*n*, 197, 198, 199,
    201, 202–203, 208, 210, 211, 212,
    214, 216–17, 218, 219, 220, 222,
    223, 224–25, 226, 228, 230–32,
    234–35
Nicaragua, 47, 55–56, 111, 112, 148,
    149, 183, 187
Nixon, Richard M., 38
NORAID (Irish Northern Aid
    Committee), xvii, 27–62, 151, 238,
    247, 248, 250, 252, 255, 256, 257,
    258
arms smuggling charges against,
    41–45, 59–62
British government's attack on, 43
British policy and, 35–36
conservative forces and, 54–55
dirty protest and, 48–49
FARA investigation of, 33–34,
    38–41, 45–48
FBI monitoring of, 32–33, 38–41,
    44, 45
founding of, 31–32
funds raised by, 35–37, 39–41,
    44–45, 57, 59–60, 61
Harrison and, 84–85
hunger strike and, 49–54, 57
INC and, 141–42
INLA and, 50–51
IRA and, 31–32, 35, 41, 43–44,
    41–47, 60–62
Irish-American politicians and, 45–46
Irish People and, 45–48
local chapters of, 34, 36–37
visa denials and, 40–41

Northern Aid Committee,
31, 34
Northern Ireland Civil Rights
Association (NICRA), xiv, xv,
27, 28
Nossiter, Bernard, 214

O'Bradaigh, Ruairi, 35, 37, 41, 60, 118,
120, 140–41, 247
O'Brien, Edna, 255
O'Brien, Fred Burns, 117, 120, 137,
142
O'Conaill, Daithi, xvii, 29–31, 32, 60,
73, 81, 91, 118, 140–41, 166, 247
O'Connell, Daniel, 27
O'Connor, Batt, 8
O'Doherty, Eamon, 96–97
O'Dowd, Niall, 255, 258
O'Dwyer, Paul, 25, 28, 42, 124, 159,
242, 244
O'Hanlon, Fergal, 30
O'Hara, Liz, 50–53
O'Hara, Patsy, 50–51
O'Higgins, Donal, 208
O'Leary, "Pagan," 16–17, 18
O'Mahony, John, 11–12
O'Neill, Thomas P. (Tip), xvi, 2,
45–46, 114–15, 122–23, 121–26,
130, 139–40, 143, 144, 145, 146,
148, 149, 150
Orwell, George, 108

Paisley, Ian, 259
Palestine Liberation Organization
(PLO), 56, 164, 197
Parnell, Charles Stewart, 14–15
Pearse, Patrick, 12–13, 18, 20
Pell, Claiborne, 187, 191
Perez, Frank, 161, 162
Petersen, Henry, 41
Philadelphia Daily News, 225, 227
Philadelphia Evening Bulletin, 36
Philippines, 189–90
Pike, Mary, 193
Polak, Louis, 204
Polish-American groups, 47
political prisoners, 48–49
power sharing, 135
press, British, 233–34
press, U.S., 196–235
   on Anglo-Irish Agreement, 232–33

August 1969 events covered by, 198
Biaggi attacked in, 220–21
on Bloody Sunday, 203–206
British propaganda reinforced in,
200, 213–14
British role as portrayed by, 197
consensus view in, 196, 213–14
"enlightened colonialism"
theme in, 199–200
on extradition cases, 192–93,
221–27
on Forum report, 231–32
human rights violations covered in,
217–20
hunger strike covered in, 230–31, 233
"inexplicable Irish" stereotype in,
198–200
on international terrorism,
223–24
on internment, 201–203
Irish-American columnists in,
227–29
Irish diplomatic service and,
230
Irish Republic in, 216–17
liberal views in, 199–200
Protestant violence
de-emphasized in, 208
religious tensions emphasized
by, 197, 198–99
republican analysis and, 197
scapegoats in, 211–21
sectarian war theme in, 206–15
sentimental persona in, 227–29
on Supplemental Treaty, 226–27
on Thatcher, 230, 231, 232–33
"Tommy" stereotype in, 200–206
UDA in, 208–14
UVF in, 209
"wildcats" in, 210–11
wire services in, 196–97
Prisoners' Aid Fund, 75
Progressive Unionist Party, xiv, 259
Protestants, 147, 151, 242
   in sectarian violence, 206–15
Prussia, 156
Puerto Rico, 111
Pyle, Christopher, 188, 189–90, 193,
227
Qaddafi, Muammar, 197
Queen Mary, 43

Quiet Man, The, 14
Quill, Mike, 75
Quinn, William, 165–70, 193, 222

racism, 241–42
Reagan, Ronald, 3, 4, 52–53, 56, 114,
    115, 129, 140, 143–44, 148, 245,
    250, 251
  extradition policy under, 154,
    160–161, 162, 163–165, 173,
    176–79, 183–84,190, 191–95
  Forum proposals and, 145
  on Irish trip, 239–40
Real IRA, xiv, 268
Red Army Faction, 192
Red Brigades, 162, 176, 192
Redick, Earl, 102–104, 107
Regan, Donald, 149
Reinhardt, Stephen, 168–169
Republican party, 155–56, 246, 251,
    252
Republican Sinn Fein, xiv, 247, 248,
    268
Reuters, 197, 210, 219
Reynolds, Albert, 251, 254, 256
Robinson, Andy, 138
rocket guns, 73
Romero, Archbishop, 63
Roosevelt, Franklin D., 23, 24
Rossa, O'Donovon, 12–13, 48
Royal Ulster Constabulary (RUC), xiv,
    4, 28, 30, 75, 139–40, 253, 367
RPG-7 rockets, 89
Russell, Sean, 21–22
Russia, Czarist, 156
Ryan, Frank, 80–81

Sackville, Lionel, Lord, 155, 156
St. Patrick's Day, 8–9
St. Patrick's Day parades, xv, 9, 25, 237,
    240
Sands, Bobby, 1, 2, 5, 6, 49, 160, 172, 230
Sands, Sean, 50, 51
San Francisco Chronicle, 203–204,
    219–20, 222
San Francisco Examiner, 219, 220, 232
Scheck, Barry, 102
Schmeisser submachine guns, 72
sectarian violence, 206–15
Senate, U.S., 2–3, 248
  Foreign Relations Committee,

148, 149,153, 155, 184,
    185–190, 194, 195, 226
Sharkey, Jim, xvi
Shultz, George, 58, 179, 183
Sikh extremists, 183
Sinn Fein, xiv, 4, 29, 32, 49, 53, 60, 61,
    91, 110, 144, 151, 246, 247, 248,
    251, 253, 254, 255, 256, 257, 258,
    259, 260, 264, 265, 267, 268
  Dail participation issue in,
    76–77, 79
  founding of, 18–19
  hunger strike and, 230, 231, 233
  liberation struggles and, 56–57
  U.S. press treatment of, 220
  visa issue and, 40–41, 117, 120,
    137–39
Sitting Bull, 16
Smith, Jean Kennedy, 254
Social Democratic and Labour
    Party (SDLP), xiv, 57, 117, 120,
    122, 144–45, 151, 197, 224, 231
socialism, 55, 57
Sofaer, Abraham, 183–87, 191–92
Solarz, Stephen, 130
Somerstein, Stephen, 193
South, Sean, 30
South Africa, 54, 55, 56, 112
Special Air Services (SAS), 172
Spence, Gusty, 259
Sprizzo, John E., 173–78, 180, 185,
    195, 222–26
Standard Tools, 93
Starr Report, 244, 245, 246
State Department, U. S., xiv, 39–40, 41,
    45, 58, 126, 130, 137–38, 139, 251
  in extradition proceedings, 160,
    162, 163, 173, 182, 183, 190
Stephens, James, 11
Stethem, Robert, 183
Stevens, Louis, 101
Stout, Charles, 137–38
Strasbourg Court on Human
    Rights, 217
Strategic Defense Initiative, 145
Sunningdale Agreement, 117, 122
supergrasses, 181, 185
Supplementary Treaty (1985),
    182–195, 226–27
Taylor, John, 69
Taylor, Peter, 233–34

Thatcher, Margaret, 3, 51, 53, 56, 115, 140, 143, 147, 173, 191n, 194, 224
  Reagan and, 240–41
  Forum's conclusions and, 144–46, 232
  in U.S. press, 230, 231, 232–33
Thomas, Jo, 235
Thompson submachine guns, 68–69, 73, 74
Thornton, John, 133–34
Thurmond, Strom, 163
Tibble, Stephen, 165, 168
Time, 198–99, 200, 201, 213, 228, 234–35
Times (London), 191
Tinnelly, Paul, 89
Tir-na-nOg, 16, 18
Tocqueville, Alexis de, 2
trade unions, 52, 75
Transport Workers Union, 75
Treasury Department, U.S., 40, 43
Trible, Paul, 188
Trimble, David, 246, 264, 266, 267, 268
Trott, Stephen, 177
Twomey, Seamus, 118
Tyrie, Andy, 138, 209

Ulster Defense Association (UDA), xiv, 58, 125, 137–38, 140, 208–14, 258, 259, 260
  in sectarian killings, 210–12
Ulster Defense Force (UDF), 258, 259
Ulster Defense Regiment (UDR), xiv–xv, 147
Ulster Democratic Party, 259
Ulster Freedom Fighters (UFF), xiv, 209–10, 211, 212
Ulster Unionist Party, 246, 256, 266, 267
Ulster Volunteer Force (UVF), xv, 85, 138, 209, 214, 215, 224
Unionists, 147–48, 198, 202, 214, 252, 254, 256, 259, 264, 266, 267
Union Leader (Manchester), 220–21
United Nations, 144
United Nations Human Rights Commission, 28
United Press International (UPI), 196–97
Uzi submachine gun, 96, 99

Vance, Cyrus, 126
Vatican, 47
Versailles Conference, 4
Vietnam War, 242n
Village Voice, 227
visa policy, 40–41,117, 120, 137–39
Vogelman, Lawrence, 102

Wall Street Journal, 191, 212, 223, 226
Washington Post, 191n, 192, 214, 226–27, 232
Washington Star, 220
Weller, George, 205–206
Westerfund, William, 43
Westmacott, Captain, 172
White, John, 8
White, John (Winslow), 95–97, 99, 100, 101, 107, 108
Wilson, Harold, 43, 120
Wilson, Woodrow, 4
Winslow, John, *see* White, John
With Michael Collins in the Fight for Irish Independence (O'Connor), 8
Woelfien, Frederick, 159
World Court, 183
World War I, 4
World War II, 22–24
Wright, Oliver, 146, 190

Young Irelanders, 10–11

Ziebel, Laurie, 106